RAZZLE DAZZLE

RAZ

ZLE DAZZLE

THE LIFE AND WORK OF

BOB FOSSE

KEVIN BOYD GRUBB

ST. MARTIN'S PRESS/NEW YORK

Toni Lopopolo wishes to thank the following people for their special efforts and cordiality: Diana Brown and Rick Felix of Turner Entertainment, Joan Pierce of MGM-UA, Yvon Kartak of MCA, Shary Klamer of 20th–Century Fox Film Corporation/ Columbia Pictures, Lee Gross, and Brian De Fiore. Also Andrea Connolly and Glen Edelstein of St. Martin's Press.

Design by Judith A. Stagnitto

Page ii photo of Bob Fosse by AP/Wide World Photos. Page vi photo of Liza Minnelli as Sally Bowles in *Cabaret* by Photofest.

Library of Congress Cataloging-in-Publication Data

Grubb, Kevin Boyd.
   Razzle dazzle / Kevin Boyd Grubb.
      p.   cm.
    ISBN 0-312-03414-8
    1. Fosse, Bob, 1927–1987.   2. Choreographers—United States-
-Biography. I. Title.
   GV1785.F67G78   1989
   792.8'2'092—dc20
   [B]   89-35077
                                                 CIP

First edition

10 9 8 7 6 5 4 3 2 1

To my parents, Royal and Sandra Grubb,
Frank Pace,
and in memory of William Como

CONTENTS

FOREWORD

Obody swayed to music, O brightening glance/How can we know the dancer from the dance?" W. B. Yeats asked in his sonnet "Among School Children" in 1927. The same year Robert Louis Fosse was born, named after Robert Louis Stevenson. Although the written word fascinated and eluded Bob Fosse throughout his career, he is remembered today for a different communication—dance—which he both performed and choreographed. It is not the classical choreography of ballet immortals that we equate with Fosse, though some might argue a Fosse dancer brings to mind as vivid an image as a George Balanchine ballerina. Nor do his dances resemble those of Busby Berkeley, Fred Astaire, or Gower Champion, dancemakers who shared the same stage and screen territories as Fosse. But one thing is certain: Fosse dancers are today the living records of his work and, in part, his life. His dancers became the dance.

When I embarked on this project, Fosse dancers were largely my *modus operandi*. Admittedly, my reason for interviewing as many dancers as possible was founded on my own experience. Having reported on dance—largely show business dance—for nearly a decade, I have learned that dancers frequently have the most insightful remarks about directors and choreographers, but are seldom given the opportunity to speak. I suppose this has something to do with the long-held belief that dancers, especially *show* dancers, articulate best through their feet. These agile beasts of burden have been the mainstay of musical theater for over a century, though their importance in shows is taken for granted until we suddenly come across a musical that does not use them (Stephen Sond-

heim's and James Lapine's productions, for example). Then, we become aware that something is missing, the element that adds exuberance and, at its best, speeds the show along its course.

If an often-heard carp at intermissions these days is that Broadway has no great choreographers to compete with imports from across the Atlantic, let's not forget that, barely a decade ago, many theatergoers were startled at the rapid ascendency of the dance musical on Broadway. With Michael Bennett's *A Chorus Line* in 1975 and Bob Fosse's *Dancin'* in 1978, the director-choreographer had finally arrived after years of aborted attempts to present dance front and center under the proscenium arch. Tom O'Horgan's *Hair* and Fosse's own *Pippin* showed directors of the late Sixties and early Seventies rearranging the hierarchy of a musical's structure. Dancers, traditionally at the bottom, suddenly became a sort of Greek chorus for the dramatic action. They slipped almost imperceptibly in and out of scenes, providing throughlines as they danced, sang, even *acted*. Although it was Michael Bennett's *A Chorus Line* that became a theater history milestone for dancers, Fosse's accomplishments were no less remarkable. He freely crossed over from stage to film and back again, proving equally proficient in both media.

Now that Bennet and Fosse are gone, the brief rise of dancers and choreographers to the ranks of principal contributors and even celebrities has ended, at least for the time being. There are the rare exceptions—a big-budget Jerome Robbins retrospective here, Mikhail Baryshnikov tackling Franz Kafka there—but the tide has washed in overseas productions bursting with every musical element but one. Do the Europeans perceive dancers as flotsam, clotting up the innovations of stage pyrotechnics? Or has show dancing, like vaudeville, come to be associated with a bygone brand of Broadway entertainment, no longer palatable to contemporary audiences? When debating the presentation of dance on the Broadway stage today, I am often reminded of the many musicals that do feature old-fashioned production numbers using dancers. While we can see dancers merrily slapping their thighs in "The Lambeth Walk" in *Me and My Girl,* or getting frisky at the Jellicle Ball in *Cats,* what do these dances contribute to their musicals' narratives? We might suspect that they are designed to be excerpted as the slick television and music video commercials that promote these two shows. Without the vitality of *human* movement, the Broadway musical has become so technically advanced that dancers are replaced by revolving stages. Today, people don't have to dance, the scenery does.

Fosse rehearsing in a studio near Broadway, 1980. *(Jack Vartoogian)*

A biography of Bob Fosse presents an irresistible opportunity to spotlight the director-choreographer. I had a fairly thorough knowledge of Fosse's work before I began the project; a year before he died I followed him for six months for an article I was writing about the dancers he had produced over the years. And while Fosse's later projects were not all dance-oriented, even nondance efforts such as *Lenny* and *Star 80* demonstrate a man wrapped around his camera like a tango dancer clenched in a passionate embrace. As Fosse himself boasted throughout his career, he was first and last a dancer.

I interviewed nearly a hundred people who worked with Fosse—set and costume designers, composers, directors, writers, actors, and, of course, dancers. From 1988 to 1989 I trotted around the United States to track down this far-flung group. Stacks of cassette tapes became mountainous, intimidating piles of transcriptions. Libraries in Chicago, Los Angeles, and New York yielded reams of clippings. There were also valuable experiences along the way that had nothing to do with note-taking. These, I think, left the strongest impressions: standing on the sidewalk outside Fosse's boyhood home on Sheridan Road in Chicago; staying in Chicago's historic Blackstone Hotel, frequented by Fosse in the Thirties when "dance stylist" Paul Draper performed there; interviewing Ben Vereen at a Catskills resort similar to those depicted not so lovingly in *Lenny;* poring over albums of photographs in the living room of Phil Friedman, Fosse's devoted stage manager for nearly thirty years, who died suddenly a few days after our interview; attending Fosse's memorial at the Palace Theatre in New York, a gathering that later turned into an end-all party at the Tavern on the Green in Central Park.

I am grateful to the number of celebrities whose glamour no doubt gives *Razzle Dazzle* added appeal, but it is disappointing that the two most important people in Fosse's life, his wife Gwen Verdon and his daughter Nicole Fosse, declined to participate. Perhaps these women, whom I had previously interviewed twice each for projects unrelated to this book, believed it was too soon after his death to get involved in something that might demand so much of their time. Or perhaps they simply feared a writer relatively unknown to them would concentrate on the more sensational aspects of his life. During the one conversation I had with Nicole Fosse about the book, she informed me she would gladly set straight all the "terrible rumors that aren't true" about her father. Obviously, she assumed my interests in Fosse were prurient.

This work is emphatically not a "tell-all" about the life of Bob Fosse—he has done that better than anyone else could in his autobiographical 1979 film *All That Jazz*—but an attempt to examine his life through the microscope of his work. His evolution from a tap dancer in stripper clubs to a Tony-, Oscar-, and Emmy-winning director-choreographer gives credence to that much-abused word, *genius,* a term with which Fosse felt profoundly uncomfortable. He remained uneasy with his success throughout his life, believing his talents were fraudulent, and that one day all the trick mirrors would be removed to reveal a man unworthy of such adulation.

Bob Fosse, Janet Leigh, Betty Garrett, and Tommy Rall in Columbia's 1955 movie, *My Sister Eileen,* choreographed by Fosse. *(Copyright © 1953, ren. 1983, Columbia Pictures Industry, Inc.)*

One fear I had about this project was that, because of the range of opinions voiced by the interviewees, the book would not paint a cohesive portrait of Bob Fosse. Although the dancers spoke with reasonable consistency about such things as his technique, auditions, and creative process, I also found people who would hotly deny he was, for example, a Svengali, and ten minutes later, feeling a bit more at ease, use the word *Svengali* to describe him. As the book began to take shape, I found these inconsistencies enormously revealing. Somewhere between the self-deprecating, soft-spoken young Chicago hoofer and the painfully candid perfectionist is the real Bob Fosse. The liberal use of quotations in this book offers glimpses of a man alternately compassionate and intolerant, hedonistic and discreet, torn between family obligations and career ambitions.

During preproduction on the film *Lenny,* a quasi-documentary on the life of comedian Lenny Bruce, Fosse, too, experienced the anxieties of trying to marshal the events of a life into a coherent picture: "I think the biography is very difficult," he told *Filmmakers Newsletter* in 1975, "but a biography of someone who was alive eight years ago is harder still. There are a lot of vivid memories—a lot of contradictory memories—of the man. The more I dug [into the life of Lenny Bruce], the harder it was to find the real man." Fosse, having controlled the reel-to-reel tape recorder in *Lenny* and conducted the on-screen interviews with actors portraying Lenny Bruce's family, friends, and colleagues, would have been the first to point out the life-imitates-art aspect that *Razzle Dazzle* shares with *Lenny*.

The strong affinity I felt toward Fosse at the onset of this work became validated during the ensuing months. So often the urge to write about someone, especially a celebrity, is motivated by preconceived ideas. We see them not as they perceive *themselves,* but as who they are in relation to *us*. Though Fosse's life undoubtedly yielded its share of surprises to me, even during his darkest hours I was struck by his unflagging desire to be truthful and his respect for language and all forms of communication.

As *Lenny* starkly depicted, people frequently react with hostility when approached about someone with whom they were close. Often people in the entertainment industry hedge straight questions, suspecting ulterior motives. This what's-in-it-for-me attitude, which I encountered from several "stars" who might have been significant inclusions in this book, reminded me why many of Fosse's closest friends were dancers and writers—people seldom found in the limelight. Not surprisingly, the dancers were the ones most willing to be interviewed. And the most helpful.

Undeniably, a biographer has the power to affect the readers' perception of a life; but finally, the biographer does not re-create this life so much as present its vagaries. During interviews a biographer experiences first-hand the fallibility of memory. I spent hours with people who had worked years with Fosse, knew what brand of cigarette he smoked, and that his favorite cocktail was a daiquiri, but could not remember if he'd ever spoken of his childhood. It is this piecing together of the puzzle that makes the arbitrariness of a biography unusually gratifying.

As brooding as Fosse's work became during the last years of his life, the man realized his enormous abilities as a comic. Anyone who's seen the Chaplinesque dancers in *Pajama Game*'s "Steam Heat" or *Sweet Charity*'s "If My Friends Could See Me Now" remembers how much mileage he got from a simple black derby or collapsible top hat. In his life, too, Fosse's tendency to self-destruct was off-set by a sort of gleeful, mischievous humor that I hope surfaces in these pages as well. To leave this book believing Bob Fosse was fascinated only with heroin-sniffing stand-up comedians and shot-gunned *Playboy* center-folds would be a terrible injustice to the life-affirming qualities in his work.

"How can we know the dancer from the dance?" Bob Fosse might have said, "Who cares as long as the number works? Give 'em the old razzle dazzle, fire up the kleig lights, and let's give the audience their money's worth. It's showtime, folks!"

Bob Fosse, about the time he co-starred with Debbie Reynolds in the MGM film *Give a Girl a Break. (Photofest)*

ACKNOWLEDGMENTS AND REGRETS

Many people offered guidance, perspective, and advice in the making of this book. I am particularly grateful to authors John Gruen and Joseph Pintauro, who, before the first words were written, suggested that I approach the biography as a novel and gave me confidence to lay fingers to keyboard.

During the research and interview phase, over a hundred dancers, choreographers, actors, writers, composers, designers, and historians were interviewed, in addition to friends and family of Bob Fosse. Many went beyond the call of duty, supplying photographs, names, addresses, and phone numbers of others to contact; theater programs and clippings; and, sometimes, a warm meal. These kind-hearted individuals include Kathryn Doby, Louise Quick, Phil Friedman, Eric Roberts, Chita Rivera, Sandhal Bergman, Shirley MacLaine, Debbie Reynolds, Ben Vereen, Juliet Prowse, Tony Walton, Robert La Fosse, Richard Adler, Graciela Daniele, Linda Palmer, John Sharpe, Gene Foote, Donald Saddler, Tom Rall, Eddie Schwartz, Kathy Henderson, Margaret Fosse, Erwin Fosse, Miriom Wilson, Jack Vartoogian, Jack Mitchell, Martha Swope, Bert Fink, and the theater department staff of the Library of Performing Arts at Lincoln Center.

I am especially appreciative of the help supplied by my colleagues at *Dance Magazine*. Thanks to Richard Philp, Marian Horosko, and Dierdre Towers. The inclusion of many of the photographs in this book would not have been possible without the consent of publishers Roz and Bob Stern and *Dance Magazine*'s late editor in chief William Como.

Other key people who have made direct and indirect (but equally valuable) contributions to this book include Miranda Ottewell, Mary Neagoy, Dr. Mae Sakharov and the Learning Center, Patrick Merla, Terry Helbing, Robert Sandla, Cathy Cook, Stan Szaro, Robert de la Haba, Catherine Olim, Maryann Peronti, Deborah Winterson, my editor Toni Lopopolo, and my agent Jane Dystel, who set the wheels in motion.

Finally, *Razzle Dazzle* owes an enormous debt to three individuals without whose assistance its metamorphosis from manuscript to book form would not have been possible. Ken Mandlebaum offered me the use of his amazingly complete library of films, videotapes, programs, cast albums, and reference books. David Daniel provided me with a job, the hours and income of which were equally essential to the completion of my manuscript. And *Wall Street Journal* copy editor Lisa Vickery lent a critical eye to the first drafts of the chapters, saving me from mixed metaphors, dangling participles, and the Aleutian Nazis.

Regretfully, not everyone interviewed for the book was included in the final draft. Although each interviewee had relevant information about Bob Fosse, often the material was unsubstantiated, or simply had nothing to add to data I already had accumulated. Nonetheless, I appreciate the time these individuals took to speak to me. Their impressions of Fosse were valuable to me and helped give shape and substance to the book.

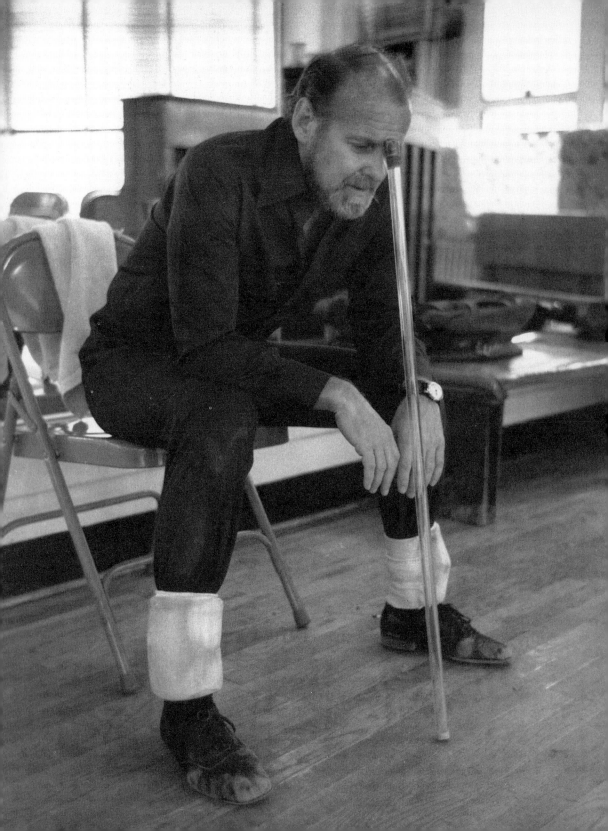

TIME STEPS: AN INTERVIEW WITH BOB FOSSE

I would never discriminate against someone's talent because they showed the poor taste to like me.

> —Bob Fosse,
> Newsweek, *1977*

The first and only time I met Bob Fosse was for an interview for *Dance Magazine* I had spent nearly three months trying to arrange. It was the spring of 1986, and both the revival of *Sweet Charity* and Fosse's first original musical in eight years, *Big Deal,* had opened on Broadway—to startlingly different critical reactions. Fosse had granted a handful of interviews prior to *Big Deal*'s critical drubbing, but he was in no mood to discuss his return to Broadway after the reviews were in. In fact, although I had followed *Big Deal* for six months—from its rehearsals in New York to its out-of-town run in Boston and back to New York again for its premiere—I had been forewarned by the show's publicists not to be surprised if Fosse declined to do the interview at all.

But once it became apparent *Big Deal* was in danger of closing, Fosse was more amenable. Through the show's publicists, he knew that I had taped hours of conversation with the dancers from both *Big Deal* and *Sweet Charity* and that my interest in him was primarily as one of the last of Broadway's *and* Hollywood's dancemakers. He was also aware that both Gwen Verdon, his wife (they separated in 1970 but never divorced) and close collaborator, and Ann Reinking, his former girlfriend and muse, had spoken to me about the article. Technicians, designers, and

(Photo by Jack Vartoogian)

Fosse's stage manager of nearly thirty years, Phil Friedman, had been interviewed as well. The only one hesitant to participate was Fosse.

The "technique" Fosse used to give me the impression he would not cooperate was probably the same one used to provoke or goad his dancers and actors into giving him the kind of performance he wanted. Many people remarked on Fosse's cunning ability to *accidentally* coax them into giving raw, realistic performances. And though some believed that the methods he used to trick them into developing their characters were flagrantly manipulative and often cruel, they also claimed it forced them to look deeper into themselves, examine their motivations, become someone else by using their own resources.

In early May 1986 I was contacted by a press agent handling the show. Fosse had consented to the interview. Could I be at his apartment the afternoon of May 15 at 3 o'clock?

My dance reporting has made me privy to the lives and work of many dancers and choreographers in musical theater; but rarely has the work of any excited me as much as Fosse's. In the years that I have watched his choreography, read about it, and discussed it with his dancers, Fosse's dances have been described variously as bizarre, burlesque, exploitational, brooding, sordid, leering, and lewd, but also brilliant, original, searing, sizzling—good box-office hype. With thirteen Broadway or Broadway-bound musicals to his credit, from 1954's *The Pajama Game* to 1978's *Dancin',* Fosse rivaled reliable hit-makers such as Jerome Robbins and Harold Prince, even his former director, George Abbott, in producing mostly successful musicals. While other directors and choreographers would have the monster hits or create seminal work, such as Jerome Robbins' *West Side Story,* Gower Champion's *42nd Street,* or Michael Bennett's *A Chorus Line,* Fosse was the one producers turned to for the requisite showstopper. He knew how to put dance front and center to camouflage a paper-thin score or a weak book. He was the eleventh-hour stage paramedic who could resuscitate an out-of-town flop and turn it into a Broadway box-office blockbuster. He was, until *Big Deal,* a sure thing.

Perhaps because my experience writing about dancers had led me to believe, like Fosse, that they are as important as a musical's other

Fosse rehearsing Kathryn Doby and Leland Palmer in *Pleasures and Palaces. (Friedman-Abeles)*

elements—in fact, sometimes *the* most important element—I did not share most critics' vociferous dismay at Fosse's last original Broadway effort. Instead of fighting over artistic control with writers, composers, designers, and producers, Fosse had had complete authority with *Big Deal,* writing the book, hand-picking the music, choreographing, and directing. Many critics failed to note that *Big Deal* was the culmination of Fosse's career as a choreographer, a total, exhausting synthesis of movement concepts he had been working toward throughout his thirty-two years on Broadway. Instead, reviews complained (rightly) that the book was bleak and unresolved and that the show lacked more than one Fosse showstopper and was constantly imperiled by Fosse's brash restyling of vintage songs from the Thirties. Still, few could argue that none of the other shows nominated in the outstanding musical category for the 1986–87 season, *Drood* and *Song and Dance,* had the singular mark of their creator as indelibly stamped on them as *Big Deal.*

Having spent over thirty years in the public eye, and used to being misrepresented in print, Fosse had made sure I had done my homework before interviewing him. I also believe he wanted to determine that, basically, I liked *Big Deal* and would give it as much consideration in the article as his more critically popular *Sweet Charity.*

After nearly six months of following Bob Fosse, I finally got the chance to meet the Busby Berkeley of Broadway.

On May 15, 1986, I arrived at his apartment at 58 West Fifty-eighth Street off Central Park South and took the elevator to number 31C. His secretary, Cathy Nicolas, met me at the door and directed me to the living room, which was, at first appraisal, spacious but unremarkable save for the spectacular north window view over Central Park. A modern, functional brown sofa was accompanied by matching chairs and a Seventies chrome-and-glass coffee table, strewn with magazines and newspapers. Though Fosse claimed he never read reviews, I saw several show business dailies on the table, and during the interview he quoted entire sentences of Frank Rich's *New York Times* review of *Big Deal.*

But further investigation revealed souvenirs from Fosse's shows scattered around the room, on the walls, and literally underfoot: neon sculptures, a silver mannequin, a gumball machine, a license plate that read "Star 80," the electric "Tango Palace" sign from *Sweet Charity,* his Oscar for *Cabaret* and an impressive clutch of haphazardly arranged Tony awards. (When I asked about his Emmy for *Liza with a Z,* he shrugged and mumbled, "It's around here some place.") These trinkets spoke as much about the man's sense of decor as they did about his work. It was like being in a museum, yet the apartment's atmosphere was casual clutter—lived-in, high-rise kitsch. Clearly, these gimcracks were not objets d'art to be displayed in curio cabinets; they defined a man who—as the Fosse-figure, Joe Gideon, says in *All That Jazz*—wakes up in the morning to his personal maxim, "It's showtime, folks!" Their brassy bluntness gave these possessions charm and appeal, a flashy, nostalgic sensibility synonymous with Fosse. Obviously, they were precious to him, emblematic of career accomplishments, cherished people, and deep personal satisfactions.

About ten minutes after I arrived, Fosse walked into the living room wearing his de rigueur black trousers and shirt, open to midchest, and comfortably scuffed black Capezio shoes. Though I had seen him from the wings during several rehearsals for *Big Deal* and *Sweet Charity,* up close he seemed slight and vulnerable, perhaps because of his ongoing back and heart ailments. Still, his body was surprisingly fit and his complexion ruddy. The gray Edwardian beard brought his chin to a point, and, when he laughed, his eyes danced mischievously. I was reminded of a middle-aged pixie.

Cathy Nicolas introduced us. I was taken off-guard by his initial shyness. "Hi, I'm Bob Fosse," he said, shaking my hand tentatively. He instructed Nicolas to retrieve a tape recorder. Thinking it was for the interview, I told him I had already brought mine, and indicated the microcassette recorder on the coffee table. "This is for me," Fosse explained. "Just to make sure nothing gets written that wasn't said. Also," he continued, "maybe I'll use it for a project." As I was to learn after his death, Fosse was nearly as ubiquitous with his tape recorders as Andy Warhol, frequently pulling one out at parties, dinners, and business meetings, always on the pretense it was for "research."

We began discussing his style. Fosse acknowledged his debt to choreographers Jack Cole and Jerome Robbins, and dancers Fred Astaire, Gene Kelly, the Nicholas Brothers, and the former tap stylist trio, Slip, Slap, and Slyde. Interestingly, he counted the late stand-up comedian Joe Frisco among his *dance* influences, which made sense considering the amount of comedy in Fosse's choreography.

In his dancers, Fosse looked first for strong ballet technique. "I try not to look at the faces in the beginning," he said. "As we near the end [of auditions], I start looking more towards personality. And, of course, in today's musicals, singing and acting is also very important. . . . Also, [I demand] a sense of humor. Rehearsals are so long and tedious and difficult. I find that if there's a sense of humor involved, a person can get over some bumpy times. To be honest, I like attractive people who aren't so terribly aware that they are attractive, who aren't looking in the mirror

all the time to see that their leotard is on straight or hitched up exactly right. People who aren't afraid to roll on the floor and make fools out of themselves."

He pointed out the distinction between his rapport with nomadic dancers—responsible for the extended "Fosse family" of gypsies—and with other choreographers': "First of all, I happen to love dancers. I think a lot of choreographers don't. They fear the dancers, and out of that fear comes hostility. . . . I was a dancer. I know how hard it is to learn a step, to keep a performance fresh eight times a week." As for the Fosse dance family, he attributed dancers' loyalty to him because, through the years, he worked to keep them employed. However, he also pointed out the necessity to use "new blood": "It's a good chemistry to have some people who have been around me and sort of know my little tricks, and then have the [laughs] innocent ones, the poor kids who don't know what they're in for."

Many of Fosse's dancers and actors have gone on to become stars under his tutelage. He spoke warmly of performers Ben Vereen, Valerie Perrine, Liza Minnelli, Ann Reinking, Eric Roberts, Sandahl Bergman, and others whose careers peaked in Fosse movies and stage musicals. "There is a kind of thrill for me in discovering people and grooming them," he admitted. "There's a small trace of Svengali in me." In the early Eighties he had considered making a movie whose reason for being would be to use his favorite actors and dancers—"everybody who had ever worked for me and done a good job." But he realized the project was mostly self-indulgent; besides, he chuckled, "I could never think of a story."

Working with people he loved was the payoff for Fosse's time. Throughout his career, he rarely had more than a year's hiatus between shows. And, by the early Seventies, he hopscotched from stage to screen and back again, never fully recovering from the physical toll of one work before beginning on another. Fosse estimated it took him two years to complete a film and a year and a half for a Broadway show. "It's always a big chunk of time," he said, "especially when I'm going to be fifty-nine in June. You start thinking about those chunks. Do I still have it in me? Can I get myself to go through it all one more time?" With bypass surgery behind him and an out-of-body experience fresh in his memory, Fosse found himself at odds with a body that refused to comply with his own dance combinations.

Bob Fosse and first wife, Mary Ann Niles, were featured dancers in the 1950 Broadway revue *Dance Me a Song*. (*Billy Rose Theatre Collection*)

In Boston, where *Big Deal* played its pre-Broadway engagement, I recall watching Fosse attempt to demonstrate a combination to the dancers. He was harnessed into a back brace for his sciatica, and every step caused him pain. Amazingly, the combination itself was fluid and clearly stated. When I mentioned that afternoon in the interview, Fosse said that his infirmities had forced him to rely upon his dancers more frequently to demonstrate—of his past and present assistants and dance captains, he spoke particularly highly of Kathryn Doby, Louise Quick, Graciela Daniele, Christopher Chadman, and Linda Haberman. All are among the progenitors of his style today. He was not content, however, to be an armchair choreographer, and invariably found himself springing up to dance.

But Fosse's deteriorating health was a secondary concern; he was wounded equally by the critics' panning of his last film, *Star 80,* and stage musical, *Big Deal.* "You never find the toll of anything until sometime later," he said reflectively. "God, in His infinite wisdom, anesthetizes you for certain periods of time. While it's happening, you never know the final results of what you've been through."

It could be said, in fact, that Fosse felt adrift as a director and choreographer in his autumn years. *Big Deal,* which he considered his best work, was fraught with hostility between Fosse and the show's producers, angry clashes with the technical crew, and the principal performers' concern that Fosse's book did not flesh out their roles. He admitted making compromises along the way to appease "the money men," and regretting it later. Mostly, however, he believed he had been misunderstood by the critics, who wield the power to close a show in New York. On this count, he was particularly outspoken: "It hurts when you get a bad review. Frankly, I don't read them anymore, but I know about them. I ask, Is it good? Is it bad? Is it in the middle? I know that they jumped on me for this one [*Big Deal*], a couple of them, anyway. But, you see, a guy like [*New York Times* drama critic] Frank Rich is such an elitist! He's so separated from the audience and what it likes. I was at the show last night and the audience was screaming and cheering. . . .

"Maybe it's just vanity or my own kneejerk reaction to bad reviews, but I believe I know more than those critics, that I'm further ahead than they are. They want traditional, old-fashioned [musicals]—here's a song, here's a dance, here's a scene, etcetera. They want *South Pacific.* They want *The King and I.* . . . John Simon [*New York Magazine*] is outside of anything that has to do with anything. I mean, he's amusing, and he's certainly sarcastic and occasionally has a fascinating sense of cruelty, but I can see how he could destroy actors so they can never go on the stage again. . . . I can understand enjoying that sense of power he must get from being the meanest of them all."

I was anxious to get his impressions of his contemporaries. What, for example, did he think of Tommy Tune's nostalgic tribute to George and Ira Gershwin, *My One and Only*? "A piece of shit," he exclaimed. What about Stephen Sondheim and James Lapine's nondance musical *Sunday in the Park with George*? "A boring experience for most people."

Fosse himself seemed irritated at his harsh indictment of his peers. "Look, I have a lot of respect for anyone who can make a musical work these days," he conceded. "Tommy and Stephen are enormously talented.

Fosse with the omnipresent viewfinder during the filming of *Sweet Charity* *(Courtesy of MCA Publicity Rights, a division of MCA, Inc. Copyright © by Universal Pictures, a Division of Universe City Studios, Inc.)*

But I loved *Big Deal,* thought I'd done a lot of wonderful work on it. [After the reviews], I stayed away from the show for a couple of weeks. I went back to see it with this fear that I was going to see something that was bad that I thought was good. . . . If you care about your work, you're always concerned that maybe you are deluding yourself, because there's a tremendous amount of self-delusion in show business. . . . But, you know, I liked it a lot. I was really proud of it. I felt so relieved, I had tears running down my face."

As the afternoon wore on, Fosse wished to bring our interview to a close. We both fiddled with our cassette recorders, changing tapes, and I was struck by how similar this moment was to the interview scenes in his film *Lenny*. At one point, when we both shut off our machines for one of his many off-the-record comments, he laughed and said, "Maybe there's a movie in here somewhere."

Before we wrapped things up, I had to ask him: "Do you really wake up in the morning and say, 'Showtime, Folks!'?"

He smiled. "I used to say it. Everybody does. Guys still greet me on the street—garbage men, policemen—they all remember it. We all have to put on to make it through the day. One time I was going to do a film, a semidocumentary, about how everyone has to put on a show, how everybody wakes up and says, 'It's showtime!' "

I thought about this on the night of June 8, 1986, while attending the final performance of *Big Deal* at the Broadway Theatre. A house full of Fosse devotees, alumni from other shows, and friends did their best to prevent the final curtain from coming down, as if applause and shouts of "one more time" were enough to keep stagehands from striking this $5 million musical by evening's end. I still carry a vivid picture of one young man, perhaps a former Fosse dancer, who carried a single red rose to the apron of the stage as the audience filed out of the theater. He placed it on the floor and walked past me, tears streaming down his face.

A year later, at Fosse's memorial service at the Palace Theatre, Loretta Devine, who starred in *Big Deal,* sang a number from the show, "Life Is Just a Bowl of Cherries." The lyrics "You work/You save/You worry so/ But you can't take the dough/When you go, go, go" seemed almost comically relevant as I thought back on *Big Deal*'s final performance. Fosse may have gone to his grave kicking about *Big Deal*'s stillbirth on Broadway, but I had the feeling that day in the Palace that his spirit was hovering above the mezzanine, delighted at this assemblage of friends, family, and fans. More than anyone, Bob Fosse knew that the show must go on. And that day, he was his own best box office.

I

FIRST STAGES

Willy: Walk in with a big laugh. Don't look worried. Start off with a couple of good stories to lighten things up. It's not what you say, it's how you say it—because personality always wins the day.

—Death of a Salesman,
by Arthur Miller

*I'm a star
And they love me
And I love them
And they love me for loving them
And I love them for loving me
And that's because none of us got enough love
  in our childhoods
And that's show biz, folks!*

—*Gwen Verdon as*
Roxie Hart, Chicago

CHICAGO, ILLINOIS

y father was closer to Willy Loman than he was to George M. Cohan. My mother always used to say, 'Keep trying,' and my father always used to say 'Goodbye.' Like Lenny Bruce says, 'nobody stays, everybody goes.' "

Fosse provided a rare glimpse into his family background when he inadvertently allied himself with Biff Loman—the son of the itinerant salesman Willy Loman in Arthur Miller's examination of the decline of the American family, *Death of a Salesman*—and Lenny Bruce in a 1974 *Los Angeles Times* interview. Fosse seldom spoke about his family. Instead, the references to Loman and Bruce—men seeking stability in an unstable world—reveal themselves in Fosse's later, self-exploratory work, especially *Lenny,* Fosse's 1974 film study of comedian Lenny Bruce, and *All That Jazz,* a thinly veiled 1979 film autobiography. More importantly, they point to a recurring problem in his own maturation: the inability to sustain stable relationships with his family and lovers.

"Do you believe in love?" Angelique (Jessica Lange) asks Fosse's alter ego Joe Gideon (Roy Scheider) in *All That Jazz*. "I believe in saying I love you," Joe replies evasively.

Despite Fosse's father's frequent absences from home, his family was close, at least until the time of his mother's death. Fosse's family was typical of many Depression-era households. Employment was not easy to come by, and men with families in the Twenties and Thirties took jobs wherever they could find them; frequently the principal breadwinners

Bob Fosse and Charles Grass, about thirteen years old, as The Riff Bros., "Tap Dancing Par Excellence."

were miles away from their families. Cyril Fosse represented the first generation of postindustrial workers in Chicago. Prior to the turn of the century, Fosse's forefathers had been farmers.

Fosse's ancestory has been traced back to 1600 by Margaret S. Fosse, the widow of Fosse's second cousin, James Russel Fosse. The patriarch, Jakob Helgeson Bolstad, was a farmer from Bolstad, Norway (the men took their surnames from their respective town or farm names), whose sons and grandsons acquired numerous farms across that country in the early seventeenth century, occasionally holding a government office, such as sheriff. Bob Fosse's great-grandfather, Lars Andersson Fosse, was one of seven brothers born to Anders Larsson Mestad. Lars had purchased a farm called "Fosse" in Norway in 1836, and when it went bankrupt three years later he was forced to sell it. The brothers immigrated to America and settled throughout the Midwest, primarily in Wisconsin and Illinois.

Isaac Lars Fosse, Bob's grandfather, lived in Chicago as that city was developing from a frontier plat into a burgeoning center of trade and industry. The city's position on the edge of Lake Michigan, its intersection with the Chicago River, and the advent of eastern transportation facilities made Chicago one of the country's most important exchange hubs. Not surprisingly, Chicago's accessibility by water—and later, rail— attracted tens of thousands of immigrants, with a heavy concentration of Irish, Germans, Swedes, and Norwegians.

As the city expanded, its families settled into neighborhoods of common ethnic backgrounds. Industrialization and the promise of higher wages within the inner city tempted many farmers to abandon agriculture. By the time Fosse's father, Cyril Kingsley, was born in 1893, an area of prairie and farmland known as Lincoln Square had been annexed by the city and quickly blossomed into a thriving community of Germans and Swedes. Ravenswood, an area within the Lincoln Square perimeters where Bob Fosse was born, was a bustling center of light manufacturing and assembling plants after World War I.

As a thriving industrial city, Chicago brought with its financial clout attendant amenities, such as vaudeville and burlesque. Vaudeville was especially popular, and young Cyril Fosse and his brother, along with two friends, tentatively pursued the footlights with a "song and spoon" act. Fosse recalled to the *Los Angeles Times* that his father "played the spoons terrifically, and he had a fine tenor voice, but he thought that was effeminate." Cyril was especially close to his older brother, Dick, and though the two men would eventually drop out of show business to pursue more traditional careers, apparently Cyril reminisced often, and fondly, about his experiences on stage.

"I think my dad idolized Dick Fosse," Bob Fosse told the *Daily News* in 1972, "and after his death at thirty-three, I became a sort of continuation of Dick in my father's emotions." A year later in an interview with the *Chicago Sun-Times,* Fosse said, "My dad, I think, kind of romanticized about me taking [his brother's] place. He was always very anxious and hopeful that I'd be in show business."

In fact, when Fosse was born on June 23, 1927, Cyril and his wife, Sarah Alice Fosse, named their son after Robert Louis Stevenson, their favorite author—perhaps hoping he would one day grow up to become a literary figure. Fosse *would* become a writer in his later career, though his screenplays and librettos were always overshadowed by his direction and choreography. Sarah, who was known as Sadie, sold magazines over the telephone, but sometimes admitted to her children she harbored a fondness for the stage. A short, heavy Irish woman who had at one time played bit parts such as a spear-carrying extra in community light operas and would launch into a Scott Joplin rag on the family piano on a moment's notice, Sadie was the matriarch of a brood of children, four boys and two girls. Bob was the youngest of the boys, and, as a preschooler, found he could win the attention of his family by staging little dances in the living room.

Young Fosse attended Ravenswood Grammar School on Chicago's North Side. The Depression's economic hardships were felt in the public school systems, with sometimes as many as forty-eight children assigned to one classroom. For a child, it was easy to get lost in the shuffle, but Bob, already accustomed to jockeying for center stage in his family, earned early recognition with his participation in children's variety shows. When he was nine, Sadie and Cyril sent him to the Chicago Academy of Theater Arts with his older sister Pat to begin formal dance lessons. Pat dropped out after a few weeks, but young Robert continued.

"I met Bob when I was eight and going to Ravenswood," recalls childhood friend Marguerite Atcher. "He was a charming little boy, very likeable and very well liked. Bob and I attended Frederick Weaver's School of Dance, which was on the second floor of a drugstore. Mr. Weaver owned the school, but it was his wife, Marguerite Comerford, who did all the work.

"When I look back on Marguerite," Atcher continues, "I realize how truly talented she was in a number of areas. She taught tap, ballet, acrobatic, ballroom—you name it. Bob was studying tap, and I took ballroom and ballet. The school would put on shows from time to time for churches and fundraising events staged by Mr. Weaver, and he had an amazing group of kids to work with. I remember one show that was patterned after the Gibson Girl revue. There were all these little girls dressed up in Gibson Girl bustle dresses dancing as the boys sang, 'Tell me, pretty maiden, is there anyone like you at home?' Bob and this other little boy named Charlie Grass would hold their hands while the girls pirouetted around them."

Cyril and Sadie encouraged Bob, as did Atcher's parents, who became avid Fosse followers, and went to see him perform in area clubs and theaters. Fosse also was exposed to adult dancers through his older brother Bud, who was a member of the 400 Club, a group for ballroom dancers. In their twenties, Bud and his wife would go to the club with Bob and Marguerite in tow, laughing as the solemn-faced tykes imitated the smooth glides and dramatic dips of the adult ballroom dancers.

From the time he entered elementary school, Bob suffered from asthma, and neither Bud nor his other brothers encouraged him to pursue professional dancing. The other boys, all strapping young men with cleft chins and broad shoulders, ribbed Bob about the tights he carried in his schoolbag and the slight speech impediment that caused him to slur certain words ("breakfast" became "breffess"). Gene Foote, who danced in many of Fosse's shows, recalls Fosse discussing his childhood as being painful because of his size. "While we were filming *All That Jazz*," says Foote, ". . . Bob opened up a little about his childhood, which was very rare. He hardly ever talked about that part of his life. He told us he had been a small, pretty boy, who had to carry little chocolate candies in his pocket to give to the bigger boys so they wouldn't beat him up."

In spite of his size and the asthma, his teachers and his parents realized Bob was fast becoming a child prodigy. By the time he entered Amundsen High School in 1941, he was dancing professionally, with Weaver booking him into area nightclubs as the star of Bobby Fosse's Le Petit Cabaret, singing, tap dancing, and telling jokes. It was the beginning of what would become a schizophrenic adolescence for Fosse, who juggled his school work and extracurricular activities such as student government, swimming, track, and Latin with professional work. "He was more involved than I think anyone realized," says Miriom Meyer, who dated Fosse during their freshman year. Adds Marguerite Atcher, "My parents really worried about the clubs he was playing in. I mean, these clubs had scantily clad dancers. I couldn't even get in them because I was underage. But my parents would see him and rave about how wonderful he was. He used to get dressed up like Fred Astaire in tails and a top hat."

By the early Forties, the Fosse family had moved from the Ravenswood district to an imposing three-story stone house on Sheridan Road in a middle-class neighborhood on the North Side. Cyril was working as a salesman for Hershey's Chocolates ("At one of my birthday parties, Bob gave me a huge bag of Hershey Kisses," says Atcher), and was rarely home. With most of her older children grown and married or fighting in World War II, Sadie turned her attention to her two youngest children, Bob and Marianne. It was from Sadie that Bob drew most of his support as a young performer.

It is doubtful, however, that Sadie knew exactly what kind of clubs her son was performing in, since most of the time she was holding down the household while Cyril was on the road. In *All That Jazz,* Fosse captures his mother's naïveté in a scene in which she is standing in the foreground in an apron at the kitchen stove, while young Joe Gideon is seen in the background surrounded by strippers in a sleazy club. Looking directly at the camera, Sadie smiles proudly and says, "He worked in all those cheap burlesque clubs, but did it bother him? Never."

"My mother misunderstood," Fosse told the *New York Times* in 1979. "She thought you could send a boy of that age into a roomful of naked women and it wouldn't bother him—because he was such a good boy. Obviously, she was wrong. She was one of the smartest women I've ever known, though. She was quite manipulative and when she died the family disintegrated."

During Bob's elementary and high school years, the family did its best to enjoy its own company, especially when Cyril was home. Bob continued to juggle school and nightclubs. Barely thirteen, he, along with another former Ravenswood pupil, Charles Grass, performed as the Riff Bros. ("Dancers Par Excellence—Offer Ultra-Modern Tap Modes") in vaudeville and burlesque shows—sharing the program with strippers and off-pitch singers—and at movie house amateur nights. Even dressed like gangly Fred Astaires, neither looked older than sixteen. Their first night as "professionals," they opened at the Logan Theater, hurried to another show at the Midland, and finished their act with a late show at the neighborhood Otto's Beer Garden. Their take for the night would sometimes be in excess of $150. Then, there was school the next day.

Surprisingly, Fosse's nighttime excursions did not affect his school work at Amundsen. He graduated an honor student and president of his class, in addition to participating in various other extracurricular activities, including the Hi-Ys, a boys' club. He was popular with the girls, dating Miriom Meyer his freshman and sophomore years, and Miriom Wilson his last year. "The minute school was over," says Meyer, "Bob was at the studio taking class. We would dance at school functions sometimes, and he was a terrible ballroom dancer. I think he thought it

was mundane. He always wanted to step out and do his own thing."

"He was completely absorbed in his dancing," recalls Bill Mazer, a friend of Fosse's at Amundsen. "During the late Thirties and Forties, Chicago had a lot of vaudeville downtown. Bob and I used to skip school, take the elevated train, and go to theaters like the Oriental and the Chicago to see Bill 'Bojangles' Robinson or Paul Draper. For thirty-five cents you could see Robinson on a variety bill. We'd stay there all day, mesmerized, and later Bob'd go back home and try to imitate his steps. He always rehearsed alone.

"The clubs that Bobby performed in, places like Cuban Village, the Silver Cloud, and Cave of the Winds, were all on the North Side. But we'd go down to the predominantly black South Side and check out the acts there. We'd hang out at this one place called the Club Delisa, watch these great tap dancers and hear really good jazz singers. It didn't matter that we were underage; the only reason more whites didn't go to the South Side was fear, and Bobby was fearless."

Fosse was concerned that not everyone at Amundsen would approve of his "night shift" gigs. Miriom Wilson says that while she and Fosse "seriously dated" their senior year, he knew she was looking for "a more stable kind of guy." I liked him for who he was as a person; I wasn't impressed by his dancing. Some of the best times we had were in the Hi-Ys, the fellows' athletic [and social] club, and the Tri-Hi-Ys, the girls' club. We'd go to dances and hayrides, or, in the summer, to the beach. He was very good-looking, and in the summer he always had a deep tan and his blond hair would get blonder. He was a very clean-cut young man.

"But the more we talked about him wanting to be an entertainer,

Fosse, about seventeen, performing at the Cuban Village, Chicago.

the more I realized it was a life-style I wasn't interested in. Bob was exposed to things most of us [at Amundsen] weren't. Today's young people think nothing of promiscuity, but I knew little about nightclubs and such, places where that sort of thing went on. And so Bob kept that part of his life from me—and probably a lot of people at school—because he knew we didn't understand it. Eventually we both decided to see other people."

One of the people Fosse saw was a waitress he met while performing with Charles Grass in Springfield, Illinois. She was in her thirties. Fosse was fifteen. Their affair lasted until her husband came back from overseas, where he was a serviceman during World War II, and accused his wife in their divorce action of sleeping with a minor, along with four other young men. Fosse was named in the divorce suit, charged with adultery. "I was panicked at the time," he told *Playboy* in 1979, "still

in high school and afraid my mother would find out. As I got older, it made a good story."

One reason Fosse was able to ease his way into nightclubs as a teenager was that World War II had depleted the ranks of legal-age performers in the city. They were overseas storming Nazis while fourteen-year-old Bobby Fosse—introduced by emcees as "Chicago's youngest"—would shuffle through "Tea for Two" in his tails and taps and deliver punch lines to jokes whose double entendres he didn't always understand. He fantasized of performing in premiere clubs such as Chicago's Chez Paris, which had a real cabana and linen tableclothes, but settled for work wherever he found it, and most often he found it in dives—the Silver Cloud and Cave of the Winds—with names far more enchanting than the clientele.

Fosse and steady high school girlfriend Miriom Geweke.

America's urban landscape in the Twenties, Thirties, and Forties had changed radically, and the strippers Fosse encountered in the burlesque clubs were evidence of a surge of permissive sexuality brought on by the rapid industrialization of Chicago. While Fosse's neighborhood, a quiet residential area on a tree-lined street of middle-income homes, appeared to be a bastion of Methodist morality, clubs such as the Silver Cloud were holdovers from pre-World War I, a time of unprecedented sexual expression. The Depression and World War II caused many once-lavish cabarets of the Twenties to close; those that survived fell into disrepair and burlesque, once a legitimate theatrical genre of satire and parody, became vulgarized.

Choreographer Donald (*On Your Toes*) Saddler, who danced with Fosse on Broadway in the 1950 revue *Dance Me a Song,* notes that the revue's popular formula of song, dance, and comedy stemmed from burlesque in its original form. "A group of actors would do a burlesque on an opera or the latest hit show," he says. "In its heyday, it was a great art form, making stars out of people like Phil Silvers and W. C. Fields. Later on, though, burlesque got lower and lower, as cheap comics were brought in telling cheap jokes. The word *burlesque* as we know it today is far removed from its original definition."

Because Fosse was exposed to burlesque at a time when it was degenerating as an art form, his affinity for it owed as much to its once-glamorous image as it did to its evolution as a sideshow of tastelessness. His later work drew from both extremes. "I've been accused of vulgarity in sections of *Dancin',*" he remarked to the *Bulletin* in 1979. "But what some think is vulgar, I think is Rabelaisian, like the burlesque shows I sometimes played in my teens. Sure there's some rough stuff, but I was raised in burlesque, so rough is part of me."

Because of cabaret and burlesque, the white working and middle classes were exposed to indigenous forms of black music and jazz, and many youths picked up on the overt and implied sexual expression found in the music of the era. On the other hand, for many the Depression signaled the end of the Twenties' permissiveness, and Roosevelt's New Deal stimulated widespread social reform and a return to fundamental family values. Young Bob Fosse was dancing in clubs that seemed caught in a time warp. Unquestionably, his sexual encounters with the burlesque dancers affected the way he would relate to women as an adult.

"The strippers were something, you know?" Fosse confessed to *Penthouse* in 1973. "Tough. Really tough. That's where my scene with women started. I mean, it was really weird. I'd sit in the back somewhere studying my Latin. I was only sixteen so I had to keep studying. Anyway, when these strippers discovered I was sixteen, they didn't believe it.

They'd wait until the emcee was about to announce my dance, and then they'd try to give me a hard-on. They'd walk out into the hallway with nothing on, or grab me and start playing with me. By the time I got out front to do my act, the only thing I could think of was covering myself."

He had an inclination toward false bravado: "I could go back to school and tell the guys stories that were at least seventy-five percent true." Still, Fosse didn't expose the subculture of the Silver Cloud and Cave of the Winds to many of his high school friends. Instead, he threw himself into Amundsen activities. "During those years," says Mazer, "Bob Fosse was loved by his teachers, his fellow students, his family, everyone he touched. People wanted to be with Bob."

Fosse was especially close to two Greek students in his class, George Foutris and Socrates Markos. Amundsen was unique in its extensive ancient languages department; consequently, the high school attracted many Greek students, despite its location in a predominantly Scandinavian and German neighborhood. Both Foutris and Markos are now deceased, but many students from their class recall that the three young men would stage outlandish concerts in which they would dress up like the Andrews Sisters and lip-sync to the trio's hit songs. In fact, after graduation, Fosse attempted to persuade Foutris and Markos to take the act on the road. "Of course, George and Socki said no," says Kiki Foutris, George's daughter. "They all knew it was Bob who had the talent."

"George was a wrestler, and he really loved Bobby," Mazer remembers. "The Greeks were mostly football players and wrestlers, while the Swedes and Norwegians ran track and were on the swim team. But for some reason, Bob just hit it off with the Greeks, and they adored him."

Many of those students who knew of Fosse's nightclub work must have found it exotic and mystifying. The genial Andrews Sisters mugging in the Amundsen auditorium contrasted jarringly with the big-bosomed boom-boom girls at the Silver Cloud. But years later, Fosse would be able to look back with a critical and often affectionate eye at the Silver Cloud, Cave of the Winds, and Otto's Beer Garden. These clubs, no longer in existence, would be immortalized as the Fandango Ballroom in *Sweet Charity,* the Kit Kat Club in *Cabaret,* the basement after-hours clubs where Lenny Bruce performed in *Lenny,* and the sleazy mud-wrestling and wet T-shirt shows staged by Paul Snider in *Star 80.* In *All That Jazz,* Fosse went so far as to re-create the actual Silver Cloud stage, complete with real-life stripper Rita Bennett.

Set designer Tony Walton, who won an Oscar for his "fantasy sequences" in *All That Jazz* and was a long-time friend of Fosse's, says, "It's hard to know to what degree burlesque dominated his early life, because the frequency with which it surfaces in his work is probably way out of proportion. Burlesque was not something he had to do because he came from a poor family. It was something he chose to do."

In the meantime, Fosse continued studying dance with steadfast determination. Across the street from the high school there was a large loft where he would spend two or three hours dancing. He began studying with Georgie Tapps, a noted hoofer-turned-teacher, who taught him how to minimize schtick and refine his dancing. Tapps showed Fosse how to work around his physical handicaps, such as his slouch, bowed legs, and inarticulate fingers. Grace is as important as technique, Tapps emphasized, and he encouraged Fosse to see as many different knds of dance as possible—ballet, flamenco, jazz, and, of course, tap.

One of the dancers whose work Fosse admired greatly was Paul Draper, remembered today for combining the upper body discipline of classical ballet with tap dancing. His philosophy of dance was defined by the relationship of the human being to the rest of the world, rather than the common notion that dance is a purely recreational form of self-expression or leisure activity. Draper, who died in 1977 at the age of seventy-one, performed with harmonica veteran Larry Adler throughout the country and was hugely popular with top-drawer supper club and nightclub audiences at places such as the Copacabana and the Blackstone Hotel, both in Chicago. Fosse tried to see him whenever he was in town. When American Dance Machine presented the PBS television special, "Paul Draper on Tap" by Camera 3, in the late Seventies, Fosse appeared as one of the show's commentators.

"I first saw Paul Draper when I was fifteen, at the Blackstone Hotel," Fosse recalled. "I had never seen such showmanship or dancing to Bach. He was the most elegant performer I'd ever seen, including Fred Astaire. Paul created magic, a kind of enchantment. He had a lot of imitators, but, no doubt about it, Paul Draper affected everyone's style."

By the time Fosse played the Cuban Village, a giant step forward in terms of club respectability, his act was polished and professionally staged. Sharing a bill with dancers in Carmen Miranda costumes skittering across the stage with bobbing head pieces made of waxed fruit, and stand-up comedians who didn't have stains on their ruffled tuxedo shirts, was indeed a career move in the right direction. "If Bobby hadn't gone into the Navy," says Bill Mazer, "he might have ended up playing in some elite place like Chez Paris. But then there was the war."

Fosse was barely seventeen when he enlisted in the Navy. It was 1945, and World War II was coming to an end. The fever of patriotism ran high across the country, and Amundsen graduates were, according to Dale Arvidson, a high school friend of Fosse's who had dated his sister, Pat, eager to enlist. "All of us knew we were going into the war," says Arvidson. "It wasn't like today when so many young men don't want to fight for their country. If you weren't in the service, it was not good news."

As a sophomore, Fosse had danced at USO (United Service Organization) shows that featured the Playboys, a group of performers that included Arvidson. Performing in American Legion halls and churches with servicemen clubs, Fosse realized that there was an enormous need to boost the morale of troops. At the same time, the young man who was president of his graduating class and voted most likely to succeed wanted desperately to get out of Chicago and travel. The Navy offered him both opportunities. He'd barely made it into boot camp when, on September 5, 1945, Allied forces defeated Japan, and V-J day was declared, officially ending the war. Fortuitously, Fosse was transferred to the Navy's Special Services entertainment division.

He performed throughout the Pacific with a company of thirteen other men, including Joseph Papp, an officer who would eventually become the New York Shakespeare Festival's artistic director. They staged topical, vestpocket editions of musicals such as *Hook, Line and Sinker*. In 1987, Papp recalled to the *New York Times,* "I saw at once that he was footjoy, carefree, jaunty. He loved to dance. On some islands he would perform in the hot sun for five or six hours. He'd go on until he nearly collapsed from the heat." When on leave, Fosse returned to Sheridan Road, or looked up old Amundsen girlfriends. Miriom Wilson and Miriom Meyer both recall a seemingly more mature Bob Fosse visiting them. "He had really grown up," says Wilson, "but that was inevitable. After all, he'd been away in the Navy. I'd been at home. We'd changed, and we wanted different things."

In 1946, Fosse returned to Chicago to attend the wedding of Miriom Meyer and, according to Dale Arvidson, was "crushed." "We sat on the fender of a car and talked for forty-five minutes," Arvidson said, laughing. "Bob was ready to end it all right there. He was so in love with that girl. I was the best man, and felt pretty bad about it all, but, looking back, I don't know why. Bob always had a girl, or two, and I guess he felt like this was the one he shouldn't have let get away." Eventually, a long-time confidante from the neighborhood, Ed "the barber" Banaka, was brought in to console Fosse's unrequited heart. "He told Bob, 'get in your car and go to Hollywood where you belong.'"

But he didn't go West. When Fosse's two-year stint in the Navy was complete, his ship docked in New York City. Hollywood would have to wait.

NEW YORK

For someone who spent a great deal of his time directing and choreographing stage and film musicals about rookies trying to break into the big time—from *Damn Yankee*'s star batter Joe Hardy to *Star 80*'s Playmate Dorothy Stratten—-Bob Fosse's own entrée into show business was remarkably unobstructed. When he finished his two-year stint abroad with the Navy, his ship docked in New York City and, with $200 in his pocket, he rented a room at Sloane House near Times Square for 35 cents a day. It was 1946, and Broadway fairly luminesced with stars performing in now-landmark shows. Among them were *Born Yesterday* with Judy Holliday, *Annie Get Your Gun* with Ethel Merman, Lillian Hellman's *Another Part of the Forest* with Patricia Neal, Eugene O'Neill's *The Iceman Cometh* with Martin Balsam, and a slight but popular revue that would be Fosse's introduction to Broadway, *Call Me Mister* with Betty Garrett.

Marian Horosko, a former New York City Ballet dancer who danced with Fosse in 1950's *Dance Me a Song,* re-creates a bustling thoroughfare of theater and employment opportunities for performers in the Forties: "Broadway at that time was very busy with shows opening and closing quickly. It gave employment to a lot of people; you could get a job fairly easily then. There were either very serious plays or revues, many of which were quite sophisticated and focused. Ballet dancers were welcomed, because if a choreographer asked you for an arabesque glissade grand jeté, you almost always could do it better than anyone who didn't

Fosse and first wife, Mary Ann Niles, when they performed an act in the early Fifties. *(Courtesy of Dance Magazine)*

have classical-ballet training. Our attitude then was that a job was a job, and since ballet seasons only lasted ten to twelve weeks a year, Broadway was what you did between seasons. The work was not bad, and you could make good money. *Oklahoma!* paid $82 a week, which were union wages set by the Theater Guild. My rent at that time for my apartment in Greenwich Village was $45 a month, so I considered myself pretty well off. I had nice clothes, went to places like the Stage Door Canteen, and did extra matinees for the servicemen."

Predictably, postwar musicals in the Forties were stamped with patriotism and military nostalgia. Composer Harold Rome had become associated with Broadway songs that sentimentalized American prosperity for the working class, primarily due to the success of a 1937 revue based on a labor union, *Pins and Needles*. Ten years later, he wrote the music for *Call Me Mister,* about army veterans readjusting to civilian life. It was Fosse's first job as a Broadway gypsy, though the production he was cast for was a road tour. Fresh from the Navy, Fosse could not have been better suited for *Call Me Mister;* he was exactly the sort of young recruit whose life inspired Rome's music. The company also included Buddy Hackett, Carl Reiner, William Warfield, Howard Morris, and another relative newcomer to Broadway, Mary Ann Niles.

Call Me Mister toured with great success for over a year, and during that time Fosse and Niles became close. She was four years older, had studied with some well-known dance teachers in New York, including Nenette Charisse and Francis Cole, and was beginning to accumulate a promising list of chorus role credentials in Broadway shows, beginning with 1945's *The Girl from Nantucket*. To a greenhorn like Bob Fosse, Niles must have seemed particularly impressive. She was not a great beauty, but had a fetching dimpled smile and green eyes, laughed easily, and held her own with the boisterous male members of the company. Most importantly, she was a crack hoofer, and Fosse was immediately attracted to her knowledge of tap and jazz dance. Marian Horosko remembers the couple in *Dance Me a Song*. "Mary Ann was dominant in the relationship, that was very plain to see."

For Fosse, who had never been able to find a girlfriend in high school fully supportive of his fledgling dance career, Niles would be the first of three wives to further his dance education. Because she was a bit older than Fosse and had a slight edge in her performing career, he looked to her for advice. From him, she sought dance direction, and the two would spend hours rehearsing tap numbers, fantasizing about an act they would take on the road when *Call Me Mister* finished touring. He began choreographing tap and jazz combinations for her, and their partnership became a pas de deux in the most literal sense. While the show was in Chicago in 1947, they decided to get married.

The ceremony at St. Chrysostom Church was attended by many of Fosse's Amundsen classmates, who recall that Niles and Fosse "looked like a Hollywood couple." There was a reception held in the theater after a performance of *Call Me Mister,* and Miriom Wilson, Fosse's former high school steady, was "overwhelmed" by his new wife and stage friends. "It was what he'd always wanted," she says. "All the glamour and the attention. Everyone in the show was very nice and friendly, but I felt so apart from them. Bob was his usual charming self, but more directed. He was definitely where he wanted to be."

The Fosse and Niles dance act was formed shortly after the two finished their stint in *Call Me Mister.* Both had worked briefly in the failed road production of *Make Mine Manhattan* with Bert Lahr in 1948, and decided that a dance act would give them stronger credibility within their profession. They followed a tradition of dance couples in the Thirties and Forties, ideally patterned after Fred Astaire and Ginger Rogers. Fosse dismissed their efforts to *People* magazine in 1979, claiming he and Niles were "a second-rate Marge and Gower Champion."

"There were a lot of dancing couples in those days," recalls Marian Horosko. "It was the end of an era when every show had a dancing couple act—brothers and sisters, husbands and wives—because you could get more work that way than as a solo act. A lot of men and women teamed up, broke up, and made other teams. Neither Bob nor Mary Ann were strong enough individually to make it solo, but, together, they were an act."

The Fosse and Niles dance team got a date at the Hotel Pierre in New York, which led to more engagements at three- and four-star establishments, among them the Plaza, the Waldorf, the Astoria, and Chicago's Palmer House. Several talent scouts spotted them or learned of them through reviews in the dailies. Soon they were making guest appearances on television variety shows, including *Hit Parade, Omnibus,* and, finally, a mini-contract with Sid Caesar for *Your Show of Shows.* Theatrical producer Dwight Deere Wiman saw them and contracted Fosse and Niles for the first Broadway musical in which they appeared as an act, in 1950's *Dance Me a Song.*

Like many Broadway offerings of the day, the show was a pastiche of loosely related scenes presented as comedic sketches, song-and-dance numbers, ballets, and dramatic scenes. Frequently, one or two stars headed the large vaudevillian cast; in *Dance Me a Song,* Wally Cox was the Top Banana, while Broadway musical-comedy star Joan McCracken handled the dance assignments. Its creative staff included writers Cox, Vincente Minnelli, Jimmy Kirkwood, and Robert Anderson; choreography by Robert Sidney; songs by James Shelton; and orchestrations by Robert Russell Bennett, all of whom were well-established in their fields.

Perhaps most interesting were the chorus dancers in some of these slight divertissements. In the Forties and early Fifties, Broadway boasted many classical and modern-trained dancers, culled between seasons, from the concert stage dance world. These included dancers who would go on to become legendary on Broadway, ballet, and modern dance stages—Jerome Robbins, Valerie Bettis, Alexandra Danilova, Nora Kaye, Bertram Ross, and Donald McKayle, to name but a few. The moniker "gypsy" perfectly describes these nomadic performers, wandering from show to show in search of a steady income or a permanent company. American Ballet Theater soloist Donald Saddler, who partnered Joan McCracken in *Dance Me a Song,* says, "Everyone worked in musicals just to exist, hoping that a little [dance] company would start up in the meantime. Or you might go into the opera ballet. It was not considered lowering your standards to go into a Broadway show."

In rehearsals for the show, it was apparent Fosse and Niles had different designated responsibilities in their act. "Watching them perform," says Saddler, "you could tell she was more experienced; she knew how to flirt with an audience. There was a more finished quality about her dancing than Bob's. He just looked so young, like he was just soaking up the limelight. She was a fabulous tap dancer. I think she taught him a lot about tap."

Of Fosse's contributions as a dancer, Marian Horosko is more critical. "Bob was very skinny with light hair—he nearly faded out of the number. His chest was sunken, and he looked a little tubercular. Whereas his dancing was limp, Mary Ann was out there every night smiling with clear taps, really selling the thing. I kept thinking she could do very well without him. I remember watching him sit on the edge of the stage slouched over and looking glum. He looked so far away and absent-minded. 'Is everything all right?' I'd ask. He'd sort of mumble 'Well, I'm a little depressed.'

"Bob's big come-on was that he seemed so helpless. You just wanted to hug him and bring him out of it. He was attractive, but not in a strong, masculine way. It was his soft, vulnerable quality that so many women found appealing. I'd watch Bob and Mary Ann and think, 'Why doesn't he give up dancing and choreograph?' because their number together was really good. It was a straight tap number with interplay between them, but he never seemed to respond to her on stage. Mary

Ann had a lot of clarity as a dancer, with wonderful changes of rhythm. Bob just seemed detached as a dancer, as though he was choreographing himself out of the number. He was keenly observant and projected intelligence. If you were performing around him, you wanted to dance a little better because he was tuning in to you. But I don't think he had a clear sense of his career at this point. For that, it seemed he looked to Mary Ann.''

Bob Fosse and Mary Ann Niles. *(Courtesy of Dance Magazine)*

Saddler, who shared a dressing room with Fosse, says his own ballet background seemed to humble Fosse, since, aside from a few lessons as a child, Fosse had focused less on classical dance than popular idioms such as tap and jazz. Throughout his life, Fosse would treat ballet dancers with respect and admiration, believing, rightly, that ballet technique is the foundation for all dancing. Many ballet dancers became the core (and chorus) of his Broadway shows, and his never-completed ballet for the Joffrey sought to reconcile his own razzle dazzle with the perfect discipline of fundamental ballet principles.

"He had a very inquisitive mind," Saddler says, "always asking questions and wanting me to demonstrate technical things to him. I would bring in books for him to look at, and he absorbed everything quickly. Opening night, I gave him a beautiful book on Picasso, which seemed to take him by surprise. I believe he liked the fact that I recognized he was talented and wanting to develop further. He had a very appealing naïveté and, at the same time, willful determination. For both of us, there was this sense that we really knew where we were in our lives at this time. We were privileged because we were doing something we loved and making a living at it. There was no question that we were going to get what we wanted."

Fosse was twenty-three when he danced with Niles in *Dance Me a Song,* and the two had been married for two years when Fosse became infatuated with Joan McCracken, one of the show's stars. Barely more than a chorus boy, Fosse was presumptuous to think she would be interested in a younger, married man—and in the same show. Examining the anatomy of their clandestine backstage romance, people in the show remarked that Fosse never really fell out of love with Niles, but that, with her, his growth as a performer had stopped. He was awed by McCracken's charisma and her knowledge of dance. More so, she was one of the first professional dancers he'd met who did not live in an insular world whose perimeters were defined by the ballet barre and seemingly endless auditions.

"Joan was the kind of woman who would come to rehearsal with a copy of Proust or Kierkegaarde," says Saddler. "That impressed Bob. She knew the poets of the day, and was married to Jack Dunphey, who was considered a serious writer at that time. Bob wanted to be part of the group she was in; to him, it must have seemed like a different world. Joan was older, the star of the show, and had this intellectual world floating around her. She was very determined, and Bob liked that, too. If she set her mind to do something, she did it."

Like Sadie Fosse, Joan was Irish, with an irrepressible spirit that helped her win pivotal supporting roles on Broadway in her early career. At fifteen, she left high school to join the Littlefield Ballet Company in Pennsylvania as its youngest soloist. She toured with the company before joining the Radio City corps de ballet, which she later left to dance with Eugene Loring's Dance Players. The Dance Players were a versatile group of performers, trained in ballet, but with a repertory embracing a number of styles. After an eight-month tour with the company, McCracken heard about auditions for a new musical called *Oklahoma!* with choreography by Agnes de Mille, and decided to try out.

Believing she was as qualified as the best ballerina in the show, McCracken audaciously asked de Mille for a soloist spot. Unperturbed, de Mille watched her auditions and determined she had the appropriate feistiness for the Girl Who Falls Down cameo. McCracken's opening night performance in 1943 generated the sort of hullaballoo Gwen Verdon would receive ten years later for her "scandalous" kicks in *Can-Can.* "You could have sopped the audience up with a piece of bread," recalls de Mille. Although larger musical-comedy roles would come with 1946's *Billion Dollar Baby* and 1952's *Me and Juliet,* McCracken would always be known as the Girl Who Falls Down. Horosko, who danced with McCracken in the chorus of *Oklahoma!,* says, "We used to tease her and call her Little Mic because she had this terrible Irish temper and could be a hard drinker."

Oklahoma! propelled McCracken out of the chorus and into the public eye. *Life* magazine published photographs of her famous pratfall from the show in a full-color spread, and, shortly thereafter, Warner Bros. signed her for a film musical, 1944's *Hollywood Canteen.* It was an enormous box-office success but did little to establish McCracken as a formidable new film dance star. Three years later, with the success of *Bloomer Girl* and *Million Dollar Baby* behind her, McCracken was picked up by MGM for a remake of the 1930 co-ed musical, *Good News.*

That movie musical, which starred June Alyson and Peter Lawford, showed off McCracken's talent to better effect in a number called "Pass That Peace Pipe." Again, McCracken's dancing was called out by critics. Despite MGM's promise of more musicals, she returned to Broadway, where she had become a darling of the press. The dailies devoted long features to her zealous dedication to ballet class; in one, she gives instructions on how to perform arabesques, *pas de chats,* and *bris* "right in your own living room." The press also gave ample space to her idiosyncratic habits, which included eating candied apples after performances and sleeping in an antique sleigh bed with a whistle chained to it, because she was afraid of living alone.

McCracken's ill-fated Hollywood career was typical of many Broadway dancers who migrated West in the Forties and Fifties. Both McCracken and Fosse would have been well-suited to the RKO musicals of the Thirties, but their talents were barely tapped by Hollywood musicals of the late Forties and Fifties. McCracken expressed her disregard for Hollywood in an insightful 1946 *Dance Magazine* article, though she chose to focus on the problems of cinematizing dance rather than political disputes. Many of her comments foretell how Fosse would revolutionize film dance, removing the restrictions imposed by hidebound arbiters of moral standards. More importantly, McCracken addressed fundamental questions of how dance should be filmed, still relevant four decades later!

"There is yet much to be discovered in the filming of dancing. . . . In the movies today dancing is a photographed reproduction of what happens on stage. Why not photograph what can't happen on stage? . . . Dancing is movement and the movies could make it move even more if the stage were forgotten, . . . I think although these ideas are not revolutionary, they are more constructive than what may be offered by some people who maybe have not thought for the movies, but worked for them."

Dance Me a Song was not a hit, but it was a pivotal show for Fosse—his first chance to perform on Broadway, and his introduction to McCracken, who was eager to show Fosse the interconnectedness between musical theater dancing and other art disciplines. Encouraged by Oscar Hammerstein to take acting lessons while in *Oklahoma!,* McCracken went on to study at the Neighborhood Playhouse with Sanford Meisner and Herbert Berghoff, and at the Actors' Studio under Lee Strasberg. Although many dancers in the Forties were encouraged by directors to study acting, McCracken's voraciousness was unusual. Eventually acting would supplant dance as her primary interest, leading many who knew her to speculate that her career might have been better regarded today had she'd stayed with musical comedies. "Hollywood was screaming for her," Agnes de Mille says. "She could have gone on to be a big star."

McCracken, too, was married when she met Fosse, but her husband, Jack Dunphey, a dancer-turned-writer she'd met while in *Oklahoma!* who was also Irish and from Philadelphia, went to South America to work for George Balanchine's American Ballet company. McCracken could not follow him because she was diabetic, and, at that time, could not get insulin in South America. Upon leaving the ballet company, Dunphey joined the Army in South America, and begged McCracken to move there.

Donald Saddler, who was friendly with Fosse, Niles, and Mc-

Cracken, says it is too painful for him to talk openly about the dissolution of Fosse's first marriage during *Dance Me a Song.* "Their lives are very private to me. It was sad and disturbing, what happened to them, and I respect them too much to go into it. I will say [the affair between Fosse and McCracken] was something we were all aware of, and it was very painful, as all these things are. It was not easy for Bob or Mary Ann."

Fosse and Niles divorced in 1951, barely two years after their marriage, and, a few months later, Fosse married McCracken, who had divorced Dunphey shortly before. The two moved into a spacious penthouse apartment with a garden terrace and, for the first time in his life, Fosse settled into a semblance of domestic tranquility, if not stability. Although Niles and Fosse did not part amicably, years later she would perform for Fosse in *Sweet Charity,* and cast members recall good-humored if acerbic exchanges between them. Like many couples in show business, both found it impossible to work as husband and wife when it was obvious they were growing in different directions. However, they never lost respect for one another's talents.

Says Marian Horosko, "Mary Ann used to tell everyone what a bad boy Bob was, although you could not believe this from knowing him. Having met all of his wives, it seemed to me he was, as a young man, looking for stronger, older, wiser women. Maybe he thought they would take care of him, nurture him. But Mary Ann and Joan ended up being big put-downs for him. Only Gwen [Verdon, his third wife] gave him the support and encouragement he needed."

Perhaps the saddest and most tragic of Fosse's marriages was that to McCracken. As with Niles, career disappointments and an affinity for alcohol would unhinge McCracken's marriage and her life.

In 1951, McCracken was hitting her stride in New York, beginning to act in dramatic roles and being pursued for musical parts on Broadway. Offstage, she was also playing Henry Higgins to Bob Fosse's Eliza, exposing him to her rarefied world of New York's intelligentsia, taking him to museum exhibitions and poetry readings. Perhaps her biggest service to Fosse's career was prodding him to study acting and dance. He began an intensive self-improvement course, using his GI bill, beginning with classes at the Actors Studio. Modern dance choreographer Anna Sokolow, one of Fosse's teachers, describes her classes as "exercises in training the body to be an instrument to express. You had to have technique, but I emphasized that technique wasn't enough." Sokolow counted Anne Bancroft, James Dean, and Marlon Brando among her pupils, and Fosse considered himself fortunate to be among them. As one of Martha Graham's original dancers, Sokolow was also considered one of the best modern dance teachers, and she remembers Fosse "and the other showbiz types" as being "really curious about different ways of expression through movement."

Joan McCracken, Fosse's second wife, in a photograph taken shortly before she died. *(Billy Rose Theatre Collection)*

In addition to Sokolow's classes, he studied under the tutelage of José Limon and Charles Weidman, but admitted in a 1975 *Dance Magazine* profile, "I was always very bad in class; it was slightly humiliating. But I did a lot of rehearsing by myself. I would go into a studio for three or four hours and just dance. So I became a semi-efficient, self-made dancer. I had a great deal of trouble with turnout [a position of the feet in which the heels are back to back] and extension [a dance movement in which the leg is extended at an angle to the body]. To compensate for this, I used to work on other areas, such as rhythm, style of movement, taking ordinary steps and giving them some little extra twist or turn. And I guess my 'style' came about mainly as a result of my own limitations as a dancer, and those limitations have forced me into a certain economy of movement."

He also enrolled in the American Theater Wing, where his curriculum included acting, diction, ballet, singing, and choreography. His arduous studying paid off; in 1952 he was hired as the understudy to Harold Lang in the title role in a revival of *Pal Joey*. When the show went on tour, he took over the role and won rave reviews (as he did when he reprised the role ten years later in a City Center Light Opera production opposite Viveca Lindfors).

While at the American Theater Wing, one of Fosse's showcase presentations was a scene from *Time of Your Life,* which he'd seen Gene Kelly perform on stage. A talent scout from MGM was in the audience, and recommended to the studio that Fosse be given a screen test in New York. The footage was sent to Hollywood, and one of the studio's musical directors, Stanley Donen, liked what he saw. Hollywood was going to make young Bob Fosse its next Fred Astaire.

HOLLYWOOD

I was looking for someone to be in a movie I never made," recalls director Stanley Donen. "It was called *Jumbo,* and I tested Bobby for the part. MGM signed him to a contract, and his first big role for me was with Debbie Reynolds in *Give a Girl a Break*." The movie, a "second-rung" musical with choreography by Gower Champion, with whom Fosse also danced, and a thin score by Ira Gershwin and Burton Lane, was a stage-door romance about three hopeful young women in pursuit of the lead in a new Broadway musical.

Lillian Sidney, who for eighteen years was responsible for developing new talent at Metro as well as preparing new actors for their screen tests, says that Fosse "did very well" on his first screen test. "Bobby had the most wonderful dramatic ability. The drama you see in his choreography and his direction was all part of that sensibility he had. But even at his young age then, he knew that he would not have the opportunities of doing all he was capable of doing in Hollywood at that time. There were already established stars for the sort of musical roles he wanted to play. But there's no question in my mind that had he arrived on the scene earlier, he would have been a big star. Even today, if Bobby would be just beginning in the business, he'd have a better shot of getting work as an actor than he did then."

Fosse's bid for stardom in *Give a Girl a Break* was a number in which he dances with a balloon. One of his favorite anecdotes was how a stunning backward flip he performs was an "accident." He had been

Ann Miller and Bob Fosse chat with Cole Porter, seated, composer of the score of *Kiss Me Kate. (Photofest)*

unable to complete the flip during rehearsals, but, once the film began rolling, he did the back flip in one take. But *Give a Girl a Break* did not break any records at the box office, and had little impact on the careers of any of its stars. Fosse considered it "a bad movie. I think it was released on Forty-second Street, and then died."

Debbie Reynolds, who recalls that Fosse was "brilliantly talented and a good, natural actor," believes, like Lillian Sidney, that had Fosse been born earlier Hollywood would have been able to utilize his dance talents to better advantage. "He was a creature of time," Reynolds says. "We were working during the decline of the star system, when musicals went out of fashion. Finally, MGM let all of us go, and we were forced to change gears to survive. Bobby started getting more involved with choreographing. I was the only one who stayed at MGM. The studio had me under contract so cheaply, it would have been ridiculous for them not to keep me."

Shortly after Fosse began working for MGM, he met his idol, Fred Astaire. Fosse frequently spoke of the encounter and of the impression Astaire made on him. Apparently, while on his first day of work at MGM, director Stanley Donen offered to show Fosse the way to the studio commissary. En route through the labyrinth of alleys, a door suddenly opened and out walked Fred Astaire. Donen introduced the two men and then engaged Astaire in conversation. While he was talking, Astaire began playing with a bent nail he spied on the ground. He moved it about a bit with the toe of his shoe, then, with an emphatic stomp of his heel, sent the nail soaring through the air and into a nearby wall. The conversation ended, and Astaire walked away.

Donen continued toward the commissary, but Fosse held back. "I'm not really hungry," he said. "First day jitters, I guess." Donen shrugged and left Fosse standing near the bent nail. An hour later, returning to the sound studio, Donen saw Fosse in the exact same place where he'd left him. Coming nearer, he noticed that the young man was intently, obsessively, attempting to repeat Astaire's trick—using his toe to launch the bent nail through the air and into the wall, over and over, until he finally succeeded.

McCracken uprooted herself from New York, and, with Fosse, moved to Los Angeles, a city she deplored, believing it offered nothing for trained dancers. Fosse's follow-up film, *The Affairs of Dobie Gillis* (1953), provided only limited opportunities for him to demonstrate his impressive, if technically limited, abilities as a dancer. Like McCracken's *Good News, Dobie Gillis* was a musical farce situated on a college campus—"Grainbelt University"—with "dance staging" (choreographers had yet to get proper billing) by Alex Romero. If Stanley Donen had hoped to groom Bob Fosse as "the next Fred Astaire" (which he claims), *The Affairs of Dobie Gillis* was not the vehicle for it. United again with Debbie Reynolds, Fosse more closely resembles a young Donald O'Connor or Mickey Rooney than Astaire.

"These were very thin musicals with lightweight scripts," Reynolds says of *Give a Girl a Break* and *The Affairs of Dobie Gillis*. "They were strictly for high school kids, like the beach-blanket films that came a generation later. Hollywood was not producing musicals for adult audiences, even though movies were still a big entertainment then. I might have done eight or ten films a year then."

Although Fosse himself marked the beginning of his film choreography with *Kiss Me Kate*'s "From This Moment On" dance, according to Reynolds, Fosse choreographed his own dances in *Give a Girl a Break*. Gower Champion was given credit for the choreography, under Donen's direction, but Fosse was allowed to stage his dances. "He had a lot of fun with his dancing," says Reynolds, "but when he wasn't dancing, sometimes he seemed a little distant. I was about twenty then, very young, and didn't have the same high goals that he did then. Bobby very much wanted to be a star, and, by all definitions of what it takes to be a star, he should have been. I was never equal to him as a dancer, even though I worked and studied hard. Years later, we were at a party and sat down and laughed at how we were when we were young. By this time Bobby was enormously successful. He told me he'd thought I was square and old-fashioned when we'd first worked together. He didn't think I was hot stuff as a dancer."

Tom Rall, a dancer who met Fosse when they danced together in *Kiss Me Kate*, MGM's 1953 musical adaptation of *The Taming of the Shrew*, believes Fosse was losing faith in Hollywood's star-making system. "He had become disappointed in his career," says Rall, "and was disenchanted with MGM. He wanted to be a film dancing star, and he realized that wasn't going to happen. He'd say, 'People keep telling me I'm going to get bigger parts, but they just keep getting *smaller*. I don't want to be an aging dancer and wear a toupee.' He was in analysis at the time, and I think he realized he could go farther being a choreographer-director."

Fosse's analysis, undertaken at McCracken's urging (she championed psychotherapy, and was one of the first dancers who believed unshakably that financially strapped performers should be provided with state-funded therapy), was pivotal to several crucial decisions he would make in the next year. Although he stayed in analysis for five years, at twenty-five, Fosse had decided his career was just about over. With no major Broadway or film credits to his name and a failed marriage behind him, he considered himself just another male ingenue. The lavish movie musicals that he had grown up with had been so commercialized by Hollywood that each new low-budget release was just one more nail in the coffin. McCracken, too, wanted desperately to be considered a viable actress *beyond* musical comedies, but could not find work in Hollywood to her liking. A year later she would be diagnosed with a heart murmur, virtually putting an end to her dancing—and her career. Undoubtedly, their joint career dissatisfactions put stress on their marriage. For the first time in his life, Fosse considered suicide.

As he told *Rolling Stone* in 1984: "I always thought I'd be dead by twenty-five. I wanted to be. I thought it was romantic. I thought people would mourn me. 'Oh, that young career.' "

Kiss Me Kate did not make Fosse a dance star, but it did turn his career around in a different direction—choreographing. He recounted to the *Sunday Record* in 1973, "My big break—and the turning point of my career—came when the studio let me choreograph a little dance for myself and Carol Haney in the film *Kiss Me Kate*. It only lasted forty-eight seconds, but it changed my life." He credited McCracken for prodding him to stage his first dance for the screen. "She's the one who encouraged me to be a choreographer," Fosse told the *New York Times* in 1973. "I was very show biz, all I thought about was nightclubs, and she kept saying, 'You're too good to spend your life in nightclubs,' she lifted me out of that, and I'll always be grateful."

One of the notable exceptions to the string of bottom-drawer musicals being churned out by Hollywood in the Fifties, *Kiss Me Kate* boasted wonderful (though relatively unknown) film dancers. In addition to its lead stars, Kathryn Grayson and Howard Keel, *Kiss Me Kate* featured a talented roster of dancers, led by the indefatigable Ann Miller and including the trio of Fosse, Tommy Rall, and Bobby Van (Hortensio, Lucentio, and Gremio, respectively), and "specialty dancers" Carol Haney and Jeanne Coyne. Both Coyne and Haney were dance assistants to two of the most powerful and talented dancer-choreographers in Hollywood. Coyne worked alongside Gene Kelly, later marrying him, and Haney was Jack Cole's assistant at Columbia, the only studio to have its own stable of dancers expressly for its films. Among the Jack Cole Dancers, as they became known, were Buzz Miller, Ron Field, Matt Maddox, and, later, Gwen Verdon. In later years, all would become renowned as teachers, choreographers, and dance stars. Fosse would later use Miller and Haney in the "Steam Heat" showstopper from *Pajama Game* and, through Haney and Verdon, become influenced by Cole's work.

Based on the popular 1948 Broadway musical, *Kiss Me Kate,* with a score by Cole Porter and musical direction by Andre Previn and Saul Chaplin, was one of few New York theatrical hits of the decade that Hollywood actually cinematized with success. Unlike earlier musicals, which were often written and directed for the screen, the musicals of the Fifties made painful, sometimes embarrassing transitions from their proscenium productions. In 1959, the year *Kiss Me Kate* was released, Hollywood had already seen the quick flops of *All Ashore* (a Mickey Rooney musical feebly fabricated after *On the Town*), a remake of *The Jazz Singer,* and the Sigmund Romberg operetta *The Desert Song.*

In the wake of their failures, studios used gimmicks such as 3-D to entice wary moviegoers to pictures that clearly had little else to offer, such as *Those Redheads from Seattle,* a 1953 musical film historian Clive Hirschhorn has aptly described as "a 3-D musical with 2-D characters and a 1-D plot."

Kiss Me Kate, choreographed by Hermes Pan and directed by George Sidney to exploit the full potential of 3-D dance, was rich in dance numbers, but audiences had already seen its basic premise countless times before; even the show-within-a-show structure (which provided twice the opportunities for lavish production numbers) failed to snare new audiences.

Interestingly, although *Kiss Me Kate*'s 3-D film dances are among the few examples of choreography actually enhanced by the technique, the film was released in the conventional print after audiences failed to respond to the 3-D version. The Golden Age of the Hollywood musical was clearly seeing the end of its halcyon days.

Pan, a highly regarded dancer-turned-choreographer, was responsible, with Fred Astaire, for most of the Astaire-Rogers film dances. But it was typical for assistants and cast members to flesh out bits of their own choreography and, sometimes, arrange entire numbers themselves. Pan remembers Fosse as "a sharp dancer, someone I knew would go far," and considers the number "From This Moment On" "one of my favorite numbers ever, one of my best." Yet it was widely known that it was Fosse, not Pan, who choreographed the critical forty-eight-second section of "From This Moment On," a dazzling display of jazz ballet pyrotechnics, in which Fosse and Carol Haney are paired in a riveting courtship dance. As Rall notes, "It's only fair to give credit where it's due. That number was Fosse's."

Students of Fosse's work may be hard-pressed to find "From This Moment On." As *Kiss Me Kate* has been edited for television, Fosse's dance with Haney has been removed, leaving many viewers to wonder what all the fuss was about. That number, and other fine examples of

Pan's and the dance cast's choreography—"Too Darn Hot," "Tom, Dick, and Harry," and Miller's and Rall's "Why Can't You Behave"—are better savored on video cassette, or, better yet, the big screen, where the dances seem less confined.

Also appreciative of Fosse's "humor and surprise" were George Abbott and Jerome Robbins, two seminal influences on Broadway, who, in 1953, were casting their creative staff for *Pajama Game,* a new musical comedy based on Richard Bissell's novel *7½ Cents,* about a wage dispute for that amount in a textile factory. An unlikely source of material for a Broadway musical, the show nonetheless had the creative guidance of Abbott and Robbins, who together had created the Ethel Merman hit *Call Me Madam* and, individually, were responsible for a veritable history of early 20th Century musicals, including *On Your Toes, The Boys from Syracuse, Pal Joey* (Abbott created the original and was responsible for the 1952 revival, in which Fosse eventually starred), *On the Town, High Button Shoes,* and *Wonderful Town.*

Abbott and Robbins saw the forty-eight-second Fosse-Haney dance in "From This Moment On" and were so taken with Fosse's choreographic inspirations that Abbott called Joan McCracken to arrange an interview with Fosse. McCracken, in fact, became the conduit through which Fosse's reputation was built; because she was a Broadway "name" and had finally achieved star status with 1953's musical-comedy smash *Me and Juliet* (directed by Abbott), Abbott listened when she told him, "Bobby is nothing like his manner. He's a very strong choreographer, even if he seems like a meek little mouse." Abbott remembers that "Joanie sounded off about Bob every time I went into her dressing room. To me, he seemed very unassuming, not very impressive at all. But she built him up like the next Great White Hope. Frankly, I wasn't at all sure he could carry a show by himself. But Jerry Robbins finally convinced me. He'd seen more of his work and said, let's take a chance."

For a short time, McCracken and Fosse enjoyed the same star billing for their respective Broadway efforts that Gwen Verdon and Fosse would have from *Damn Yankees* on—McCracken in her new hit musical, Fosse, the twenty-six-year-old wunderkind, choreographing his first show for preeminent stage director George Abbott.

Shirley MacLaine, who danced in the chorus of *Me and Juliet,* says that Abbott approached all the gypsies in the show and asked them to

Fosse and Carol Haney perform "From This Moment On" from *Kiss Me Kate.*
(Copyright © 1953, ren. 1981, Loew's Inc. Metro-Goldwyn Films)

contribute 35 cents to a new show about a union. Previously, MacLaine had known Fosse only through McCracken, with whom she worked in a class McCracken had established.

"Joan had formed an actors' group for dancers," MacLaine recalls, "and we would meet between matinees on Wednesdays and Saturdays, with Joan serving as the acting coach. We would try on the experience of what it was like to speak, not just move. I was about eighteen, and Joan liked me for some reason. She said I had acting talent. I had never even considered such a thing, particularly with the emphasis on comedy and drama."

While Fosse would launch his career as a choreographer in *The Pajama Game,* McCracken began her withdrawal from musical comedy the same year. She already had performed to strongly favorable reviews in Clifford Odets's *The Big Knife,* then played Sally Bowles in a regional production of John Van Drutten's *I Am a Camera,* based on Christopher Isherwood's *Berlin Stories,* later adapted by Fosse in his film treatment of the Broadway musical, *Cabaret.*

In 1954, following the smash success of *Pajama Game,* Fosse would rejoin Abbot and Robbins, and the musical score team of Richard Adler and Jerry Ross, for *Damn Yankees,* which starred Jack Cole's dancer-assistant, red-haired Gwen Verdon, as the temptress Lola. For Fosse, it would begin a five-show association with Verdon, earning her three Tonys, which would span twenty years. The Broadway hits were offset by a rocky marriage and, eventually, a separation. For McCracken, it would be the beginning of the end of her career—and her life.

When she was diagnosed as having a heart murmur in 1954, Mc-Cracken retreated further away from musicals and concentrated on dramatic acting; but producers were reluctant to cast McCracken in nonmusical projects. She began to drink heavily, despite the fact that it only aggravated her diabetes and heart condition. After a now-forgotten appearance in Jean Cocteau's 1958 *Infernal Machine,* McCracken ostensibly retired from show business. Legally, she was still married to Fosse, but it was known he was seeing other women, and McCracken did not try to stop him. Instead she pursued painting, but was constantly frustrated at her finished work, and gave it up. Friends found her ill-tempered and abusive, especially when they inquired about Fosse's whereabouts. Despite rumors that Fosse had "abandoned" her, it was widely known that McCracken, upon learning of her debilitating illness, encouraged Fosse to continue his growth as a choreographer, without her if necessary.

By 1960, McCracken was seriously ill. After attempts to get work in New York as a stage actress, she left the city and relocated to the Fire

Island Pines community, a stretch of sand bar three hours from Manhattan where she had a summer home. The island, accessible only by ferry and helicopter, is primarily a summer community, its homes not insulated for eastern winters. At the end of the summer in 1961, McCracken refused to return to the mainland; by November she was the only resident left on the island, despite efforts by local authorities to remove her. She and a companion remained alone on the snow-swept island as winter set in. A semi-invalid, McCracken died of an apparent heart attack in the Pines at age thirty-eight in November of 1961, though some newspaper accounts of her death claimed she succumbed at her Manhattan apartment.

Bob Fosse (left), Tommy Rall, Bobby Van, and Ann Miller perform "Tom, Dick, and Harry" in the 1953 MGM film *Kiss Me Kate. (Copyright © 1953, ren. 1981, Loew's Inc. Metro-Goldwyn Films)*

It was a lonely end for "The Girl Who Falls Down," and her death haunted Fosse all of his life. In Fosse's obituary in the *New York Post,* Gwen Verdon—who became his wife in 1960—was quoted as saying "[Bob] can have half a million in the bank, all the Tonys, Oscars, and Emmys one human can amass in a lifetime, and all he lives with is the fact that Joan McCracken died so young on him."

The unravelling of Fosse's personal life kept him from fully enjoying his "overnight" success with *The Pajama Game.* But after years of struggling for success as a dancer, Fosse realized Hollywood could not provide him with the roles he needed to be considered the next Astaire. Niles and McCracken had educated and encouraged him; he would parlay their accumulated years on stage into choreographic inventions which also drew from his own burlesque days and his early work in film and on stage. If he still suffered from severe bouts of insecurity and depression, which would stubbornly remain until the day he died, by the early Fifties he was ready to showcase his still-developing choreography, both on the proscenium stage and the wide screen.

For Bob Fosse, son of a closet hoofer and torch-bearer of a long tradition of vaudeville dance, the Fifties and Sixties would provide opportunities for him to "catch up" with already-established choreographers of his day—Jack Cole, Jerome Robbins, Gower Champion, Agnes de Mille, and Michael Kidd. He would (in the most literal sense) move the work of these mostly-Broadway dance makers forward, redefining the role of dance on stage, unabashedly using it as a narrative device, from which the other components of a musical—the score and book— would extend. He would revolutionize not only the stage, but screen musicals as well, borrowing from his knowledge of cameras in those early MGM musicals he later criticized ("no wonder I went back to the theater," he told the *Los Angeles Times* in 1985).

Fosse's career achievements paralleled his growth as a sensualist, a man increasingly open to experiencing the pleasures of life, more freely offered as his cachet on Broadway and in Hollywood increased. It is safe to say that while Fosse likely "played the field" during his early twenties in New York and Hollywood, his relationship with women was not fully put to the test until he married Verdon in 1960. In his life, no one would affect him so profoundly as she. As he vacillated between family man, Casanova, and esteemed film director, it was Verdon—and, later, their daughter Nicole—who would cause him the most happiness and, by no fault of Verdon's, the most despair.

II

THE BIG BREAKS

A new town
Is a blue town
A who-ya-know-and-show-me-what-ya-can-
    do town
There's no red carpet at your feet
If you're not tough
They'll try to beat ya down
In a new blue town

. . . Since that first day when I said, "Hi,
    town"
They damn well tried to make me say,
    "Goodbye, town"
But I won't leave until I make it my
    town. . . ."

> —*"A New Town Is a Blue Town"*
> *by Richard Adler and Jerry Ross,*
> *from* The Pajama Game

THE PAJAMA GAME

Bob Fosse drew his early inspirations as a dancer from a variety of sources. His salad days as a burlesque performer in Chicago, the movies of Fred Astaire, and his early flings with second-rate Hollywood musicals and Broadway revues not only shaped his dance technique, but also created an aesthetic sensibility that continued to develop throughout his life. The second stage of his career—from 1954's *The Pajama Game* to 1957's *New Girl in Town*—was profoundly influenced by his relationship with legendary director George Abbott. It was also during this time that he met Gwen Verdon, who was as important as Abbott in showcasing and shaping his style.

Only twenty-six when he was hired by Abbott to choreograph *The Pajama Game,* Fosse had already staged dances for a revue workshop called *New Faces of 1952,* which was seen by a number of Broadway "insiders," including Jerome Robbins, a gifted dancer and promising choreographer who worked with Abbott.

While *The Pajama Game* wasn't considered a revolutionary musical per se, Abbott is generally credited as changing the face of the Broadway musical after the first quarter of the century, and *The Pajama Game* is a marvelous example of an archetypal Abbott show. It is indicative of the kind of musical that attracted record numbers to his shows and allowed him to be his own longest-running hit. In fact, almost every year from 1926 until the late Seventies, there was at least one Abbott production on Broadway; in 1939, there were six.

Favorite Fosse dancer Carol Haney in *The Pajama Game*'s showstopping "Steam Heat." *(Courtesy of Dance Magazine)*

As a director, Abbott was cool and shrewd. In 1955, *Time* magazine described him as acting "about as theatrical as the vice president of a savings bank." Already sixty-five when he directed *The Pajama Game,* he was far from lethargic; he jettisoned long-winded books and fussy production numbers, getting to the heart of the story and using songs and dances that fueled the plot, rather than belaboring it.

Abbott says that "Fosse came to me highly recommended, although I had not seen any of his work. Among the dancers, he was very popular, and many of those who knew him, including Joan McCracken, claimed he was the best thing to come along since peanut brittle. Jerry [Robbins] had seen his dance in *Kiss Me Kate,* and said, 'Let's hire this guy.' But I wasn't so sure. So the arrangement was that Jerry would assist me as director of the show, and if Bob didn't work out, Jerry would double as choreographer. Fortunately for everyone, Bob did work out. No one was disappointed."

"Jerry wanted to break into directing," Fosse recalled to the *New York Times* in 1973, "but in case I fell on my face, they put him on as co-director. I did all the dances, but I failed in a couple of the songs, and Jerry came in and staged them. Watching him was the greatest lesson I ever had. I think he's an absolute genius."

Although Fosse went into *The Pajama Game* believing he was a Hollywood reject, under his short-lived contract with MGM he had learned the art of bluffing his way through auditions. When he learned he was being considered to choreograph what would be his first Broadway musical, he made up an impressive list of credits, hoping to wow Abbott and Robbins. "I lied myself into the job," Fosse told *Rolling Stone* in 1984. "But that's what I thought you did in show business. I thought that's how you showed you had confidence." And to the *Los Angeles Times* he confessed, "I freely admit I stole every step from Astaire and Kelly and others."

Buzz Miller, one of the three dancers in Fosse's "Steam Heat" showstopper from *The Pajama Game,* recalls that Robbins approached him about finding a choreographer for the show and asked his opinion. Miller had performed in the *New Faces* review choreographed by Fosse, and also knew him through Joan McCracken, who starred with Miller in 1952's *Me and Juliet.* "I don't mean to take credit for Bob getting the job," says Miller, "but I did suggest to Jerry that he go see *Kiss Me Kate,* which had that fabulous 'From This Moment On' number in it."

John Raitt and Doris Day (center) cavort to the title song in the Warner Bros. film adaptation of *The Pajama Game. (Photofest)*

Once he began, Fosse sequestered himself for eight weeks during preproduction, choreographing the show alone in a studio. He was determined not to embarrass himself in front of Abbott and Robbins. He told *After Dark* magazine nearly twenty years later, "The most difficult thing for me, because I'm slightly shy and inhibited, was to get up in front of people and try to *create* for them."

Fosse's insecurities as a choreographer stemmed back to his disdain for the Hollywood choreographers whose work, he believed, was often less accomplished than that of their assistants and dancers. When he was peforming a solo act as a nightclub dancer in the early Fifties, Fosse hired choreographers to provide him with dances, but always ended up using his own material instead. "I had very little respect for choreographers until I decided to go into it myself," Fosse told *After Dark*. "Then, suddenly I had a *lot* of admiration for anyone who can line up eight girls in Las Vegas and have then turn around and make a circle. That takes more talent than most people think!"

"Steam Heat" is perhaps Fosse's most fondly remembered Broadway dance, and, like so many phenomenally popular dances, its inception was quite by accident. Richard Adler, who, with Jerry Ross, was responsible for *The Pajama Game*'s score, recalls, "Bob did a ballet for the opening of Act II, a long, complicated thing that Abbott hated. He was looking for something on the order of what you would see at an amateur night during a union meeting, featuring some of the factory employees. Fosse came to me and said, 'Do you have any songs that might be appropriate?' I told him no, then I said, 'Maybe I do, but I hate it.'

"About three years before that I wrote a song in a bathroom. I was a young, compulsive idiot in those days, and would set up these little writing exercises for myself, like sitting in a bathroom until I wrote a song about something in it. I considered the toilet, then thought that would be in bad taste. Frank Loesser had just written this song about a faucet dripping, so that eliminated the sink. Then, suddenly I heard the radiator go on, and the *fsssst!* sound followed by the clanking of the pipes inspired me. That's how I came up with 'Steam Heat.' "

Fosse loved the snatch of the song Adler played for him, and began work on the number immediately, completing it in three days. "When it was finished," says Buzz Miller, "he threw about a million steps at us, and Carol [Haney], who was Bob's link, would pick them up like a magnet. He'd show us something and Carol would go 'uh-uh,' meaning she hated it, or 'ah-ha!'—it works! Bob loved that kind of feedback. He was so good to work with because he really wanted you to be great. Bob didn't have an ego problem."

From left, Buzz Miller, Carol Haney, and Peter Gennaro perform "Steam Heat" from Broadway's 1954 hit *The Pajama Game*. *(Will Rapport)*

Fortunately, Fosse had recruited some of the best dancers around for *Pajama Game,* including Buzz Miller, Peter Gennaro, and Carol Haney. "According to Bob," remembers Abbott, who said Fosse took the job only on the condition that he could hire Haney, "that girl was Marilyn Monroe. He said she was going to be a star." Fosse was prophetic on that count, but it was as much his choreography, especially in the numbers "Steam Heat" and "Hernando's Hideaway," as Haney's performance in them that rocketed her and Fosse into Broadway's firmament.

At this formative stage in Fosse's career, Fosse's lack of ego, his willingness to let dancers contribute to the creative process, permitted a fresh exchange and encouraged everyone to work at maximum potential. Watching "Steam Heat" today, Fosse's choreography remains the model to which many of his later dances can be compared. Here, he states his vocabulary plainly—knees turned in or out, locked ankles and pigeon toes, slouched back, forward-thrust hips, and pinched wrists—and fully exploits the humor in these Chaplinesque combinations. Attired in stovepipe trousers, black zoot suit jackets, bow ties, and bowler hats, Miller, Haney, and Genarro are three little tramps with a message ("C'mon, union, get hot!"). Although numbers such as "Hernando's Hideaway" are perhaps funnier, and others, including "Once-a-Year-Day," show off Fosse's ability to choreograph large groups, "Steam Heat" exemplifies the George Abbott less-is-more approach to musical staging. The number's leanness sets off each dancer's personality; simple accoutrements, such as the derbys, take on the importance of toe shoes in a ballet.

Shirley MacLaine, Haney's understudy, believes that "Bobby's choreography was sort of a natural extension of his own complicated psychology. His steps were brilliantly convoluted, though it was hard to get off on them. I have this secret psych-pop assessment that that's why so many of his dancers got injured trying to satisfy those brilliant convolutions. He wasn't interested in clichés. His unpredictability turned the tables while you were dancing, which made his work technically difficult, and his dancers injury-prone."

Ironically, it was Haney who succumbed first to an injury in the show. The second night, while warming up, she pulled a ligament and MacLaine went on, in perhaps the most well-documented story of an understudy vaulted to stardom in show business history. Earlier that day, the twenty-year-old MacLaine, who had lopped off her long, red braid in order to have the same pixieish haircut as Haney, was riding on the subway and wrote a note to the stage manager that she was quitting the show. She was tired of being a chorus girl and believed she would never go on for Haney. Before she could turn the note in, MacLaine was informed that she was going on for Haney that night.

"Of course, Shirley made mistakes," says Miller of that fateful performance. "She'd hardly learned the part from Carol before she had to go on. I don't even think there had been a full rehearsal with Shirley. But she went out there and did it like there was no tomorrow. She was pretty terrific. Both Peter [Gennaro] and I were proud of her."

"It was scary," MacLaine laughs at the image of her trembling chorine in 1954. "The cast was lined in the wings wondering what I would do. I didn't know if the songs were even in my key; I'd never heard myself sing them. There were all these things to worry about. Except the dancing. That wasn't a problem. Somehow I did it. I remember thinking

Helen Gallagher, who replaced Carol Haney, performing *The Pajama Game*'s "Hernando's Hideaway." *(Talbot)*

that the cast knows what I'm doing wrong, but the audience doesn't. The only thing on my mind was that I would drop the hat during 'Steam Heat.' I was thinking about that frigging hat, which is what you do when you're a dancer, and dropped it. I muttered 'shit!' picked it up, and went on. At the end of the number, I walked out with Buzz and Peter, and they peeled off and let me take the applause by myself. I was extremely lonely."

And extremely lucky. When *Pajama Game* opened the night before, May 13, 1954, the last musical of an otherwise uneventful 1953–54 Broadway season, word quickly circulated that George Abbott's new musical was a shoo-in for the Best Musical Tony Award. Notices were especially fine for Haney, whom *New York Times* theater critic Brooks Atkinson called ". . . a comic dancer of extraordinary versatility." Thomas R. Dash of *Women's Wear Daily* wrote, "One of the thrills of last night's opening was watching the birth of a new star in the musical-comedy firmament. Not since Gwen Verdon and [Zizi] Jeanmaire captivated New Yorkers with their febrile talents has anything like this been seen."

But when theatergoers and talent scouts packed the 46th Street Theatre the following night to see what all the fuss was about, they were greeted with the announcement: "Ladies and gentlemen, at tonight's performance, the role usually played by Carol Haney will be played by—" The sighs and groans were so loud that Shirley MacLaine's name was all but inaudible. In the audience that night were producers Hal Wallis and Bob Goldstein, who had come expressly to see Haney. Prepared to be disappointed when she did not appear, Wallis was instead mesmerized by the red-headed fireball who commandeered the stage. MacLaine was almost instantaneously plucked from the cast and flown to Hollywood. Wallis gave her a screen test, and Shirley MacLaine's future as a film actress was sealed. Haney resumed her role after MacLaine's departure.

Although Fosse was still married to McCracken while *The Pajama Game* was in production, it was apparent to everyone who saw them together that their marriage was not stable. "According to Carol," says Buzz Miller, "the night she was injured, he came up to her dressing room and had intimate relations with her, and it's my impression this was not an isolated incident. I was so shocked when she told me that I changed the subject. I didn't want to hear any more about it. I think he carried on with the chorus girls from all of his shows; this is not supposition so much as theater folklore. To my knowledge, he had girls on call in all of his shows."

Adds Richard Adler, "There is nobody who knows anything about Fosse who doesn't know about his sex life. He made it very public; he just didn't care. How he portrayed himself in *All That Jazz* is playing down what he was really like. This man was sexually insatiable."

The Pajama Game proved to be Haney's only starring role before a sudden illness claimed her life in 1964. While filming the movie version of *The Pajama Game,* Haney collapsed several times from physical exhaustion. Diagnosed as diabetic, she thereafter concentrated on choreographing. Like McCracken, her frustration resulted in drinking, especially after her 1955 marriage to actor Larry Blyden ended in divorce in 1963. As a choreographer, her Broadway credits included the productions of *Flower Drum Song* and *Bravo, Giovanni* as well as the considerably more popular *She Loves Me.* Her last show was 1964's *Funny Girl* with Barbra Streisand. On May 5, 1964, she became ill at her home in Saddle River, New Jersey, and died five days later, at age thirty-nine, of bronchial pneumonia in New York Hospital.

Capitalized at $250,000, *The Pajama Game* went on to run 1,063 performances, earning $1,365,941 on its investment. In fact, the show might have gone on to an even longer run had the 46th Street Theatre not been reserved for George Abbott's next musical, *Damn Yankees,* which would be created by most of the same staff responsible for *Pajama Game,* including Fosse. When no other theater could be obtained, the show was closed; but only six months later, it was back on Broadway in a production staged by the New York City Center Opera in May 1957 (the same year the film version of the show was released, also choreographed by Fosse). Although the cast was entirely different, the revival garnered equally favorable reviews.

Through the years since, *The Pajama Game* has proven one of Abbott's most enduring musicals. In the original production John Raitt and Janis Paige played the romantic leads, with a subplot concerning the travails of Carol Haney's character and her jealous boyfriend, played by Eddie Foy, Jr. The exemplary cast would be matched by the 1957 Warner Bros. film, in which the lead players reprised their stage roles with the exception of Paige, whose plunky character, Babe Williams, went to Doris Day. Babe was a coveted female character for musical-comedy actresses, alternately shrewd, funny, pragmatic, and sexy—other actresses who played Babe in subsequent productions include singer Julie Wilson and, in 1966, Liza Minnelli.

DAMN YANKEES

efore embarking on the dances for *Damn Yankees*, Fosse returned once more to Hollywood to choreograph and star in Columbia's 1955 film musical *My Sister Eileen*. Of his early films, *My Sister Eileen* is undoubtedly one of the most important in his development as a director-choreographer. Although some consider it his last bid to become the heir apparent to Fred Astaire and Gene Kelly, it seems more likely Fosse was beginning to concentrate on his choreography rather than his performing. *The Pajama Game* had suddenly made him an in-demand choreographer, enough to attract the attention of Columbia Pictures's president Harry Cohn, who signed on Fosse for *My Sisten Eileen*.

Tom Rall, who danced with Fosse in the picture, says, "Back then, if a studio wanted a talented choreographer, they went to New York to get him. Hollywood had a lot of hacks, choreographers who didn't really know what they were doing. Word got out that Bob's dances for *The Pajama Game* were wonderful, and suddenly it was like he had a new career. Also, it helped that he'd had a film background. He came into *My Sister Eileen* with a basic of idea how dances should be filmed."

My Sister Eileen was originally based on Ruth McKinney's short stories about Ruth and Eileen Sherwood, two sisters from Ohio who move to a basement apartment in New York's Greenwich Village. At the time the stories first appeared in the *New Yorker* in the late Thirties, they were immensely popular, recounting the young Midwesterners' acclima-

Lola (Gwen Verdon) performs her best seduction dance on rookie baseball player Joe Hardy (Tab Hunter) in "Whatever Lola Wants" from *Damn Yankees*. *(Photofest)*

tion to the then-bohemian Village and its eccentric "fringe dwellers." By 1940, the stories began the first of many stage and screen adaptations when a Broadway stage comedy, *My Sister Eileen,* opened, later presented on television starring Rosalind Russell. Betty Comden and Adolph Green wrote another version of the story for the 1953 Broadway musical *Wonderful Town,* featuring Leonard Bernstein's score, which ran for 559 performances. Two years later, *My Sister Eileen* was remade as a film musical for Columbia Pictures, starring Janet Leigh and Betty Garrett as the two sisters, Jack Lemmon as a magazine publisher, and Fosse and Rall as the women's suitors.

As adapted by Blake Edwards and Richard Quine, *My Sister Eileen* presented the bizarre, often humorous encounters between the young innocents Leigh and Garrett and the "criminal element" of Greenwich

Fosse's first film assignment as choreographer was *My Sister Eileen,* in which he also co-starred with Janet Leigh. *(Copyright © 1953, ren. 1983, Columbia Pictures Industry, Inc.)*

Village. Although the score by Jule Styne and Leo Robin was not one of the film's best assets, Fosse's choreography bolstered even the weaker songs. His vaudeville antecedents surface in the dances for "Conga," while Broadway's razzmatazz exuberance shines in "Give Me a Band and My Baby."

Conceiving the dances for the movie did not take Fosse long, but he was concerned that they translate well on film. He worked closely with cameraman Richard Klein, who explained to Fosse about different lenses and the effects they would have on shooting a dance. He would create an imaginary camera frame with his fingers and peer through it to determine perspectives. "Bob wanted the dances to be a cut above a lot of the stuff that Hollywood was putting out," says Rall. "I still don't know how he did some of the choreography for the numbers he was in. Basically, he wanted to invest the dances with humor and create strong showstoppers. He came up with some interesting ideas for some not-great songs."

While choreographing *My Sister Eileen,* Fosse had the first of many disagreements in his career with studio executives who believed they knew how to stage effective dances better than the choreographer. Attempting to challenge the precepts of film dance, Fosse experimented with different concepts, not only pertaining to how dance should be filmed, but also how to integrate it into a storyline or present dances that didn't look formulaic.

According to Tom Rall, one day Harry Cohn came into the studio to see a number Fosse had worked on tirelessly, and was not happy with the results. "We had been beating ourselves to a pulp on this dance," says Rall, "and we were anxious for him to see it. We thought he'd really be pleased. When we were finished, he waved his hands and said, 'You guys got it all wrong. People wanna see the old soft shoe.' Then, he got up and did a soft shoe for us. It made me really angry, and Bob and he left to talk it over. Bob came back a few minutes later and said, 'I can't believe it. He wants us to put sand on the floor and do a soft shoe!' "

It was hard for Fosse to fathom that Cohn, who had employed Jack Cole to create many of the ethnically influenced, sexually suggestive dances for Columbia in films such as *Gilda* and *The Thrill of Brazil,* wanted him to stage a soft shoe. In retrospect, Rall believes Cohn was testing Fosse. "He was the head of the studio, and he wanted to make sure we knew who was the boss. Cohn was the kind of guy who had to get up and tell you how to do something. I don't think he expected us to actually do it that way." And they didn't. In the end, Fosse's own choreography won out.

Fosse hardly had time to relish his work on *My Sister Eileen* when he was called back to New York in 1955 to begin work on *Damn Yankees* on Broadway. *Damn Yankees* was an important project for Fosse for a number of reasons. Although his dances in *Pajama Game* received fair notices, many reviewers spent more ink on Haney's performance in numbers such as "Steam Heat" and "Hernando's Hideaway" than on the man responsible for them. *Damn Yankees* gave Fosse an opportunity to prove he was a four-square choreographer, capable of creating truly innovative dances with his own signature. Shortly before he died, Phil Friedman said, "I was always surprised at how insecure Bob was with his successes. He was always waiting for someone to call him a fraud, because deep in his heart he suspected he was not as talented as everyone said he was. Once, during *All That Jazz,* a reporter asked him about his early days choreographing *Pajama Game* and *Damn Yankees.* In both cases, Bobby attributed the fact that the dances were hits to Carol [Haney] and Gwen [Verdon]. In fact, he said that if it wasn't for Gwen in *Damn Yankees,* his choreography might not have been recognized."

Unquestionably, the combustible pairing of Fosse and Verdon in *Damn Yankees* was responsible for the smoldering sexuality in not only that musical, but in all of Fosse's work for the next thirty years. If indeed Fosse was nagged by deep-seated fears of failure, Verdon validated his choreography as only Haney had done previously. Fosse's second Broadway musical would demonstrate that *Pajama Game*'s choreography was no fluke.

Using the same creative team as *Pajama Game, Damn Yankees* went into rehearsal in early 1955. Once again, George Abbott turned to a popular novel of the time, Douglass Wallop's *The Year the Yankees Lost the Pennant,* and adapted it into a Faustian tale about America's most ardent baseball fan and his reincarnation as a long-ball hitter.

In the story, the middle-aged fan of the ailing Washington Senators baseball team claims that he would sell his soul to see his beloved Senators beat those "damn Yankees." He ends up doing exactly that when Satan (using the pseudonym Mr. Applegate) appears, identifiable only by his red socks and tie and the ability to pluck lighted cigarettes from the air. Applegate tells the man he will transform him into a twenty-two-year-old slugger named Joe Hardy in exchange for his soul at the end of the season. With an average of .460, Hardy becomes the world's greatest long-ball hitter and almost single-handedly ressurects the Senators to make them a contender for the pennant. Despite Hardy's newfound superstardom, he misses his wife, whom he had to leave in order to become Joe Hardy. To keep him from straying back to her, Applegate offers the luscious Lola, played by Gwen Verdon, to distract him. The 172-year-old witch performs her seduction dance, "Whatever Lola Wants," on Hardy, but clearly he is a man who was serious when he took his vows "to love, honor, and obey," and he rejects her. In the final inning of the pennant game between the Senators and the Yankees, Applegate transforms Hardy back to his former self just as he is making the catch that will put his team in the World Series.

From left to right, Al Lanti, Eddie Phillips, and Timmy Everett as three Washington Senators in Fosse's "Shoeless Joe from Hannibal, Mo." baseball "ballet"—from the original company of *Damn Yankees*. *(Fred Fehl Photo, courtesy of the Phillips family)*

Fosse conceived a range of dances that illustrated his diversity as a choreographer, from the acrobatic "baseball ballet," "Shoeless Joe from Hannibal, Mo.," to what became one of Gwen Verdon's most famous dances, "Whatever Lola Wants." The breadth of his work in *Damn Yankees* shows a man in the midst of developing his personal style as a choreographer. The back flips, somersaults, and barrel turns in "Shoeless Joe" are examples of acrobatic dancing harking back to traditional large-group production numbers (including Fosse's own "Once-a-Year-Day" from *The Pajama Game*).

On the other hand, Verdon's character dance, "Whatever Lola Wants," permitted Fosse to stretch out as a choreographer and pick up where he left off with the teasing sexuality of "Steam Heat." Verdon, with her Jack Cole technique, invests the number with pseudo–East Indian hand gestures and faux-flamenco foot stomps (the influence of Latin social dances is evident in many film and stage musicals of the Fifties). The ethnic embellishments add to the exoticism of Lola. In her form-fitting black skirt, red hair afire, Verdon stalks all-American-looking Stephen Douglass (as Hardy) with determined abandon. " 'Allo, Joe, it's meee-ee," she peek-a-boos coquettishly, and, when that approach fails to woo him, she staggers forward like a tipsy Kewpie doll, all pouty and pigeon-toed. Bridging burlesque with Jack Cole's jazz dance technique, Fosse and Verdon kept Lola's striptease exciting without resorting to vulgarity. Off come two gloves, a skirt, and a pair of lace panties as Lola arabesques through her routine in a skin-tight black corset as if she were en pointe in a Balanchine ballet. As *New Yorker* drama critic Wolcott Gibbs wrote of Verdon following *Damn Yankee's* premiere on May 5, 1955, "[Verdon is] the most entrancing femme fatale I've seen in years." The public agreed. "Whatever Lola Wants" became a popular jukebox single across America and Lola made the cover of *Time* magazine.

Yet another dance highlight was "Who's Got the Pain," a mambo variation danced in the later film version by Verdon and Fosse. Although Fosse did not perform the role on Broadway, Richard Adler recalls one evening Fosse stepped in for the dancer who usually played the role. "Suddenly you saw it," Adler remembers, "that magical oneness between a choreographer and his star dancer. I was mesmerized." Indeed, when Fosse and Verdon danced "Who's Got the Pain" in Warner Bros.'s 1958 film version of the musical, there appears to be an intuitive understanding between them. Not only are their bodies in almost perfect sync throughout the mambo send-up, the two share a jolting physical rapport as partners that transcends their slight characters. "Who's Got the Pain," the only time Fosse and Verdon appeared together in a motion picture, boasts two under-used film dancers at the peak of their professions.

Verdon's rise to stardom on Broadway occurred almost by accident as, in fact, did her entire career as a dancer. Her theater program biographies and press releases present a suitably theatrical background: She was born in January 1925 in a $12-a-month bungalow in Culver City, near the MGM Studios, where her English father worked as an electrician. The Verdon lineage included several performers. Her great-great-grandfather was a Shakespearean actor in a British repertory company. Her great-grandfather was an English "step-dancer," and her mother, a vaudeville dancer and ballerina who owned her own dance studio.

"[My mother] told newspapermen that her own parents were strolling players in England," Verdon said in an *American Weekly* interview in 1959. "They weren't. It was just that Mother was nervous and thought that if she said something crazy the newspapermen would go away. They didn't, of course, so she said I was born in the shadow of the MGM lot in Culver City, which is also untrue, but has been repeated in every story written about me, including my biography in my own theater program."

At two, Verdon had a hernia operation, which was shortly followed by a series of other ailments, culminating with a severe case of rickets. It left her knock-kneed and pigeon-toed ("a perfect Fosse dancer," she would later jest), and she was forced to wear a cumbersome pair of corrective therapy shoes laced up to her knees. Schoolchildren taunted her with "Boots Verdon," but her mother was determined that Gwyneth

Gwen Verdon burst into Broadway's firmament as Claudine in Cole Porter's 1953 musical *Can-Can.* *(Courtesy of Dance Magazine)*

Evelyn Verdon would one day dance. She enrolled her daughter in dance classes, some taught by dancer Marge Champion's father, after tearing up a doctor's letter recommending that the child's legs be broken and reset to straighten them. Thus, the therapeutic use of dance to heal and strengthen was put to the test on a three-year-old.

Just as Fosse fought against his own physiological handicaps—asthma and stuttering—as a child dancer, Verdon, too, found that show dancing provided opportunities to perform without the precision of a ballet dancer. She learned the buck-'n'-wing and the waltz clog and, before her fourth birthday, was entertaining adults at an MGM Christmas party hosted by actress Marion Davies. By six, she acquired the billing "Baby Alice, the fastest little tapper in the world" at the Shrine Auditorium. At thirteen, her measurements were already 36-24-36, and with the right makeup she projected the image of a young adult. A year later, claiming she was twenty-two, Verdon appeared at a San Diego club as half of a ballroom team called Verdon and Del Valle. Between performances she went to burlesque houses to watch clowns in baggy pants, fascinated by the "little tramp" character. Later, her characters would become deeply indebted to the French clown, Pierrot, and Harlequin, the sixteenth-century commedia del l'arte character who is the prototype for many circus clowns and burlesque comedians.

As a minor, the precocious Verdon encountered many of the same hair's-breadth sexual encounters with drooling patrons that Fosse experienced as a teenager with the wanton strippers in Chicago. Unlike Fosse, who projected the precious appearance of a child dressed up in his father's tails and top hat, Verdon's look was startlingly adult. When she danced at Hollywood's lush Florentine Gardens, her mother stuffed the fifteen-year-old into a rubber bra and panties, and applied a makeup of gold powder and glycerin. The well-endowed redhead and her mother were intent on conjuring a provocative golden-girl mystique. Between classes at a school for professional children and her dance engagements, she modeled swimsuits on Venice Beach.

But her designs to become a professional show dancer ended abruptly at seventeen, when she met and married handsome, blond James Henaghan. Henaghan was older, a minor gossip columnist on Louella Parson's staff, a sometime-screenwriter, a literary agent (for Mickey Spillane), a promoter (later, for John Wayne), and a man with all the right connections. Verdon thought him erudite and impressively informed about the entertainment industry. After they married, she accompanied him to openings, met famous people, and enjoyed the "perks" of entertainment journalism, but she stopped dancing when she became pregnant. Henaghan no longer took her with him to cover events, and frequently stayed out all night.

"He was a drinker," she revealed to the *New York Times* in 1981, "so he would wind up in Kansas City not remembering how he got there. My son was born in March, and on New Year's Eve I said, 'That's it' and I went home to mama. I took my child, my dog, and my cats and left."

It was a pivotal decision in her life. Before leaving Henaghan, whom she would soon divorce, Verdon had began writing his column for him on the nights he was too drunk to attend performances or type his reviews. Her crash course in journalism resulted in an assignment by the *Hollywood Reporter* to review a performance by Jack Cole's dance troupe. Cole's act reminded Verdon of all she had given up to become a housewife and mother, rekindling her ambitions to be a professional dancer; after the show she promptly went backstage and asked him for an audition.

If not for Cole, it is unlikely Verdon would have gone on to achieve fame as a dancer; without his instruction, many now-immortal stage and screen musical actresses probably would not be remembered as dancers today. Cole was the first choreographer working in Hollywood to revolutionize dance in both technique and content, though today he is little known outside the circles of concerned dance historians, fans of cult musicals, and a smattering of dance students fortunate enough to know his work and technique through the classes of his protégés. Fosse first met Verdon, who was then Cole's assistant, at an audition for a Hollywood film to be choreographed by Cole. "Bobby, who was dancing

Choreographer Jack Cole's ethnic, sexually charged dances influenced Fosse later in his career. Here Cole appears in a studio photo by Maurice Seymour. *(Theatre Collection/Museum of the City of New York)*

with his first wife, Mary Ann Niles, auditioned," recalled Verdon to the *Daily News* in 1975, "but he didn't get the job. Bobby Van did. And then we met again in Hollywood when I was working with Jack on *The Merry Widow* and Bobby was waiting for Fred Astaire to retire, so he could take over."

Part of Cole's brilliance was his ability to tap a performer's natural rhythms and build on them. His choreography was modern with a twist; ethnic dances figured importantly in his work. Borrowing from Indian, Cuban, African, and Oriental dance traditions, Cole interpolated thousands of years of indigenous cross-cultural dances with contemporary jazz in the four decades in which he developed as one of Hollywood's most powerful choreographers; his work was adventurous, exotic, sexual, and emphatic. Cole was also unusual in that he supervised the camera work for his choreography and despised choreographers such as Busby Berkeley, whom he believed "used people like wallflowers" in his dances. As a result, he became an in-demand choreographer for female film stars who did not know how to dance and required a choreographer who was familiar with the camera. Rita Hayworth, Betty Grable, Jane Russell, Mitzi Gaynor, and especially Marilyn Monroe learned their footwork under Cole's supervision. When he was too busy to work with them one-on-one, he delegated the responsibility to his assistants, later to include Carol Haney and Verdon.

Verdon's first job for Cole marked the beginning of a tumultuous six-year working relationship with him, a tenure that remained uninterrupted until her first non-Cole musical, *Can-Can,* made her a star almost overnight. "My first concern was that I had to make a living," Verdon reflected on her status as a single parent to the *New York Times* in 1981. "If anything came up at Fox Studios [where Cole served as general dance director], I'd do it. I sang a song about prunes once. I would dub in the sound of footsteps in movies. [She and Carol Haney provided the tap sounds for Gene Kelly.] I took any and every job that came along. I was lucky—they always kept me busy."

Indeed, until the second phase of her career began with 1953's *Can-Can,* Verdon performed with Cole at nightclubs she laughingly claimed were run by "Murder, Inc."; had small dance roles in a string of movie musicals; taught a galaxy of movie stars how to dance; and performed in short-lived shows on Broadway choreographed by Cole, including *Bonanza Bound, Alive and Kicking,* and *Magdalena.*

Like Joan McCracken and Carol Haney, Verdon's experiences as a Hollywood dancer were not always happy ones. Although Marilyn Monroe said of Verdon's abilities as a dancer to *Family Circle* in 1957, "If

Gwen can't teach you a routine, you're rhythm bankrupt with incompatible feet," she predicted accurately that "Gwen's such a fine dancer that Hollywood may never think of her as anything else." Verdon disappeared abruptly from United Artist's *Gentlemen Marry Brunettes* after the Motion Picture Producers' Code determined her prologue dance was "too sexy" and her outfit "too brief." The film's equally well-proportioned co-stars, Marilyn Monroe and Jane Russell, escaped the scissors. It was a bitter irony that Verdon, who coached them, was never seen in the film.

Richard Adler says of her appearance in the movie version of *Damn Yankees,* "Tab Hunter [who played Joe Hardy] was almost perfect looking, like he could have been made by magic. But according to the Hollywood tradition of that era, Gwen's face wasn't pretty enough to make her a star. At that time, Hollywood was still into a narrow definition of 'pretty.' I always thought Gwen was terrific looking, but when most people thought of her then, it was for that figure. Wow!"

Although she dated some of Hollywood's leading men of the day, including Danny Kaye, Verdon's driving ambition was to break out of small dance roles and away from the title "assistant to." She first met Fosse while under contract with 20th Century–Fox, where she and Grable danced in *The Farmer Takes a Wife* with pie plates on their feet. Fosse was working as a dancer for MGM, and McCracken was living on the West Coast with him. Although Hollywood employed hundreds of dancers and choreographers for its film musicals of the Fifties, dancers who worked regularly soon became familiar with their competition at rival studios. "All dancers always collect," Verdon told the *Hampton Newspaper Magazine* in 1986, referring to a commonly held notion that gypsies stick together. "It doesn't matter if you become a choreographer or a director, if you've been a dancer, dancers collect—and cook and eat."

Verdon knew Fosse was married to McCracken, "who was my idol. She was the first dancer I ever saw do a play and *not* dance." It seems likely Verdon was as fascinated by Fosse's relatively famous stage wife as she was with his own reputation as a dancer and fledgling choreographer. But, in the early Fifties, their relationship amounted to mutual admiration. It would not be until 1955, when Fosse began working with her in rehearsals for *Damn Yankees* on Broadway, while he was still married to the infirm McCracken, that their partnership began.

Verdon's association with Cole kept her steadily employed until she scored her first triumph in the 1953 Cole Porter–Abe Burrows Broadway smash *Can-Can,* starring the French actress Lilo. Invited by choreographer Michael Kidd to audition for the show, Verdon flew to New York believing she had little chance of landing the part. She already knew the

can-can, having danced it in Cole's ill-fated choreography for *The Merry Widow* the year before, and Kidd and the producers were looking for a strong, sexy dancer to play the role of Claudine. But she was a relative unknown, despite her numerous film appearances, and no one knew if she could sing or act.

Her inhibitions increased when Lilo and her manager-husband began cutting Claudine's dialogue, until Verdon only had eight lines and her dances were reduced from seven to four. Lilo even arranged to have Verdon offstage at the end of three of them so there would be no applause. Clearly, the star felt threatened by the supporting actress's magnetism on stage. The coup de grace was the truncation of Verdon's stage name, Gwenyth Verdon, to Gwen for the marquee of the theater. Incensed, she gave notice and prepared to leave after a four-week run. "I was so unhappy I wanted out," Verdon told Rex Reed when he interviewed her for the *New York Times* in the mid-Sixties. Of her remaining dialogue in the show, Verdon said, "By the time we opened all I remember saying was, 'Oh, Boris!' eight times and 'What's on the menu?' I don't really blame Lilo. She was the star and I was stealing her show. In the theater, that's like another woman in a marriage triangle."

Verdon's numbers in *Can-Can* were hugely appealing to audiences, especially an Indian dance and "The Garden of Eden Ballet." On opening night, after her second number, the chant "we want Verdon" rose from the orchestra. Verdon, who was already dressing for her next number, was hustled back on-stage to take a solo bow. She was wrapped only in a Turkish towel, but her *dishabille* added to her seductive image. Verdon extended her contract, and *Can-Can* kicked up its heels for 894 more performances. At twenty-eight, a divorcée with a young son to raise by herself, Gwen Verdon (she kept her marquee name) was a star.

If George Abbott was indirectly responsible for ushering the choreography of Bob Fosse onto the Broadway stage, he played an equally important, if unintentional, role in the pairing of Fosse and Verdon in *Damn Yankees*. He and producers Frederick Brisson, Robert E. Griffith, and Hal Prince decided early into the development of the script for the show that Verdon would be cast in the siren role. "She's a complete jewel," Abbott told *Time* in 1955, "quick, indefatigable, cooperative, and objective. . . . She'll rehearse for hours and never complain. And though she has a mind of her own, she never questions any decision."

Newlyweds Verdon and Fosse appear on a CBS musical salute, "The American Musical Theatre," in April 1960. *(Courtesy of Dance Magazine)*

Indeed, Verdon took to Lola with complete enthusiasm, so much so that Abbott gave her more dialogue as Fosse expanded her dance routines. Fosse was in awe of her and a little intimidated by the credits she had amassed since working with Jack Cole. Like Mary Ann Niles and Joan McCracken, she was older than he (by four years) and had the professional dance training he lacked. She, in turn, was impressed by his work in *The Pajama Game* and felt an affinity for him as a former gypsy dancer. She also admired his wife enormously. Obviously, there was much to catch up on since the first time Verdon and Fosse had met during a Jack Cole audition in Hollywood. During the first weeks of rehearsals they became friends, and Verdon latched on to Fosse's style, which "fit" her like a glove. To Fosse, she imparted much of Jack Cole's dance philosophy, and the choreography Fosse developed for her eventually became a collaborative effort. Soon, they were convening outside the theater over dinner about rehearsals.

"The happiest times I ever had with Gwen," Fosse told the *New York Times* in 1971, "were when we were working together. They stimulated all sorts of things. I mean, they were fun, we had our own jokes about rehearsals, and we had something in common. I think it even affected sex."

Although he had a new love interest and a new show to buoy his spirits, other concerns, such as his ill, untenable wife and the irascible George Abbott, kept Fosse in a constant state of anxiety. In addition to creating Verdon's dances, he was also responsible for the rest of the show's numbers, which Abbott eliminated with a wave of his hands if he disapproved of their showiness or questioned their relevance to the book. Fortunately, because Fosse was a baseball fan, his close observations of the game lent an authenticity to the "Shoeless Joe" "baseball ballet." Richard Adler's hoedown rhythm permitted him to expand on the intrinsic "choreography" of the game. Fosse appropriated the motions of pitching, batting, fielding, and sliding, even tapping the comic potential of the game's "props" in an acrobatic feat where one player juggles a group of bats.

Banking on New York's reputation as a baseball town, the producers spared no expense when it came to recreating the look and feel of being in an actual stadium. Bright stadium lights lit not only the stage, but also the orchestra, and hot dogs were sold at intermission. A curtain was made of 1,775 baseballs donated by the A. G. Spalding Co. It cost $2,444, and was seen only briefly, during the overture.

Damn Yankees opened on May 5, 1955, at the 46th Street Theater with Verdon, Stephen Douglass (as Hardy), and Ray Walston (as Satan/ Applegate) leading the cast. Among the supporting players was character actress Jean Stapleton as a nosey neighbor and devout Senators fan. The $250,000 musical initially had a difficult time meeting its weekly $33,000 operating expenses, despite generally favorable reviews from the dailies' critics. In general, *Damn Yankees* was considered less sustained than *The Pajama Game,* though the stars—especially Verdon—and Fosse garnered raves. The Richard Adler–Jerry Ross score received several drubbings from music critics, but it was eminently hummable; songs such as "Heart," and "Whatever Lola Wants" have become Broadway standards. Radio announcers had a tough time spitting out the controversial title when playing selections from the cast album. In order to get around having to say the "D" word—at that time banned by the FCC on its airwaves—disc jockeys called it everything from "Dum Yankees' to "Dim Yankees" to the Bronx equivalent of the former Brooklyn team known as "Dem Bums"—"Dem Yankees."

Damn Yankees would be the first of many Fosse shows to elicit controversy over its sexy dance numbers. In April 1964, some ten years after the show opened, an Ionia, Mi., Episcopal rector excommunicated a couple who had criticized his objection to a dance sequence in the local high school production of *Damn Yankees*. Reverend Raymond Berlein, the rector, called Lola "salacious and immoral." In the mid-Seventies, Fosse's much more "salacious" choreography in *Pippin* also caused a furor to erupt in several public high schools, whose superintendents were pressured by parents to censor many of the "lewd and unbecoming" dances in the schools' productions of the musical.

Such controversy seems tepid by today's standards, but undoubtedly the sexual intrigue behind Fosse's dancers and his dance star, Verdon, contributed to *Damn Yankees'* eventual—and considerable—profit. Whether it was the score, baseball, Verdon, or a combination of the three, *Damn Yankees'* batting average at the box office eventually improved, and it has gone on to be another of George Abbott's biggest success stories, playing 1,030 performances in its original production. In 1981, *Variety* reported that the show had returned $1,317,500 to its investors for a 263 percent profit.

Although *Damn Yankees* has played around the world in hundreds of productions ranging from high school musicals to major revivals, the success of the show has always rested on the collaborative efforts between director, cast, and choreographer. An April 1967 General Electric television presentation of *Damn Yankees* starring Lee Remick and Phil Silvers exemplified everything that goes wrong when that fragile thing called a Broadway musical is Hollywoodized out of proportion. Fortunately, the George Abbott–Stanley Donen film production of *Damn Yankees* did not lose sight of those seemingly small appeals of the stage musical that made it a hit.

Verdon and Fosse in the mambo "Who's Got the Pain?" from *Damn Yankees*. *(Photofest)*

The Warner Bros. film adaptations of both *The Pajama Game* (1957) and *Damn Yankees* (1958) are close approximations of their original stage versions. Composer Richard Adler believes that "neither film expanded enough; they stuck too close to the plays." But for musical buffs too young to have seen the original Broadway productions, the films preserve the exuberant optimism found in many Fifties Broadway musicals and present a cavalcade of stars—Doris Day, Tab Hunter, Gwen Verdon, Ray Walston—at their peak. For Fosse, both films gave him further opportunities to familiarize himself with dance cinematography. The aerial shots of the "Once-a-Year-Day" picnic number in *The Pajama Game* permit audiences to view Fosse's impressive large-group combinations from a perspective unavailable to audiences watching the action on a proscenium stage. As the camera swoops down on the dancers, pivots around them, and comes to rest on Carol Haney, mugging sweetly in her own solo, we see the makings of video dance—choreography that is as much about the camera as it is about what's in front of it.

By the end of the Fifties, Fosse had arrived as a formidable Broadway choreographer. Unquestionably gifted, he was the first to admit he could not attribute his success merely to his own instincts, since much of his choreography developed through collaboration with his dancers. Through the ceaseless campaigning of Joan McCracken in the early Fifties, Fosse's work was seen by influential Broadway and Hollywood producers, directors, and choreographers.

Fosse's greatest teacher in his evolution as a choreographer during the Fifties was George Abbott. And though Fosse's work would change dramatically by the late Sixties, his work with Abbott from 1954's *Pajama Game* to 1959's *Redhead* provides a blueprint for what, in later years, were dances that bore a distinct Fosse signature.

Of equal importance to Fosse's choreography was Gwen Verdon. Her contribution spills into his personal life as well. By 1960, they would marry and their collaboration would result not only in a string of hits, including *Damn Yankees, New Girl in Town, Redhead, Sweet Charity,* and *Chicago,* but a daughter, Nicole, as well. As Phil Friedman says, "Gwen became a star because of *Can-Can,* but Fosse established her with *Damn Yankees.* Otherwise, she might have been an also-ran, like Joan Mc-Cracken, Carol Haney, or Mary McCarty—women on the edge of stardom who never made it. Because of the work Bob gave her in *Damn Yankees,* she went over the top."

Verdon's Jack Cole training was well spent on Fosse's choreography, though by the time she would star in *Sweet Charity* a decade later, the Fosse style was light-years from his more genteel work in the early Abbott musicals. Friedman, Cole's assistant for many years, believes Fosse was profoundly affected by Cole's choreography. "I think Cole was the nucleus for everything Bobby did. It influenced him terribly. Cole used more ethnic dance than Bobby, but they both achieved that sexuality in their dances."

Today, Abbott claims, "Whatever Bobby learned from me, I don't know. He might have discussed it with other people, but he and I never talked about it. We didn't have that kind of relationship. Bobby was not a fellow who shared happiness." But, on the basis of their joint endeavors, Abbott and Fosse formed an allegiance responsible for some of the most noteworthy American stage and film musicals of the Fifties. When Fosse eventually broke away from Abbott, he used his knowledge of Abbott's approach to stagecraft to carve out his own niche as a Broadway and film director.

III

IN LOVE WITH THE FLAME: THE VERDON-FOSSE YEARS

The way it happens is the way it happens. I mean, who knows where I'd be if it weren't for Gwen?

—*Bob Fosse,*
Penthouse, *1973*

ALL THAT DANCE

rom 1956's *Bells Are Ringing* through 1966's *Sweet Charity*—Fosse's turning-point musical—Broadway witnessed the evolution of a provocative and prolific choreographer. Borrowing freely from his knowledge of minstrelsy, vaudeville, and burlesque, Fosse perfected his closed-in, lurid style of slithering innuendo to such a degree that, by the early Seventies, dancers leafing through *Backstage* pretty much knew what was required of them for a Fosse audition.

During that formative decade from 1956–1966, of the eight musicals he worked on in different capacities, few are remembered as hallmarks of the American musical theater. In fact, one—*Pleasures and Palaces*—never made it to Broadway, and another—*The Conquering Hero*—closed barely a week after it opened. They did, however, permit Fosse to explore new directions as a choreographer, or, more accurately, to return to old musical forms and revamp them.

Fosse's work during this decade is also remarkable for the creative output inspired by Gwen Verdon. It was Verdon who made demands to *Redhead*'s producers that Fosse be her choreographer *and* director in that show. Only Jerome Robbins and Fosse could lay claim to the credit "director-choreographer" during the Fifties. Without Verdon's intervention, it seems likely Fosse might have waited a few more years—if not another decade—for his shot at directing a show. The Verdon-Fosse liaison did not disappoint. From *Damn Yankees* through *New Girl in Town*, *Redhead*, and *Sweet Charity*, Verdon won three Tony Awards for her

Gwen Verdon *(Courtesy of Dance Magazine)*

musical–comedy work in Broadway shows choreographed by Fosse, and was nominated for a fourth. When she and Fosse married in 1960, it cemented an artistic collaboration.

To appreciate Fosse's accomplishments at this time, it is important to have a general understanding of the sort of musical–theater dances that came before his arrival on Broadway. If any twentieth-century choreographer had a historian's fascination with dance antiquities, it was Bob Fosse.

That his dance material harks to the past is no secret to anyone who recalls the "Mu Cha-Cha" from *Bells Are Ringing,* the "Uncle Sam Rag" from *Redhead,* or the "Rich Kid's Rag" from *Little Me.* In fact, as Fosse matured as a choreographer, his more contemporary work dovetailed Broadway jazz dance with old-time vaudeville, such as "Magic to Do" from *Pippin,* "Me and My Baby" from *Chicago,* and "Recollections of an Old Dancer" from *Dancin'.* More than any other Broadway choreographer, including Gower Champion, Fosse realized the appeal of a George M. Cohan style of show, presented as something quite contemporary; his ability to borrow heavily from these music-hall traditions without creating derivative pop-up facsimiles of show dances remains one of his greatest accomplishments.

Traditionally, dance in musical theater has served to communicate to the melting-pot audiences of Broadway. (Today's audiences are much more homogenous, not surprising given the price of theater tickets today.) Dance conveys emotion without words, and, from its very beginnings in American revues of the late eighteenth and early nineteenth centuries, show "hoofing" was used rather amorphously as the glue that held the other components together. Olios, pantomime, toe dancing (a bastardized form of ballet), "legomania" (a full leg extension), and acrobatic and eccentric dancing all titillated audiences while demanding little intellectually. Up until the Thirties, vaudeville relied almost exclusively on these popular dances.

The first person to change the face of dance in the Broadway musical significantly was George Balanchine. Trained at the Russian Imperial Ballet School and, later, a choreographer with Serge Diaghilev's Ballets Russes, Balanchine invested his nightclub and Broadway choreography

From left to right, Ray Walston, Gwen Verdon, and Bob Fosse, with their respective Tony Awards for 1955's *Damn Yankees. (Gary Warner)*

with a narrative that was heretofore unheard of for musicals. His "Slaughter on Tenth Avenue" ballet for Richard Rodgers' and Lorenz Hart's 1936 *On Your Toes* startled audiences with its nonverbal communication of the storyline, and his musical theater translation of *Scheherazade,* "La Princess Zenobia," was a sophisticated send-up of the classical ballet. Just as Broadway musicals in general were retiring the wormwood conventions of mindless musical revues featuring dancing "lovelies," so were Broadway dancemakers eschewing rote dance numbers. *On Your Toes* redefined the role of the "dance director" when Balanchine insisted that he be credited as a "choreographer," with total conception and artistic control of dances fully incorporated into the book and score. A dance director's responsibility was primarily to rearrange dances to the satisfaction of the director and musical arranger; the choreographer's position was more autonomous.

Seven years later, choreographer Agnes de Mille's dream ballet, "Laurie Makes Up Her Mind," in 1943's *Oklahoma!* began a musical-theater trend. De Mille refused to pander to the assumed ignorance of the audience where ballet was concerned. *Oklahoma!* boasted dignified, professionally trained ballet dancers whose every lift, arabesque, and port de bras conveyed the musical's intentions as effectively as the book and score. Later, her considerable achievement in moving from choreographer to director paved the way for a new era in musical theater defined by the director-choreographer.

Jerome Robbins further defined the new breed of multipurpose showman in 1957 with *West Side Story*'s credit "conceived, directed, and choreographed by"; two years later, *Redhead* bore the words "Entire production directed and choreographed by Bob Fosse." The new generation had arrived.

Next to Jack Cole, Gower Champion (*Bye Bye Birdie; Hello, Dolly!; 42nd Street*) comes closest to capturing the love of vintage hoofing embodied in Fosse's early work. While Cole's work was heavily influenced by ethnic dance, Champion was the torch bearer of the Busby Berkeley tradition of show dance. But whereas Champion remained true to the spirit of Broadway at its most innocent and naïve, Fosse's later choreography intentionally corrupts old-time Broadway and vaudeville shows, especially evident in the cynical number "Razzle Dazzle" from *Chicago*.

For Balanchine, de Mille, and Robbins, stage musicals provided a springboard to a more "legitimate" form of dance expression, the ballet. And, indeed, all of them forged new careers that, in many ways, far surpassed what they might have accomplished on Broadway. But Cole, whose expansive dance vocabulary indicates he might have had a career as illustrious as Balanchine's, de Mille's, or Robbins's, clung tenaciously to the promise of commercial stardom in films and stage musicals that offered only glimpses of his enormous talent. Champion and Fosse simply knew their limitations. "The musical is my field. I create especially for the musical theater and I couldn't cross over to the City Center and do a ballet like Jerry [Robbins] can . . ." admitted Champion in 1964. Fosse had similar reservations. When *Dance Magazine* pressed him on his always-in-the-works ballet for the Joffrey in 1975, he said, "One of my great fears . . . is that I don't know if I could sustain a dance work of any length. I think whatever I do—whether it's good or bad—is best said in four or five minutes, maybe six; and about the maximum I've ever sustained a number was about seven minutes. . . . I don't know whether I can hold the stage longer than that."

BELLS ARE RINGING

Fosse's apprenticeship as a musical-theater choreographer ended with two shows, 1956's *Bells Are Ringing* and 1957's *New Girl in Town*. The directorial team of George Abbott and Jerome Robbins had splintered after *Damn Yankees,* but Fosse continued to work with them individually. With Robbins, he co-choreographed *Bells Are Ringing;* under Abbott's direction, he choreographed *New Girl in Town*. Between the two stage musicals, Fosse went to Hollywood to choreograph *The Pajama Game* and *Damn Yankees*. Barely thirty, he was already shuttling between coasts at a pace that would not slacken until he died.

Bells Are Ringing confirmed Fosse as a Robbins protégé. Theater critic Clive Barnes told *Rolling Stone* in 1984, "Fosse is post-Robbins, who was the first to see dance in terms of direction." But Fosse never put himself in the same league. "[Robbins] talks to God," he told *Rolling Stone* in 1984. "When I call God, he's out to lunch." For both choreographers, *Bells Are Ringing* provided numerous opportunities to infuse a particularly slight storyline with high-voltage dances. The musical's other mark of distinction was its cast, led by the effervescent Judy Holliday, playing a benevolent switchboard operator who gets involved with the lives of some of her callers. Also starring were Charlie Chaplin's son, Sidney Chaplin, Jean Stapleton, and Peter Gennaro, one of the era's best specialty dancers, who would later become a choreographer as well. *Bells Are Ringing* boasted an all-star creative team, with a score by Jule Styne and book and lyrics by Betty Comden and Adolph Green.

From left to right, co-choreographers Jerome Robbins and Bob Fosse discuss staging ideas for 1956's *Bells Are Ringing* with composer Adolph Green. *(Roderick MacArthur)*

Comden and Green had written the show expressly for Holliday, who had last appeared on Broadway in their *Revuers*. Since then, she had rocketed to stardom in Hollywood, winning an Oscar for her performance in *Born Yesterday* and establishing her particular kooky screen presence in other films depicting her as a timid, bubbling blonde with a piping voice who is always a lot smarter than everyone else thinks she is.

Holliday's dizzying, madcap eccentricities provided Robbins and Fosse with ample opportunities to choreograph dances that explored the storyline's knockabout brand of boulevard comedy, even if, as Fosse told *After Dark* in 1972, "Judy Holliday really had no feeling for dance whatsoever." Because Robbins was then associate artistic director of New York City Ballet and had just completed his first film. *The King and I,* as well as a new ballet, *The Concert, Bells Are Ringing*'s choreographic responsibilities were largely delegated to Fosse, who came up with marvelously witty dances. "Hello, Hello, There!," in which Holliday ingratiates herself with some typically dour-faced straphangers in a Bay Ridge, Brooklyn, subway train, would be reprised some years later in another subway scene in *Sweet Charity*. "The Midas Touch" was a throwback to Fosse's nightclub days, and affectionately spoofed a mishmash of gaudy chorus girl routines in a fictitious dance den called the Pyramid Club. Ten years later he would update Fifties nightclubs to Sixties discotheques in *Sweet Charity*'s "Rich Man's Frug."

The standout dance of *Bells Are Ringing*—"Mu Cha-Cha"—was performed by Gennaro, Holliday, and Ellen Ray. It revisited the same Latin-dance territory explored in Carol Haney's showstopping, tango-like "Hernando's Hideaway" from *The Pajama Game* and Fosse and Verdon's "Who's Got the Pain?" mambo in *Damn Yankees*. Here, Gennaro, playing a dancing delivery boy with an eye on the comely Holliday, shows her the joys of dancing a mambo, and soon she is thrusting her pelvis and pumping her arms like a blonde Carmen Miranda. Although the number did little to progress the narrative, it did serve to bolster the prevailing lunacy of Holliday's character. Fosse had already proven he could create stars from his dances, as evidenced in performances by Haney and Verdon in past projects. The coming decades would see him molding dance stars out of Shirley MacLaine, Liza Minnelli, Ben Vereen, Ann Reinking, and Sandahl Bergman. If a musical's box-office clout rested partly on its star turns, Fosse was fast evolving as Broadway's Svengali.

Budgeted at $360,000, *Bells Are Ringing* was an immediate hit with the public and most critics, primarily on the basis of Holliday's performance. Brooks Atkinson of the *New York Times* called the plot, ". . . one of the most antiquated of the season . . . on the level of a routine vaudeville show," but conceded that Holliday was exemplary as the harried switchboard operator and that the choreography ". . . provides the regulation good ballet numbers."

A box-office stampede overtook the Shubert Theatre the next day, where, for the following week, there were daily queues of over a hundred people. The show quickly built up an advance of over $1 million, and when Holliday left nearly two years later, *Bells Are Ringing* had sold over $5 million worth of tickets. Through the years, Holliday's character, Ella Peterson, became a star vehicle for a host of other musical-theater actresses, including Jane Russell, Peggy Cass, June Havoc, Julie Wilson, Shelly Winters, Janet Blair, and Betty Garrett. But Holliday has remained most associated with the role, no doubt because she also co-starred, with Dean Martin, in Vincente Minnelli's rather static 1960 MGM film musical of the show, with unremark-

able choreography by Charles O'Curran. *Bells Are Ringing* was Fosse's third consecutive hit show.

Judy Holliday and Peter Gennaro rug-cut with Fosse's "Mu Cha-Cha" in *Bells Are Ringing. (Billy Rose Theatre Collection)*

NEW GIRL IN TOWN

Bob Fosse had just completed choreographing the screen version of *The Pajama Game* when he began work with George Abbott on *New Girl in Town* in 1956. Verdon, who, after two years, was still starring in *Damn Yankees,* had been cast in the lead role in what was presumably the dramatic musical translation of Eugene O'Neill's Pulitzer Prize–winning play about a fallen woman, *Anna Christie.* Abbott, who had adapted other classics into musicals before, including Shakespeare's *Comedy of Errors* as *The Boys from Syracuse,* spent six weeks writing the book while composer Robert Merrill wrote eighteen songs in eleven days. Verdon and Fosse, who had been living together, worked tirelessly on the dances-in-development.

"Bobby and Gwen spent much of the summer by themselves working on a number ("The Red Light Ballet") that was set in a whorehouse," recalls Abbott. "It was obvious they'd worked hard on it; in fact, all of us appreciated that Bobby had gone to extremes to come up with something imaginative. But I didn't think the dance worked. I thought the reaction of Anna to the whorehouse should be one of repugnance, but Bob and Gwen made the whole thing look glamorous. The tone was all wrong, and I told them so. I don't think either of them liked me for a while after that," he said, chuckling.

New Girl in Town was the first musical Verdon had done that allowed her to demonstrate her proficiency as an actress, achieved principally

Fosse and Verdon rehearsing in a studio for *New Girl in Town. (Billy Rose Theatre Collection)*

though numbers such a waterfront ball, the infamous "Red Light Ballet"—which arrived on Broadway considerably toned down from its original form—and "On the Farm," in which Anna recounted her history of being sexually abused as a child on her family's Minnesota farm. There were, of course, lighter numbers as well. "There Ain't No Fleas on Me" indicated Fosse's fondness for steamer-trunk props, such as straw hats and canes, while "Roll Yer Socks Up" proved he could choreograph an old-fashioned, rousing production number in the grand tradition of the music hall circa 1900. All of the dances were significant because they fleshed out Anna's character, and since Verdon was principally a dancer, Fosse used choreography to create her role.

Ultimately, it was Verdon and Fosse who made *New Girl in Town* a hit. Critics largely agreed that Abbott's book cheapened its source, sometimes embarrassingly. When, at one point, the actor George Wallace as Mat Burke learns of Anna's past and gasps, "You slut . . . you dirty slut!" audiences could be heard sniggering. Verdon's triumph was that

Scenes from Fosse's controversial dance, "The Red Light Ballet," from 1957's *New Girl in Town,* starring Gwen Verdon. Director George Abbott forced Fosse to tone down the sexually explicit dance before the show opened on Broadway. *(Billy Rose Theatre Collection)*

her already-established comic flair gave levity to the script's feeble attempts at shock-drama. And, when she danced, it didn't matter what show Verdon was starring in; audiences would have come to see her in anything.

Many people believed Fosse was riding on the coattails of Verdon's enormous box-office appeal, and that it was she, not Fosse, who was responsible for her dances. But, claimed the late Phil Friedman, Fosse's long-time stage manager, "That's just not true. But whenever Fosse choreographed for a dancer, man or woman, he used the qualities that that person had in order to create the very best that could be delivered on stage. So when he was choreographing for Gwen, he used her best qualities—the line, the big kicks, the Jack Cole squiggles—she could do anything. Bobby interpolated the best things she could do in his own choreography for her."

She had worked steadfastly to erase audiences' perception of her as a "flame-haired, green-orbed" siren in toe shoes, even going so far as to bleach her hair blonde. She told the *New York Times* in 1957, "The first thing is always my red hair. . . . I thought, 'Never mind the color of my hair.' Some day I'll turn gray, and I want to be remembered as good, not just flame-haired."

Studying with acting coach Sanford Meisner, she applied her own tormented childhood to Anna's fear of discovery and recrimination. "I was crippled when I was little, and I wore special black shoes. I could see people look at me and think I was pretty but still think I was crippled. And even after I was able to take those shoes off, I was afraid something would stick out and give me away. For Anna, I'm trying to be a lady, but now people look at me and still think I'm a prostitute. Something gives me away."

That "something" became Verdon's trademark as much as Fosse's sexually convoluted choreography. Having worked together in only two shows, Fosse and Verdon had already defined what would become Verdon's alter ego, the hard-luck, well-intentioned bad girl who wears her heart on her sleeve—or, as in *Sweet Charity,* tattooed on her arm—and talks with her feet. For if any musical stage dancer could convey through dance the passionate extremes of a woman in love, it was Verdon. From Anna's near-crucifixion as a whore in *New Girl in Town* to Roxie Hart's defiant "nobody walks out on me!" murder of her estranged lover in *Chicago,* Gwen Verdon's characters are paradoxes. However sexually experienced they may be, these women remain romantic neophytes.

Nearly twenty years after *New Girl in Town,* Verdon examined her collection of Charity Hope Valentines in a *People* magazine profile. "When it comes to love, those girls I've played are naïve and pure. They are looking for someone to really love. But they aren't bright and they haven't been brought up in a family situation that enables them to evaluate. As for the prostitutes, well, they're 'loved' every 20 minutes, or what substitutes for love in about 90 percent of American homes—I'm pretty cynical about that."

Proof that Verdon had arrived as a formidable musical actress occurred abruptly while the show was trying out in Boston. Sidelined with the flu, Verdon was replaced by *four* understudies; one read Anna's dialogue and sang, three other women performed the dances.

Although *New Girl in Town* paid off its $200,000 investment, earned an estimated $72,000, and enjoyed a lengthy run, like *Bells Are Ringing,* the show was really a thinly veiled excuse to show off the merits of its star and choreographer despite an inconsequential book and score. Certainly, it did not harm the careers of anyone involved, though attempts to revive the show have been rather fruitless. When New York City's Equity Library Theater, a musical repertory company that specializes in reviving old shows, staged *New Girl in Town* in 1975, it jettisoned the dances completely, thus negating both Anna's development as a character and Fosse's dance narratives. The revival left audiences who had not seen the original musical wondering how such minimal musical merits could have been responsible for a show that won Verdon, co-star Thelma Ritter, and Fosse Tony Awards.

New Girl in Town is most significant as Fosse's first effort as a Broadway choreographer without the assistance of Jerome Robbins. The dances succeeded because of Fosse's invention and Verdon's execution. Together, they became the Alfred Lunt–Lynne Fontanne of musical theater. Their off-stage affair fueled their creative outpouring. As Verdon continued to win accolades as a Broadway star of Mary Martin–Ethel Merman stature, she never let anyone forget that it was first Jack Cole, then Michael Kidd, and now Bob Fosse who had exploited her considerable talents as a dancer. And when Verdon was approached by producers Robert Fryer and Lawrence Carr to star in a musical set in a London waxworks, she agreed only on the terms that Fosse would choreograph *and* direct her.

"When they were getting *Redhead* together," Fosse told *Penthouse* in 1973, "she simply said, 'He's my director. *Bob Fosse's my director.'* Can you believe that? I'd never directed, but she believed in me . . . insisted. And because of her I was able to do it. Gwen's got to be one of the greatest performers. I mean, the *greatest* . . ."

REDHEAD

By 1959, only a few choreographers could claim they had also *directed* Broadway musicals, and Fosse was one of them. Along with Agnes de Mille and Jerome Robbins, he was part of a group of dancemakers who believed the line between directing dancers and the rest of a musical's cast had become all but invisible through the years. Director-choreographers maintained that movement was the wellspring of dramatic situations. By the Eighties, with the arrival of third-generation choreographers such as Michael Bennett and his assistant Bob Avion, Tommy Tune, and Graciela Daniele, dance's reason for being on the Broadway stage had been drastically altered. *Dreamgirls,* for example, boasted four columns of on-stage lighting towers that Bennett had "choreographed," which were as integral to the progression of the narrative as the book, music, and dances. The notion of putting a set as well as the dancers in motion transformed the theatrical landscape.

"Being *just* a choreographer had its drawbacks as well," Fosse reflected to *Dance Magazine* in 1975. "I would find that the director had the final say. And in my early days I objected strenuously to some of the ways that shows were going. But the only way to control this was to be the boss and to make the show all of one fabric. There's such an advantage to having the control, as director-choreographer; the power is enormous."

Fosse's requisite derbies, white gloves, and spats won over audiences in 1959's *Redhead,* starring Gwen Verdon, center. *(Billy Rose Theatre Collection)*

Although it is doubtful Fosse, then in his thirties, would have become a director without the intervention of Gwen Verdon, his debut was undeniably auspicious. First, there was the material. *Redhead* was fanciful pink-champagne-and-black-tights fluff, lending itself almost completely to song-and-dance numbers. The plot concerned an English spinster named Essie Whimple (Verdon), an apprentice in a turn-of-the-century London waxworks modeled after the famed Madam Tussaud's. Spoofing Victorian thrillers, the show's book presents a red-bearded (hence, the title) assailant, reminiscent of Jack the Ripper, who slinks through the waxworks strangling unsuspecting young women with purple scarves. Verdon's love interest, who transforms her from a wallflower into a prancing, pink-haired sprite, is Richard Kiley, who may or may not also be the villain. The mock-ominous mood of the show is established immediately when the waxworks serves "tea and spirits of ammonia" to its patrons after unveiling its latest Chamber of Horrors exhibit.

Although its setting was original, *Redhead,* written by Dorothy and Herbert Fields, could not find interested producers for nearly ten years. The script had been offered to several stars in the hopes they might bankroll the show themselves, or take it to a producer. But Ethel Merman, Beatrice Lillie, Mary Martin, Celeste Holm, and Gisele Mac-Kenzie all declined. At one point, Irving Berlin was commissioned to write the score, but he, too, backed out and Albert Hague was hired. When Verdon was given the script, she felt that to make the show work for her own special abilities, she would need a director sensitive to her strengths as a dancer, and recommended Fosse to producers Richard Fryer and Lawrence Carr. They agreed on the basis that she would perform in the backer's auditions, which she did.

Choreographer Donald McKayle assisted Fosse on the dance numbers. He recalls that, at the time of *Redhead,* Fosse was "very interested in this thing called choreographing. He even took classes in it offered by Anna Sokolow. He told me she once said she didn't like his choreography. But he saw that as a challenge to become better. He was highly competitive, a man driven by a desire for excellence. He rented a studio next to the Edison Hotel, where he also kept a room. We'd rehearse there late into the night. Fosse always had a cigarette in his mouth. There was sort of a groove in his lip where it sat. I don't ever remember him dragging on it. He just kept working until there was an ash about three inches long on it, then he'd snuff it out and stick another one in his mouth."

Gwen Verdon *(Photofest)*

By the time *Redhead* arrived on Broadway in February 1959, it had gone through an estimated sixty rewrites and a few hundred revisions. When librettist Herbert Fields died during production of the show, writers Sidney Sheldon and David Shaw were brought in to assist his sister Dorothy Fields. It was generally agreed the musical's Achille's heel was the book; composer Albert Hague recalled to the *Newark Evening News* in 1959 that during *Redhead*'s frantic out-of-town rewrites in New Haven, ". . . it got to be so we used a different color binder for each script that was changed. Four times we ran out of colors and had to use numbers."

Technical problems and Verdon's bouts with illness threatened to postpone the $300,000 show repeatedly. While in Philadelphia, a jail-cell set crashed during a performance, pinning all Verdon's toes and one instep to the stage. Five doctors in the house came to the rescue, but she insisted on finishing the number. Fosse was livid. "I saw him try to attack a guy who'd had a few beers and dropped a set on my feet," Verdon told author Glenn Loney in *Unsung Genius*. "[The man] was a stagehand in *Redhead*. I've seen Bob get deranged . . ."

Donald McKayle says that Fosse and Verdon had evenly matched tempers. If there was never any question who was in charge of the show off the proscenium, onstage, everyone knew that Gwen was the star. "Gwen was the first person I'd ever worked with who always had *two* follow spots on her," says McKayle. "Sometimes, if she liked a particular actor or dancer enough, she arranged so that the spots sort of fell on them too, like they were part of her light."

At five feet four inches and 125 pounds, Verdon fought constantly to keep her weight up during the nearly three-hour-long show. She was frequently ill and claimed to lose several pounds at each performance. When a reporter from the *New York Tribune* interviewed her in her dressing room one night, he noted she consumed "a double orange juice, a glass of milk, a cup of hot chocolate and gobs of whipped cream, several pieces of candy, a chicken sandwich. . . . Before the show, incidentally, she had had a roast beef dinner, a milkshake with egg and assorted vitamins. During the show she swigged at a honey bottle."

It was a necessary diet. The dances Fosse had devised for Verdon were enormously strenuous. They were also some of his best to date. If, as critics indicated, the choreography in *Redhead* at times called too much attention to itself and Verdon, while Fosse's overall direction seemed to abandon the book and the score, the dances succeeded on their own terms. "Uncle Sam Rag" parades an entire history of American music-hall dances as perceived by the very proper British. "Erbie Fitch's Twitch" resurrects legomania; Verdon strutted on stage in Charlie Chaplin baggy pants, a bowler hat, and cane. The end of the first act concludes with an ambitious, full-scale dream ballet embracing popular entertainments from French cabaret to a circus strong-man act. In one of the funniest dance moments, in the cluttered waxworks, the strangler is chased in a burlesque of the Keystone Kops.

Buzz Miller danced with Verdon in "The Pickpocket Tango," playing a jailer who is accosted by Verdon in order to get his cell keys. "I think she is coming on to me," Miller recalls, "but it's really the keys she's after when she's got her hands all over me. It was a charming number. Bob had been in a room for six weeks rehearsing it. He never set a rehearsal time with us. He'd just take us in the back room and give us some steps. There was always a wealth of possibilities." Sixteen years later, Fosse would draw from "The Pickpocket Tango" for *Chicago's* "Cellblock Tango."

"What I got from Bob Fosse was direction like I've never had in my life," Verdon told the *New York Times Magazine* in 1959. "I was way out on a limb though. I thought, either I have no taste at all or I'll please some people who will be amused or entertained by what amuses or entertains me."

Redhead proved to be yet another monstrous hit for Fosse and Verdon, though this victory was particularly sweet because it was Fosse's first credit reading "entire production directed and choreographed by." *Variety* predicted, "If there has been any lingering doubt about Miss Verdon's star status, this show should remove it." And though its book was universally faulted, *Redhead*'s staging and Verdon's star appeal generated a tremendous box office. The show had a $1 million advance before it opened, and, the day after, 750 people stood in line outside the 46th Street Theatre to purchase tickets. *Redhead* ran for over a year before beginning a national tour. United Artists reportedly had tagged Verdon to do a screen version of the show; this picture was never made, but *Redhead* went on to win five Tony Awards in 1959, including outstanding direction and choreography. In addition to clinching the Tony for outstanding actress in a musical Verdon won a Grammy for her vocal work on the *Redhead* cast album.

THE CONQUERING HERO

G wen Verdon had no desire to marry again after her divorce from Henaghan, but she did want to have a child with Fosse. While *Redhead* was playing in Chicago in 1960, they clandestinely wed. She described the Evanston, Ill., ceremony to the *New York Times* in 1981. It "was in a place I looked up in the telephone book. The justice of the peace had a living room decorated like a chapel and a record playing 'Oh Promise Me' or something on that order."

Verdon and Fosse refused to confirm the marriage for five months, primarily because Fosse's second wife, Joan Mc-Cracken—recently divorced from Fosse—was seriously ill, and it was no secret that he and Verdon had been keeping company for some time. But the press had its ear to the gossip grist mill, and learned of the marriage a few days after the ceremony. Shortly thereafter, while Verdon and Fosse were dining at New York's Harwyn Club, photographers besieged them, and the next day rumors of their wedding were in most of the dailies.

Two years after Fosse and Verdon were wed, Verdon spoke candidly of how performers were obliged by their profession to compromise their personal lives to their craft. "[Performers] tend to marry between the afternoon and evening shows," she told the *Daily News*. "They bury their parents on weekends so they don't miss being on stage, things like that. When my mother died, I didn't go to her funeral. I was in *Damn Yankees* and couldn't leave." Verdon ostensibly "retired" from the stage after the

Fosse rehearsing a war dance for 1961's *The Conquering Hero,* his first Broadway flop. (*Billy Rose Theatre Collection*)

marriage to devote herself to raising a family. She and Fosse began trying to conceive a child, but Verdon was counseled by doctors not to get pregnant because of her age, though she was only thirty-four. Fosse, on the other hand, was told by his physician that he had "slow sperm"; adoption was advised.

Meanwhile, Fosse was engaged to direct and choreograph what would be his first flop, *The Conquering Hero,* based on the 1944 Preston Sturges film *Hail the Conquering Hero* about a marine who is undeservedly given a hero's welcome when he returns home from fighting overseas. Although the show is little remembered today, *The Conquering Hero* was a landmark show for choreographers. Fosse was dismissed halfway through its out-of-town tryouts, in Washington, D.C., by producers unhappy with his work because they believed a battle number he'd choreographed made soldiers look effeminate. It was the first time he'd ever been fired from a show. He was advised by his attorney, Jack Pearlman, to remove his dances from the production. Fosse declined on the basis that critical opinion of the early performances of the musical indicated the choreography was *The Conquering Hero*'s highlight.

Instead of withdrawing his choreography, Fosse asked for a letter from the producers guaranteeing that if one of his dances was used, it would be presented in its entirety and not "in some mutilated form." When the producers refused this request, Fosse offered a compromise. If his two lengthy ballets were preserved intact, he wrote them, they could do whatever they wanted with the remainder of his work. When *The Conquering Hero* opened at the ANTRA Theatre on January 16, 1961, the *New York Herald-Tribune* noted, ". . . there's a dance quite early that . . . suggests a whole new profitable vein for musical-comedy choreography. . . . Nothing is labored here, the uncredited choreography is all very deadpan and all very funny." "We wondered who directed the swift and galvanized dances, which looked to us like the work of Bob Fosse," offered the *Newark Evening News.*

Upon Fosse's termination, rumors began circulating that he had left the show due to artistic differences. In order to dispel such reputation-damaging accusations, Fosse sent a telegram to the *New York Times* on December 14, 1960, barely a month before *The Conquering Hero* was to open on Broadway, explaining his release from the show and his plans to seek immediate action for the protection of his choreography through the American Arbitration Association. Fosse requested, and was rewarded, a mere six cents in damages. The amount of money, he reasoned, was irrelevant. What was at stake were the rights to his own material.

Verdon and Fosse at New York's Harwyn Club, 1960, a few days after they clandestinely wed. *(AP/Wide World Photos)*

Fosse's minor contretemps succeeded in calling attention to the plight of choreographers whose work, however instrumental to the formation of a musical, is often most vulnerable to violation. It would not be until 1976 that a revised copyright act designated pantomime and choreography as subject matter suitable for copyright in the United States. Today, no Fosse musical produced after 1976 may be staged without adhering to the original choreography unless the producers have written permission from the Fosse estate. Thus, *The Conquering Hero*'s arbitration against the show's producers was a landmark victory.

The show itself, however, was another matter. When *The Conquering*

Tom Poston (center) starred as an unjustly honored war hero in 1961's *The Conquering Hero. (Billy Rose Theatre Collection)*

Hero opened on Broadway, its *Playbill* conspicuously omitted credit for either director or choreographer. Though Albert Marre had been called in as director when Fosse was fired, and Tod Bolender supervised the choreography, neither man received credit in the New York program. Their absence would seem to indicate that the producers realized Fosse's work was still recognizable. Years later, when Fosse was called in to "doctor" ailing musicals out of town—such as Harold Prince's *Grind,* starring Ben Vereen—some reviewers could not help noting that Fosse's touch was evident. Unfortunately, even the most inventive choreography could not salvage *The Conquering Hero*'s ailing book and score; it closed after only eight performances. Because of his legal actions against the show, Fosse was the only member of its creative staff who escaped artistically unscathed.

HOW TO SUCCEED
IN BUSINESS...

A fter *The Conquering Hero*'s disaster, Fosse made two strategic and discerning moves in 1961. The first was to return to the stage as a performer in a revival of *Pal Joey,* produced by the New York City Center Light Opera Company; the second was to stage the musical numbers from *How to Succeed in Business Without Really Trying*.

Pal Joey, of course, was the Richard Rodgers and Lorenz Hart musical that had put Fosse on the map as a promising musical-theater actor and dancer in a 1952 Broadway revival. In fact, Fosse's performance in a summer stock production of the show in 1954—which he also choreographed—attracted the attention of several Broadway scouts, and it is largely believed that it was Fosse who was the catalyst that sparked *Pal Joey*'s subsequent revival.

Nine years later, Fosse had grown into the role perfectly. An ambitious, fast-talking performer/entrepreneur who makes up for his lack of business savvy with brazen, audacious charm, Joey appears to have been tailor-made for Fosse. *Pal Joey*'s protagonist flagrantly uses his good looks and ability to think on his feet to seduce a number of well-groomed, sometimes well-heeled women, one of whom is so smitten with him that she invests her considerable assets in a club called Chez Joey. Playing Joey also solidified Fosse's position as a jack-of-all-trades showman; not only could he choreograph and direct, but he still found

Office workers suffer caffeine withdrawal in Fosse's hilarious "Coffee Break" dance from *How to Succeed in Business Without Really Trying. (Billy Rose Theatre Collection)*

time to headline a major musical revival. Reporters were drawn to the busman's-holiday angle of the story. Theater historians have noted that Fosse's performance ranks alongside those of the best Joeys, including Gene Kelly, Harold Lang, and, in the film, Frank Sinatra.

Fosse parlayed his singing, acting, and dancing into musical staging when he was invited by producers Ernest Martin and Cy Feuer, the team responsible for bringing *Guys and Dolls* to Broadway, to consult on the dances in a new musical called *How to Succeed in Business Without Really Trying*. Based on a 148-page best-seller by advertising agency vice president Shepherd Mead, *How to Succeed . . .* made its first appearance on stage as a comedy by Jack Weinstock and Willie Gilbert. Feuer and Martin optioned it, brought in veteran Broadway musical librettist Abe Burrows to collaborate on the book, Frank Loesser to write the score, and Hugh Lambert to choreograph. The story concerned the adventures of a business-savvy window washer (Robert Morse) who, by reading Mead's book, learns how to claw his way to the top of the World Wide Wicket Company, Inc. Its president (Rudy Vallee) is won over by the young go-getter, as is most of the company, only to later discover the power-hungry monster they have created. *How to Succeed . . .* was a pre-*Doonesbury* skewering of free enterprise, and, especially in some of its Fosse-staged dances such as "Coffee Break" and "A Secretary Is Not a Toy," satirized what have become signposts of corporate America.

Explaining his involvement in the landmark show to *After Dark* in 1972, Fosse said, "I came in late on *How to Succeed. . . .* They were already in rehearsal. They had a young man doing the choreography. The director and the producer were vain enough to think they could do all other staging. They got into rehearsals and discovered they needed help. They already had the song, 'Coffee Break,' but they just didn't know how to stage it. I took it to its extreme, treating coffee as if it were a drug—as though people needed a coffee fix. The show was like a cartoon anyway, careful exaggeration was in order for the dance. And I thought: I can go as far as I want with this because the need for coffee in the morning can be, for some people, really quite desperate."

The resulting dance depicts office employees' "desperate" reactions when they learn the daily coffee trolley is out of caffeine. Their hysteria converges in a dance number that is less a traditional Fosse production number than a caustically funny illustration of what happens to the body's nervous system when it is deprived of its daily stimulant. The dancers' spasmodic gesturings and facial contortions fit snugly into the musical's consistently frenetic pace. Part of the show's enormous appeal stemmed from its creators' abilities to keep the action believable even

Robert Morse (left) and Rudy Vallee in the Pulitzer Prize-winning 1962 musical comedy *How to Succeed in Business Without Really Trying.* *(Billy Rose Theatre Collection)*

when the day-to-day operations of a Fortune 500 business are given a slapstick treatment. "The main problem," Fosse told *After Dark,* "was to make everything seem like it was possible, even remotely. They had to seem like people in an office."

Fosse's acute observations of the business world are reflected in "A

Dictation *en l'air:* Fosse's "A Secretary Is Not a Toy" number from *How to Succeed in Business Without Really Trying.* From left to right: Tracy Everitt, Donna McKechnie, Nick Andrews, Rosemarie Yellen. *(Courtesy of Dance Magazine)*

Secretary Is Not a Toy," which humorously rebuffs the mistreatment of women in the officeplace; "The Yo-Ho-Ho," a spoof of TV ad jingles; and especially "The Brotherhood of Man," an effective if mean-spirited climax to the show that assaults the fraudulent camaraderie of back-slapping corporate men. If, in fact, Fosse the dark humorist rears his head with "The Brotherhood of Man" in *How to Succeed . . . ,* his attitude toward hypocrisy was tame compared to the dances he would construct for his post–*Sweet Charity* film and stage musicals. Uncredited in the program, Verdon came in as Fosse's dance assistant on the show.

Donna McKechnie, whose first show with Fosse was *How to Succeed . . .* (in which she was in the chorus line), says she was amazed at how Verdon, a star in her own right, threw herself into assisting Fosse on the dances. "I could hardly get over the fact that this was the star of stars getting sweaty and saying, 'yes, Bobby; yes, Bobby.' They were married, and I was so impressed at how they worked together. They would go home every night and do their homework on the show. Gwen had some charming stories about how they'd jump all over the bed rehearsing steps. I had this mental picture of them hopping all over their furniture choreographing."

How to Succeed . . . became one of Fosse's most successful shows. Aside from Morse and Vallee, its cast included Bonny Scott, Charles Nelson Reilly, and Virginia Martin, all of whom had rarely been presented in better form on Broadway. Vallee capitalized on his appeal as a Twenties and Thirties crooner, at one point cupping a hand over his mouth like a megaphone to warble the song "Ah, There." Audiences were delirious. The show won the 1961 Pulitzer Prize, only the fourth time the coveted award was presented to a musical or play, and, during the first year of its three-and-a-half-year run at the 46th Street Theatre, was consistently sold out. When it closed in 1964, *How to Succeed . . .* had notched 1,418 performances and grossed over $10.5 million. In addition to the Pulitzer, it also won seven Tony Awards and the Drama Critics Circle Award. More than the awards, the show was significant for Fosse in that, for the first time in his career, his dances were acknowledged as being fully integrated into the musical. "The book, songs, staging, designs, and performances are all of a piece," wrote the *New York Times*. The producer of *How to Succeed . . . ,* Cy Feuer, would be responsible for a number of future Fosse projects, including the milestone film musical *Cabaret*.

LITTLE ME

Producers Cy Feuer and Ernest Martin, fast acquiring a string of hits to their credit, were intent on optioning more musical properties. In November 1961, Patrick Dennis, whose novel *Auntie Mame* spawned the long-running Broadway musical *Mame* with Rosalind Russell, wrote a parody of the pompous "as-told-to" star autobiographies called *Little Me*. His heroine was the manipulative, self-centered, would-be film star Belle Poitrine, considered to be so untalented that one of her husbands, the head of Metronome Pictures, kills himself after viewing her latest picture. Neil Simon was enlisted to adapt the book and Cy Coleman wrote the music with lyrics by Carolyn Leigh. Producer Cy Feuer was responsible for the book's direction, and Fosse handled the musical staging.

Simon's novel approach in his adaptation was to create two Belles, one younger (Virginia Martin), one older (Nancy Andrews), and one man who would play all of her husbands and lovers (Sid Caesar). The story of a wanna-be star who rises in the world when she becomes a fallen woman is played against her relationships with Caesar's characters—among them an adolescent, an eighty-eight-year-old skinflint, a Prussian film director, and a straw-hatted, singing boulevardier. The zaniness of Simon's characters is exemplified by Nobel Eggleston, one of the suitors, who goes to both Harvard and Yale, studies law and medicine, becomes a World War I flier who shoots down forty-six enemy planes—twenty-seven in the air, thirteen on the ground, six in the factory—and is

Little Me's funniest dance was Fosse's "Rich Kid's Rag," which sends up the pretentiousness of the idle rich. *(Billy Rose Theatre Collection)*

elected governor of both North and South Carolina. His absolute perfection is equaled only by his complete lack of happiness or self-worth. Unable to do anything wrong, Nobel gets no satisfaction out of doing anything right.

It was a tour de force comic role for Caesar, who had, in the Fifties and early Sixties, achieved considerable fame from his popular television comedy shows. *Newsweek* put him on the cover in 1962 surrounded by his assorted personas in *Little Me*. Other cast members included old burlesque comedian Joey Faye and specialty dancer Swen Swenson.

Swenson, who had studied at the School of American Ballet and with modern dancer-choreographer Merce Cunningham, recalls that he was asked "out of the blue" to audition; Fosse had seen him seven years earlier on stage and remembered him. At a second audition he was given "I've Got Your Number" to learn. "They told me they were looking for a cross between a Clark Gable and a Frank Sinatra," explains Swenson, "but after I went and learned the song, I found out it was being dropped. Apparently, they just couldn't get it to work in the context of the show and had given up on it. But it turned out to be the hit of the show."

The incident was one of many flare-ups between Fosse and lyricist Carolyn Leigh, who refused to cut any of her lyrics to accommodate Fosse's choreography. "She was one of those people who is extremely talented but she could be very insensitive about what she said," recalls Swenson. "If anybody made the slightest—I mean *slightest*—criticism about her work, she became traumatized." Adds Phil Friedman, who stage-managed the show, "When Bob wanted to cut a number from *Little Me,* Carolyn went into hysterics. Bob had this whistle he wore to get the dancers' attention, and she took it and ran out into the street, blowing on it unremittingly to get a cop's attention. She finally found one and told him to arrest Bob and close the show. Those are the kind of collaborative things Bobby constantly had to fight diplomatically, but with strength."

Although Fosse never lost his temper with dancers onstage, the police whistle he used was designed to cut through the general melee of auditions and get dancers organized in as orderly a way as possible. "I couldn't figure him out at first," says Swenson. "The first thing he said to me the night we started to work together was, 'You know, you're going to hate me when we're through.' And then there was that damn whistle. I wasn't sure if he blew it at me what I'd do. But it never happened. In fact, when we finished the number, he said, 'I haven't worked with anybody like you since Carol [Haney] and Gwen.' "

In "I've Got Your Number," Swenson played a lascivious Chicago

nightclub owner who se-
duces Belle with his sexy
striptease, a Chippendale's
act ahead of its time. The
number paid homage to burlesque strippers who didn't
take *everything* off, thus leaving the audience with some
anticipation. Plus, there was
the provocative twist of having the stripper be a good-
looking *man.* "It stopped the
show dead," says Swenson.
"Women were constantly
rushing toward the stage. I
knew this was the kind of
number you get once in a
lifetime."

Swenson recalls an inci-
dent that reveals the freedom
Fosse gave to dancers whose
instincts he trusted. One
night while the show was
playing a pre-Broadway engagement in Philadelphia,
the show's orchestra seemed
sluggish during "I've Got
Your Number," and Swenson

JACK MITCHELL
NEW YORK

devised some fill-in choreography to accommodate the slow tempo.
"Fosse ran backstage after I was finished," says Swenson, "and asked if I
remembered what I'd just done. He loved it and said, 'Keep it in.
Whenever you feel like it, whenever there's something you want to add
or embellish, go ahead and do it. I'll tell you when to stop.' He gave me
great freedom."

In retrospect, Swenson sees "I've Got Your Number" as an example
of effectively staged, sexually charged Fosse choreography that became
coarser in his Seventies musicals. "There is a sexual element to everything
he did," says Swenson, "and 'I've Got Your Number' worked because it
teased the audience without getting too low and vulgar. I think Fosse

Swen Swenson in *Little Me. (Jack Mitchell)*

was fascinated with lowlife, and it was disappointing to me that, as years passed, he became less restrained about expressing it. When I saw that ballet class number ['The Dream Barre'] in *Dancin'*, I was embarrassed for him."

Little Me also brought into Fosse's life two dancers who would be instrumental in his career and life: Kathryn Doby and Leland Palmer, both of whom auditioned for the national production of the show in 1963. Doby, who became Fosse's assistant on the film *Sweet Charity* and continued to dance and work for him through *All That Jazz* in 1979, says there were "hundreds and hundreds of dancers auditioning for him. It was his name and his reputation. And he was different; dancers got excited because he had a different style. He liked pretty girls; you would never find unattractive girls in any Fosse chorus. Beyond the fact that they had to be able to do his style, he looked for something that was sexually attractive to him. Good bodies. Nice long legs."

"In *Little Me,* I remember Bob as a real live wire," says Palmer, who played Fastrada in *Pippin* and Audrey in *All That Jazz.* "If he saw a dancer he admired, he pursued her. Very early on Bob told me I was special. 'You're not pretty, but your dancing and personality are lovely,' he said. But it was a problem [for chorus girls] to get involved with Bob."

Palmer recalls that the day she auditioned, Fosse was particularly edgy because of an incident that had occurred between him and a young woman who had tried out for the show earlier in the day. At Fosse's memorial service in October 1987, Neil Simon humorously recounted the incident. "It was the dancers' call and there were easily two hundred dancers to see that day. Bob sat on a stool at the center of the stage, his back to the orchestra seats where I was sitting alone, watching. Each dancer would put his or her dance bag at the side of the stage, then when called by name, would simply come out, do a long run, a leap, a twist and a jump in the air. Maybe more, but not much. . . . And Bob would either say, and always graciously, 'Please stand with the group on the right' or, 'Thank you very, very much.' . . . After about a hundred dancers had leapt across the stage, one very attractive but very nervous young lady came out, prepared and then did her run, leap, twist and jump and landed with a great smile on her face, looking at Bob for approval and a contract. Bob said, again graciously, 'Thank you very much.' The girl stood stunned. She didn't move, literally for minutes. There was dead silence in the theater. She walked over quietly, picked up

Sid Caeser (center) as a nightclub proprietor in Neil Simon's 1962 musical comedy *Little Me*, with musical staging by Fosse. *(Billy Rose Theatre Collection)*

her dance bag and said to Bob, 'No one says thank you to me' . . . and proceeded to pummel Bob with her heavy dance bag, hitting him so hard, she knocked him off the stool. Two stage hands pulled her away into the wings. Bob got back on the stool, smoothed back his hair and said, 'Ladies, no more dance bags on stage, please.' "

By the mid-Sixties, Fosse's reputation of being something of a Svengali was well known, and *Little Me,* in which Fosse strode around the stage with his whistle and appraised the anatomy of his gifted female dancers, represents the height of his self-indulgence. When a reporter from *Theater Arts* slipped backstage to observe rehearsals in November 1962, he described Fosse as ". . . probably close to being middle age, but he looks like a sub-teen Parisian street urchin ready to run from the *flics.* His gaunt, unlined face would be the delight of a New Wave director. His slightly stooped skinniness is accentuated by bone-tight trousers and a coat-sweater that manages to look baggy and form-hugging at the same time. A raffish cap is so much a part of his head it could have been born with him: Fosse's own cradle cap."

That "cradle cap" not only added to Fosse's look of studied rumpledness,but also camouflaged his own pink scalp. It was, in fact, his vanity that was responsible for the now-famous bowler hats and derbys used in so many of his dances. "I think I first used hats because, when I was very young, I began losing my hair," Fosse told *Dance Magazine*'s Richard Philp in 1975. "I thought, 'Well, a hat will cover that up.' So I became very adept at dancing with a hat on, taking it off, putting it on quickly, and so forth."

Coming on the heels of Fosse's biggest hit, *How to Succeed in Business Without Really Trying, Little Me* seemed like another foolproof musical. Producers Feuer and Martin had high hopes for the show; Neil Simon, Cy Coleman, and Fosse prayed for a hit. Though New York City was in the midst of a newspaper strike, all the first-night critics attended the show. Simon recalls its opening night, November 11, 1962, at the Lunt-Fontanne Theatre, "I was standing with Bob and Cy Coleman at the back of the house . . . and Sid Caesar, who otherwise gave a brilliant performance, coughed on each of his first three laugh lines . . . causing, obviously, no laugh on his first three laugh lines. I looked at Cy, Cy looked at me, and then we both looked at Bob. Bob very simply put his arms down at his sides, closed his eyes . . . and fell backwards, every part of his body hitting the floor simultaneously . . . a perfect Ten at any Olympics. . . . He hardly moved on the floor, except to moan very quietly. . . . And then, a few minutes later, a very hostile and inebriated man got out of his seat, walked up the aisle on his way to the men's room, turned to us and said angrily, 'This is the worst goddamned show I've seen since *My Fair Lady.*' . . . Bob laughed until he cried."

So did audiences. *Little Me* received generally glowing reviews, except from the *New York Times,* whose critic, Howard Taubman, lamented, ". . . not a great musical or even a consistently engaging one." Strangely, the show was only moderately successful on Broadway, running thirty-three weeks and never fully recouping its $400,000 investment. A subsequent London production in 1965 also failed to stir any long-term interest at the box-office, closing after 406 performances.

Swenson believes the failure of the show to ignite the box office was the fault of those who determined how *Little Me* would be advertised. "Because of the newspaper strike, the reviews weren't out the next day. But when the strike finally finished, I remember the first papers to hit the stands were two feet thick, and shows like *Oliver* and *Stop the World, I Want to Get Off,* which had also done well with the critics, had two-page spreads." *Little Me,* Swenson claims, was barely acknowledged. "It was only word-of-mouth that kept people coming." (Producers Feuer and Martin did not wish to comment on Fosse or any of his shows for this book.)

Little Me was revived briefly in 1981 by Neil Simon, who told the *New York Times* he believed ". . . it was not done properly the first time," and estimated that 40 percent of the show was new. Victor Garber and James Coco split the roles originally played by Sid Caesar. But the sight gag of one actor harnessed to multiple roles was what made the original production memorable; consequently, the revival lost some of the comic wallop of its predecessor. A 1984 London revival staged by John Sharpe more closely followed the staging of the original production.

PLEASURES AND PALACES

The next four years found Fosse shuttling from one musical project to another—*Funny Girl,* in which he cast Barbra Streisand in the role that launched her career, Alan Jay Lerner's *On a Clear Day You Can See Forever,* and Frank Loesser's last show, *Pleasures and Palaces.* He discussed this series of disappointments with *Penthouse* in 1973. "Seriously, about ten years ago I was really hot. Then I went on a show called *Funny Girl*—I cast Barbra Streisand for that, in fact—and stayed on that for about seven months. But then I had trouble with Ray Stark, the producer. It really had nothing to do with Ray at all; it was something that I built up in my mind. So I quit and went to Alan Lerner's *On a Clear Day You Can See Forever* for fourteen months. I didn't make a nickel on either of those projects. A director usually works for a piece of the box office. If the show closes, or doesn't open, he can work years for virtually nothing. With *On a Clear Day* Alan was having some kind of domestic trouble and he just wasn't writing. So I sat there—wondering what to do. I decided that *if* I was a director, then I had to work. I couldn't develop my craft just by sitting around for two years; I had to get to *work* with actors. So I took the first show that was offered me."

The show was *Pleasures and Palaces,* and it drew to an uneventful close the first half of Fosse's career on Broadway. It was another daunting experience, marked by daily friction between Fosse and his collaborators, composer Loesser, and librettist Sam Spewack. The production team of

Fosse rehearsing a Russian-inspired dance for his 1965 musical, *Pleasures and Palaces,* which closed out of town. *(Billy Rose Theatre Collection)*

Feuer and Martin told Fosse that Loesser, responsible for the music in *How to Succeed in Business Without Really Trying,* had written a new score, and asked if he'd be interested in directing a musical based on it. Fosse was so anxious to get back at the helm as director that he agreed without reading the script or listening to the music. "Once I heard the score and read the book, I knew we had trouble," Fosse told *Penthouse.* "But I still thought I could pull it off. It's that Jack Armstrong quality."

The show was a comic opera based on Spewack's Broadway comedy, *Once There Was a Russian,* which folded after one performance in 1961. The story concerns John Paul Jones' visit to Russia during the reign of Catherine the Great in 1787. To impress the Westerner, Catherine orders army officer and personal favorite Prince Grigori Aleksandrovich Potemkin to construct a faux American village (an elaborate multipurpose set was designed by Robert Randolph); a subplot concerns Potemkin's affair with a love-hungry woman named Sura. The cast was an odd lot, led by British actress Hy Hazell as Catherine, American John McMartin as John Paul Jones, British classical actor Alfred Marks as Potemkin, and American actress Phyllis Newman as Sura. It was unrealistic to expect that this hodge-podge of trans-Atlantic accents and acting styles could transport audiences to eighteenth-century Russia; even Fosse fumbled over the script's and lyric's attempts at Russian dialects, telling Loesser on the first day of rehearsals, "You should have Stanislavsky to direct this, not a simple Norwegian boy."

Fosse recruited dancers from many of his former shows—including *The Pajama Game, Redhead,* and *Little Me*—for the $450,000 *Pleasures and Palaces*. In the chorus were Kathryn Doby and Leland Palmer from *Little Me*. "I remember that there were always people coming in to work and fix it," says Palmer. "There was a lot of drama; a lot of sadness. . . . He was trying to establish himself as a director. Bob had a lot of personal feeling invested in it."

As is typical in many failed Broadway musicals, the source of *Pleasures and Palaces'* problems was ineffective communication. "We were all doing different things," Fosse told *Penthouse.* "Spewack was doing a Shavian comedy, Loesser was doing an opera, and I was doing a Russian version of *A Funny Thing Happened on the Way to the Forum.*" Indeed, when the *Detroit News* reviewed the show out of town, the show's choreography was described as ". . . a cross between *A Funny Thing Happened on the Way to the Forum* and the Moiseyev folk dancers," even though Fosse had recognized the dangers of imitating Russian folk dance; "I hope to do this show without a single Kazatsky," he told the *New York Herald Tribune.* "That's the one where you get down and kick from the knees. But it will be pretty hard. Every time you get on those fur-topped boots, you step right into it."

In fact, when rehearsing the dancers in a military number that opened the show, Fosse exchanged his familiar black Capezio jazz shoes for a pair of marching boots. Kathryn Doby says, "Bob always had a thing for rhythm and different sounds. He used stamps and claps and slaps [in the number]. The curtain went up and you saw a dark stage with one big staircase on it, which was supposed to be the Palace wall. . . . The number started backstage, where you heard stamps and claps. . . . Then people started marching on stage. Some of the boys had solo sections, strong jumping stuff. But the beginning, with just the sounds, was terribly exciting."

While in Detroit, it quickly became apparent the show was in serious trouble. American musical actor Jack Cassidy replaced Alfred Marks as Potemkin; constant rewrites kept the actors busy relearning their dialogue. Fosse was unable to develop a consistent comic tone for the show, which was further weakened by Loesser's undistinguished score and Spewack's ponderous book. The producers quietly decided to close the show before it moved to Broadway.

Leland Palmer recalls that after the dancers learned that the show was closing "everybody grouped together and did a parody for Bob to cheer him up. We tried to go out with a little celebration."

Elaborate costumes, sets, and a Frank Loesser score couldn't save *Pleasures and Palaces* from a transparent plot. *(Billy Rose Theatre Collection)*

"There was a number called 'Tears of Joy' that he had a lot of trouble with," says Doby. ". . . [T]he closing notice went up on a Tuesday, and there was a notice for a rehearsal of 'Tears of Joy' on Thursday, but since the show was going to close on Saturday, they were going to cancel the Thursday rehearsal. Because Bob had almost finished 'Tears of Joy,' the whole cast got together on that Thursday to rehearse it, even though everybody knew *Pleasures and Palaces* was history. But we all showed up and he finished the number. It was wonderful how the whole cast was rooting for Fosse to finish it. . . . [There] was something about Fosse, his own personal charisma, his determination not to give up on that show—even when it seemed hopeless he had a need to perfect it."

Although the beginning of the Sixties threatened to nullify Fosse's early achievements in his Fifties musicals, his personal satisfactions from his choreography in *How to Succeed in Business Without Really Trying* and *Little Me,* along with his marriage to Verdon, helped him to weather this fallow period in his career. In 1962, Verdon—already a grandmother from her son James Jr.—and Fosse began adoption proceedings that were interrupted when Verdon discovered she was pregnant. "Gee," Fosse said with amusement some years later in the *Los Angeles Times,* "we were ready to try fertility pills, but discovered the best way to hasten a pregnancy is to start adoption proceedings."

The baby girl, born in March 1963, was named Nicole Providence, the first name taken from a character in F. Scott Fitzgerald's *Tender Is the Night,* the second name proffered by lyricist Dorothy Fields because, she reasoned, it was providence that had intervened when doctors had told Verdon and Fosse they might not be able to have children. Because Verdon was assisting Fosse on his shows, Nicole frequently was brought along on the road with her parents. Verdon told *Family Circle* that Nicole uttered her first word while in a hotel room. It was, apropos for the offspring of two Broadway stars, "bellhop."

Despite Fosse's failure with *Pleasures and Palaces,* he already had his next project lined up. Joining people he felt comfortable with from past shows, including Neil Simon and Cy Coleman, Dorothy Fields, John McMartin, and Gwen Verdon, he began work on what would become *Sweet Charity*. It marked the beginnings of a new, bolder, more self-assured approach to creating a musical comedy, and heralded the second phase of Bob Fosse's Broadway career.

IV

THE FOSSE-FELLINI CONNECTION

Looking inside me
What do I see?
Anger and hope and doubt
What am I all about?
And where am I going?

> —*"Where Am I Going?"*
> *by Cy Coleman and Dorothy Fields,*
> *from* Sweet Charity

SWEET CHARITY

Of Bob Fosse's fourteen stage musicals, the most enduring is *Sweet Charity*. *The Pajama Game, Damn Yankees, Bells Are Ringing, How to Succeed in Business Without Really Trying,* and especially *Pippin, Chicago,* and *Dancin'* enjoyed longer runs, but *Sweet Charity,* which ran a respectable (and financially successful) 608 performances, remains one of Fosse's greatest achievements. It telegraphed the direction that his choreography and thematic concerns would take in future projects, exposed him to collaborators at the peaks of their professions, introduced him to his mentor, Federico Fellini, established him as a film director, and featured Gwen Verdon in her most spectacular role since her debut in *Can-Can* thirteen years earlier. *Sweet Charity* delineated the Fosse aesthetic forever in the public's and critics' minds. Its repercussions as a stage smash and film flop were equally responsible for Fosse's development as an auteur.

Sweet Charity's germination began some twenty years before it arrived on Broadway in 1966. Fledgling Italian director Federico Fellini, esteemed director Roberto Rossellini, and script writer Tullio Pinelli developed a story for Italian film star Anna Magnani in which a street-walker standing in Rome's Via Veneto becomes infatuated with a charismatic male movie star who cruises around the area in a Cadillac. Ultimately Magnani, who was to have directed the project, rejected it. The story remained dormant until Fellini used it for his first wide-release film, *The White Sheik* (1952), which opened to critical acclaim.

Gwen Verdon in "If My Friends Could See Me Now," from *Sweet Charity*. *(Courtesy of Dance Magazine)*

In this picture Cabiria, a sympathetic prostitute, makes her first appearance. Fellini cast his wife, actress Giulietta Masina, who played the role beautifully. Cabiria was based on abstract streetwalker characters Fellini had observed. Then, while shooting *Il Bidone* in 1955, he befriended a prostitute named Wanda, who lived in an abandoned water tank near the ruins of the Roman aquaduct. Living in poverty, Wanda reluctantly accepted Fellini's offers of food in exchange for information about her life and her livelihood. Isolated from the rest of the world, Wanda epitomized Fellini's recurring theme of the lonely individual.

Fellini expanded the small role of Cabiria in *The White Sheik* to become the core of *Nights of Cabiria,* the neorealistic story of a prostitute's romantic disenchantments—and the archetype for *Sweet Charity*. A straightforward, unflinching account of Cabiria's search for ideal love in a corrupt world, *Nights of Cabiria* opens with Cabiria being robbed of her savings and dumped in a river by a man she believed loved her. Half-drowned, she manages to get back to the concrete shanty she lives in ("bought and paid for with my own money," she says proudly) on the outskirts of Rome. While at work one night, Cabiria meets a movie star outside a club. He has argued with his beautiful girlfriend and, in an act of retribution, decides to claim Cabiria as his date for the evening. They go to another club and then back to the movie star's lavish home. Cabiria thinks her dream romance is about to begin; but when the girlfriend unexpectedly returns, Cabiria spends the rest of the night in the star's plush bathroom. The next day she attends a religious pilgrimage, and later is hypnotized and humiliated in a seedy vaudeville theater. That night she meets Oscar, a quiet, self-deprecating man who seems genuinely interested in her. Cabiria quickly steers their courtship to marriage, sells her house, and offers him her money. But on the eve of their wedding, he robs and abandons her. Although the ending is heartwrenching ("Kill me, kill me," she implores Oscar, preferring to die rather than live in a world without love), Fellini offers a final, redemptive scene: Cabiria, walking alone, encounters a group of young people serenading along a country road. They include her in their merriment, and, again, her faith in humanity is restored.

Nights of Cabiria became a huge international success, and went on to win the Academy Award for best foreign film of 1956.

Giulietta Masina as Cabiria in Federico Fellini's *Nights of Cabiria,* which inspired Fosse's stage and film productions of *Sweet Charity. (Courtesy of MCA Publicity Rights, a division of MCA, Inc. Copyright © by Universal Pictures, a Division of Universe City Studios, Inc.)*

Fosse first watched *Nights of Cabiria* in a small art theater in New York. The film served as a catalyst; it helped spur him to explore more realistic subjects, to break away from the formulaic musical comedies of the Fifties like *Pajama Game* and *Damn Yankees*. Although Fosse's choreography appealed to an adult sensibility in its provocative posturings and combinations, pre-*Charity* shows, such as *Redhead* in 1959, were tethered to the conventions of tried-and-true musical formats. By the time he choreographed and directed *Sweet Charity,* Fosse was ready to leave behind the constraints of an earlier theatrical era. *Nights of Cabiria,* with its low-budget production and gritty subject matter, might seem an unlikely choice for an established Broadway director-choreographer to pursue,

but given Fosse's own checkered showbusiness background and Gwen Verdon's previous stage roles ("sexpots," she called them fondly), the film had immediate appeal. Both Fellini and Fosse were fascinated with street life, and used their actress-wives to explore characters who clung to the hope of a better existence, seemingly unshakable in their optimism.

In fact, of all of Fosse's contemporaries, only Fellini would examine the lurid, brutal, tantalizing side of the entertainment industry as recurrently. From *Variety Lights'* traveling theater mise-en-scènes to the homosexual actor and salacious dancers in *I Vitelloni,* Fellini's early films capture the insular world of the music hall (be it a cabaret or a theater) with the same knowingness of Fosse's *Cabaret, Lenny, All That Jazz,* and *Star 80.* Later Fellini efforts *(The Clowns, Amarcord, And the Ship Sails On . . . , Ginger and Fred)* delve further, juxtaposing entertainment and corruption, religion and art, power and performance.

In an interview in the *New York Times* shortly after *Sweet Charity's* Broadway debut, Verdon recalled Fosse's introduction to *Nights of Cabiria:* "One night we had nothing to do, so we went to see that Fellini film, *Nights of Cabiria.* Well, I just hated it—so depressing—but Bob, he's the movie buff in the family, just loved it. He couldn't sleep. So he woke me up at 6 A.M. with a nine-page Americanization of it, and he got me all stirred up. We changed her from a prostitute to a dance-hall hostess, because in New York the whores are either elegant with posh lives—then nobody would have any sympathy—or they're bums—then nobody would care. I guess people will compare me with Giulietta Masina, or be disappointed because the show has an unhappy ending. American audiences always want you to get the fella and eight kids in Scarsdale, but how many people actually end up that way?"

Explaining why he had altered the main character from a prostitute to a taxi dancer, Fosse told the *Times,* "There is something ugly about a prostitute in this country. It's all right in Italy. I wanted to get the nearest thing to a prostitute, a promiscuous girl who sold something for money—a dance, her understanding, conversation, something."

With his rough draft of the story, Fosse and Verdon convinced the production team of Robert Fryer, Lawrence Carr, and Joseph and Sylvia Harris to pay Fellini $25,000 for the legitimate theater rights to *Nights of Cabiria.* Fosse flew to Italy to discuss the project with Fellini, who wished him well but expressed no interest in becoming involved with the musical.

Back in New York, Fosse and Verdon enthusiastically planned field trips to various taxi dance halls, also known as tango palaces. For weeks Fosse scoped them all, adopting the disguise of a curious out-of-towner inveigled by the dance dens' promises of "charming hostesses at bargain prices." On the back cover of his script book for *Sweet Charity,* Fosse taped a photograph of the now-gone Orpheum dance hall during a police raid. As he continued to revise his script, he returned to the photo periodically. Its vivid depiction of the once-stately Orpheum gone to seed and the equally tawdry taxi dancers inspired the Fandango Ballroom, the locale of *Sweet Charity*'s showstopping "Big Spender." More importantly, the dancers in the photograph looked frightened and vulnerable, like Cabiria during the movie's police raids of the streets she walked. The photograph conveyed the women's fear of sudden exposure to a world that condemned their life-style, a fear Fosse hoped to instill in his heroine Charity.

From left, Gwen Verdon, Helen Gallagher, and Thelma Ritter in *Sweet Charity*'s fandango, "There's Got to Be Something Better Than This." *(Courtesy of Dance Magazine)*

During the six months he frequented the dance halls, Fosse found more groping than dancing. "The girls are anywhere from eighteen to fifty years old," he told the *Times*. "They are very interested in you and attentive. I never told them I was doing research for a show. None of them would have guessed. It just wouldn't have occurred to them."

As *Sweet Charity*'s book evolved, Fosse included Verdon on his excursions. She accompanied him twice, noting that the "palaces" were open from noon to 4 A.M., and that the "girls" charged $6.50 per half-hour. (When his research was complete, Fosse estimated he had spent $150 collecting material in the dance halls.) But the dancers resented Verdon's presence with her husband, so she decided to go undercover and work as one of them. Although in her forties and a grandmother, Verdon was at the peak of her career. Years of dance training had kept her body firm and supple, and her handsome face was fair competition to women half her age. She worked in a tiny, dark upstairs hideaway dance hall on Broadway as a dance hostess, where she and the rest of the women were protected by wooden dividers from the men until one of them paid for a dance.

"Some of the girls seem to be arrested in time," she told the *Times*. "They wear their hair like Lana Turner did years ago or they look like Betty Grable. Some of them are still wearing wedgies." The younger women, she believed, found something romantic in the faded grandeur of the dance hall.

Shortly after the musical was announced, the producers decided that the show would re-open the historic Palace music hall as a legitimate theater. The Palace's last "legit" show had been 1959's *Redhead*, which starred Verdon and was directed and choreographed by Fosse. To accommodate the production, the Palace went under an extensive renovation; over $50,000 was spent converting it from its previous status as a second-rate movie theater. A looming white elephant surrounded by the sleeker Times Square cinemas, the Palace's last picture show was 1965's *Harlow*, accurately assessed by the *New York Times* as "rock bottom entertainment."

That same year the Nederlander Organization purchased the Palace for $1.6 million (a then-record amount for a legitimate theater) plus a yearly ground rent of $63,000. For *Sweet Charity*, a high-speed elevator was designed, rising ten flights above the stage to newly designed dressing rooms (the theater's old dressing rooms had been removed to expand the backstage area). Because Fosse wanted to establish intimacy with the audience, the Palace's second balcony seats, still the highest from the stage of any Broadway theater and justly called the crow's nest by box-office employees, were not used, limited a capacity house to eight hundred orchestra and six hundred first-balcony seats.

Sweet Charity was slated to open in December 1965, but the theater's restoration forced the show to postpone its New York premiere until Saturday, January 25, 1966. The Palace finally opened in renewed splendor, truly deserving of its name. The dominant color scheme was red: plush red velour seats; red baroque paneling on the ceiling; red, black, and burgundy carpeting with a motif of Greek lyres and wreaths woven into it; and walls covered in gold- and cream-colored damask, with lighting provided by crystal chandeliers seven feet high and five feet wide. *New York Times* cultural reporter Vincent Canby described the Palace's facelift as "garish grandeur."

Of course, the hoopla surrounding *Sweet Charity* had as much to do with the show's successful out-of-town tryouts, the cast, and the artistic staff as it did with Fosse, Fellini, and the Palace. Originally, the show was to be in two parts: the first being the reworked *Nights of Cabiria,* the second, an original work by Elaine May called *Robbers and Cops.* Eventually May's script was dropped because it too strongly resembled another Broadway-bound musical, *Drat the Cat!* (which had only a brief run before closing), and *Sweet Charity* was expanded to two acts.

Following Fosse's and Verdon's dance-hall excursions, the show went into rehearsals in September 1965. Fosse, using the pseudonym Bert Lewis, was credited as the author, Dorothy Fields, who had co-written the book and lyrics for *Redhead,* was the lyricist to Cy Coleman's score—the first electronic music heard in a Broadway show. Robert Randolph designed the set and lighting, and fashion designer Irene Sharaff created the show's 150 costumes. It was an extravagantly talented group of collaborators.

Almost as soon as the score was written, it became sought after among contemporary vocalists, and once the show opened out of town, word of mouth spread that it was brimming with potential hits. Even songs cut out of town from *Sweet Charity,* such as "Pink Taffeta, Sample Size 10," achieved a certain cult notoriety on the cabaret circuit. Another, "Poor Everybody Else," popped up in 1973's *Seesaw,* staged by Michael Bennett. "Big Spender" was introduced by Peggy Lee at the Copacabana in New York before the show opened on Broadway. Once *Sweet Charity* was a bona fide hit, other singers who rushed to record selections from the score included Perry Como, Tony Bennett, Sarah Vaughan, Robert

Goulet, Sylvia Simms, Al Hirt, and Barbra Streisand. All of this insured substantial profits for Capital Records, the major investor of the $400,000 show.

Sweet Charity began Fosse's long-time romance with the typewriter. Determined to prove he was not *just* a dancer, Fosse found that writing was a different kind of exercise than going alone into a studio and choreographing a dance. Eventually he would excel, in films such as *Lenny* and *Star 80,* at interview-style scriptwriting, which served these starkly shot, confrontational projects well. *Sweet Charity,* for all its innovations, was still very much a conventional Broadway musical, and Fosse's early drafts proved insufficient to bolster the Coleman–Fields score and transport Fellini's characters to American audiences.

In October 1966 Neil Simon was brought in to assist Fosse on the book. Then billed as a "contributing writer," Simon already had earned the nickname "doctor" for rewriting shows in trouble. At the time *Sweet Charity* was in rehearsal, Simon had two hit comedies running on Broadway, *Barefoot in the Park* and *The Odd Couple,* and was considered a gifted young comedic writer. He and Fosse shared a similar perspective on the story, since much of Simon's humor stems from the same working-class, day-to-day travails that beset Fellini's characters. It was Simon who was responsible for "lightening up" Charity with memorable lines such as "She runs her heart like a hotel; guys check in and out all the time," and, when Charity sizes up the guests at the posh Pompeii Club, "I'm the only one here I've never heard of." Although the book was roundly attacked by critics as being paper-thin and inconsequential, Simon's drollery locked into Fosse's choreography unobtrusively, keeping the show buoyant without calling attention to itself. By November Simon was given full billing as author and "Bert Lewis" disappeared from the credits.

Along with his creative team, Fosse had assembled a sterling cast for the original production of *Sweet Charity.* Verdon's dance-hall chums, Nicki and Helene, were played by Helen Gallagher and Thelma Oliver, both well-known musical actresses (Gallagher was an alumni from both *The Pajama Game* and *Redhead*). Dyan Cannon auditioned for the role of Ursula, the movie star's girlfriend, but bowed out to marry Cary Grant. The role eventually went to former Miss America Sharon Lee. John McMartin played Charity's beau Oscar, going on to play him in the 1969 film as well. Making her Broadway debut, Ruth Buzzi played the Good Fairy and other minor character roles. Lee Roy Reams, best known for his tap dancing in *42nd Street,* and Ben Vereen also had small parts in the show. By November, casting was complete.

Because Verdon and Fosse had so thoroughly researched their subject, rehearsals progressed rapidly as *Sweet Charity* began to take shape. When the show opened out of town for a two-week run in Philadelphia, it was an immediate hot ticket, garnering unanimous raves from the local critics. The dailies reported that in Philadelphia police were called into the Shubert Theater at 10 A.M. the morning after the reviews came out to supervise a line of prospective ticket buyers pushing their way to the box office. The stampede became a riot, and the box office was closed temporarily until the pandemonium subsided. The show sold out its run, with scalpers getting $200 a ticket (on Broadway, top ticket prices at the time were $9.50).

As with all show tryouts, *Sweet Charity* went through a number of alterations before moving on to Detroit and New York. Before arriving in New York, Sharaff's costumes were drastically redesigned by Fosse. Reams recalls a confrontation between Fosse and Sharaff in Philadelphia that illustrates his sometimes-stormy relationship with collaborators and explains the origins of the now-famous plain black dress Charity performs in throughout the show.

"During the Philadelphia run," Reams says, "Gwen had a different costume for every scene. When she'd rehearsed in New York, she wore a black slip and carried a purse with a rope for a handle, since Bob wanted her to have a swayback look. But out-of-town one of her costumes was a lime green dress with a purple slip underneath. It was designed in the fishhook style, with a very tight bodice that flared out at the bottom.

"We started rehearsing 'Big Spender,' and the girls came out in very glittery costumes; their hairdos were huge. It was clear Fosse hated the costumes. He got hysterical and said, 'I can't see my number! The clothes are overpowering it. They're too bright, too shiny. They're not seedy enough. They look too new. I can't see my choreography!'

"Sharaff stormed down the aisle with a big group of sketches, threw them in his lap and said: 'Here, you son-of-a-bitch! These are the costumes that you approved in New York, and these are the costumes you are seeing today. Look at the sketches!' Well, Fosse had the clothes spray-painted to tone them down—these are dresses that cost thousands of dollars—painted right over the sequins, ripped off the frilly trims. He had all of Gwen's costumes taken back. He said, 'I want her in a plain black dress, and she'll wear it the entire time.' "

Kathryn Doby, one of the taxi dancers in the "Big Spender" number, remembers the incident. "I was wearing a gorgeous paisley print," she says, "and every single pattern on it was sequined and beaded. I'd never seen anything like it in my life. They should have kept it and put it in a museum. But it was on me—a chorus girl—and when you looked at the number you couldn't see anything but that one costume. The focus was supposed to be on the stars, not on the costumes. There was no time to make more costumes, so Fosse had Irene Sharaff take that costume and put it on a dummy. She sprayed it, and sprayed it, and sprayed it until there was practically nothing left of the original. You could see the agony on her face."

Nearly everyone in the original company of *Sweet Charity* was impressed at the meticulous detail behind Sharaff's work, and, to a man obsessed with minutiae as Fosse, her creations were probably equally magnificent. But the fact was, they were inappropriate for the wear and tear of the choreography. Tights split. Accessories such as gloves proved impractical for fast costume changes. Seams stitched with silk thread popped onstage. "By the end of 'Rich Man's Frug,' " Reams recalls, "all the men were in tatters. It was embarrassing." While Sharaff's designs wowed buyers on Seventh Avenue, on Broadway her *Sweet Charity* costumes best illustrated the vast differences in creating for the fashion elite and designing for the stage. When *Sweet Charity,* the movie, was made, famed Hollywood designer Edith Head took over the costumes.

Patricia Zipprodt, who won a Tony for the 1986 revival's costumes, believes Fosse's experience with Sharaff exemplifies his lack of trust in collaborators. When she was approached by producer Stuart Ostrow to meet with Fosse to discuss costumes for *Pippin,* Zipprodt says Fosse was still smarting from the costume catastrophe with Sharaff six years earlier. "Bob discussed Irene's costumes with me," Zipprodt says. "He looked at me and said, 'Do your costumes look like the sketches?' and I said, 'Yes, as a rule, they look quite a bit like them.' He said, 'Well, with Irene Sharaff, she showed me a sketch and it had seven little circles, indicating seven sequins. But on stage I couldn't see the costume, those sequins were so blinding.' "

Despite Fosse's outbursts at Sharaff, the Philadelphia run progressed smoothly, and the Verdon–Fosse team again proved a magical combination on stage and at the box office. "They thought alike," Kathryn Doby observes. "It was uncanny. Bob would be explaining something to her and before he finished, she would already be doing it. Fosse would start moving, and Gwen would go with him and finish it. When you work with someone a long time you do it inadvertently. By the time I worked with him on *Dancin',* I was doing it too. It got into my body."

Many dancers in the company would hang around and observe Fosse and Verdon during their breaks, just to try and understand their collaborative genius. "To watch Bob and Gwen at work!" remarks Reams. "I used to just hide and watch. They were both in love with each other's talent. The joy on Bob's face when he would come up with something and she would execute it was unequaled. She worked so hard, all day long, and in numbers she wasn't even in. It was a totally dedicated relationship. Bob would say, 'Oh, that's not good,' and Gwen would say, 'But, Bobby, it's wonderful.' And he'd say, 'But everything I do looks good on you. I can never tell if it's really any good or not.' And it's true; anything she did she made look good. She was his greatest example as a choreographer."

Many dancers who worked with Fosse and Verdon in *Sweet Charity* on stage and on film remarked that the project represented a turning point for him choreographically and thematically. Technically, his dances became more fractured. He began experimenting further with smaller groups of dancers. Combinations structured around eight- and sixteen-bar phrases were split almost infinitesimally. Two dancers would begin a combination, followed by two more four bars later, and two more four bars after that. The effect was that of constant reverberations, with the dances becoming hypnotic in their repetitions. During rehearsals, Fosse would choreograph four combinations of eight bars each on the dancers. Each one would be assigned a separate combination. Counterpoint combinations followed: A dancer would begin combination one at bar one, number two on bar four, number four on bar three, and so on.

"I've never found any choreographer as precise as Fosse," Kathryn Doby says. Dana Moore, the lead frug dancer in the 1986 revival of the show, recalls an incident in which Fosse became furious at her for changing the tone of her character. "One of the things he was a real stickler about was that he wanted me to have my chin down," she recalls. "He explained that the whole dance is a tease, and, to him, the chin down was a much more teasing, seductive look. I remember one time he came to see the show in L.A., and he was so upset with me he could hardly talk. I was mortified; I didn't know what I'd done wrong. It turned out he was mad because I was *smiling* on stage. He said, 'It's not about smiling and selling it! I should never see your teeth. There's always a smile in your eyes, but you've got to be cool—aloof and sophisticated. You would *never* smile or show your teeth!'"

Sweet Charity marked more than just a technical advancement for Fosse, however. Within the dances quake deep sexual tremors reflecting the Sixties' uninhibitedness; they represent Fosse's own desire to express pent-up desires. The Latin syncopations in "There's Gotta Be Something Better Than This" percolate slowly and build to an exuberant declaration of independence. As the lyrics urge, "I'm gonna get up/I'm gonna get out/I'm gonna get up, get out/And do it!" The quasi-flamenco choreography—with its foot stomps and hand claps—ranks among Fosse's most dramatically effective and visually exciting dances.

So does "Big Spender," with its line of dancers stretched over, under, and straddling a partition barre. The women's drooping cigarettes, pointing fingers ("Hey, mister, do ya speak French?"), and deadpan stares are overstated theatricalizations of the actual dance-hall hostesses

Taxi dancers line up for the "Big Spender" number from *Sweet Charity*. From left: Charlene Ryan, Chita Rivera, Paula Kelly, Renata Vassily, Louise Quick. *(Courtesy of L. Quick)*

whom Fosse and Verdon observed. Who but Fosse would have found in their knock-kneed ungracefulness moments of choreographic brilliance?

"He believed dance had been approached from every angle," recalls Gene Foote, a Fosse dancer who later became a director, "and so he was constantly searching for new ways of presenting movement. He used to watch people with physical imperfections walk down the street and try to pick up the rhythm. Later that day, he'd take their afflictions and re-create them as a dance."

His uncommon, colloquial dance vocabulary produced a great deal of humor in his work. "If My Friends Could See Me Now" presents a teasingly sexual Charity as she discovers the possibilities of a pop-up opera hat she scrunches shamelessly between her legs and snaps open on her derriere. In all these dances, as well as "Rich Man's Frug" and "Rhythm of Life," Fosse was following his sexual impulses as a chore-ographer. The innocent pas de trois between Carol Haney, Peter Gen-naro, and Buzz Miller in *Pajama Game*'s "Steam Heat" had progressed to intricately patterned combinations in the orgiastic religious frenzy of "Rhythm of Life."

"I think *Sweet Charity* was a bridge between the style Fosse had in *Pajama Game* and *Damn Yankees* and what became *Pippin* and *Chicago*," believes Reams, who also danced in the film version of *Sweet Charity*. "Suddenly, he became whatever his sexuality was. His choreography reflected that. People were doing more suggestive dancing. Males and females became one body, like in *Pippin;* there was a lot of unisexuality, where it was difficult to tell which sexes were which.

"Bob was built like a question mark—slumped shoulders, the thrust-ing pelvic area. So when he danced, everything became a pelvic thrust. His early work wasn't so pelvic-oriented; it happened during and after *Charity*. Body formations changed, became more intimate. Everything was extremely subtle. He choreographed down to the little finger. You would get into a position and the slightest little move would become so important. He focused his choreography brilliantly."

Sweet Charity crystallized Fosse and Verdon's artistic relationship and, during its run, they became *the* couple profiled in celebrity columns and lengthy feature articles. By the time the show got to Detroit's Fisher Theater around Christmas 1965, *Sweet Charity* was an unqualified smash. When it arrived on Broadway on January 29, 1966, *Charity* hysteria was at a pitch reserved today for Andrew Lloyd Webber extravaganzas.

The day before *Sweet Charity*'s opening, Fellini, who knew of Ver-don's work and saw the parallel between his wife Masina's roles and those Fosse had directed for *his* wife, gave Verdon a cornetta—a curved horn that is the traditional symbol of good luck. Interestingly, Fellini's latest film, *Juliet of the Spirits,* starring Masina, was playing next door to the Palace at the Embassy Theater.

Thanks to generally favorable reviews out of town (most New York reviewers touted Fosse's choregraphy and Verdon's dancing but were harsh on Simon's book and Coleman's score) and strong word of mouth, the show was an immediate sellout through July. Verdon's black slip and rope-handled purse appeared on everything from program souvenir books to shopping bags in Times Square.

Commenting on that season's Broadway choreography for the *New York Times,* however, dance and theater critic Clive Barnes wrote: "Mr. Fosse's choreography for Miss Verdon gives her gamine charm its full chance. The remainder of the choreography is extraordinarily slick and perfectly empty of true choreographic interest. . . . [He] reduces movement to robot simplicity and [has] a whole group of dancers performing eccentric, often jerky, movements with the mechanized perfection of Swiss cuckoo clocks." Today, Barnes seems to have been reacting against a new wave of Broadway choreography ushered in by Fosse; at the 1986 revival, by contrast, he was enthusiastic. *Sweet Charity* replaced Agnes de Mille's and Jerome Robbins's story ballets with street-oriented choreography—the pugilistic fists in "The Heavyweight," the taxi dancers in "Big Spender"—and, aside from technical advancements, Fosse presented sometimes shockingly frank poses—splayed legs, raised buttocks, jutting breasts, pelvic thrusts—Chaplinesque comedy, and even plaintive "recitation" numbers ("Where Am I Going?").

New York Herald drama critic Walter Kerr astutely described the Janus-faced Fosse in his review of the show. "*Sweet Charity* doesn't want real lightness of heart. It wants a wriggling little worm of pathos to take up residence inside all the brass band bravura, it wants a slight shade of ruefulness to modify the 6/8 beat, it wants audiences to be a wee bit sorry that all the gaiety isn't so." Yet, despite the downbeat ending, in which Charity is again assaulted and abandoned by her lover, Fosse injects a note of ironic humor to save the moment from becoming morose. "He always looked for the humor in violence," says Gene Foote. "Charity gets pushed in a lake twice! Now, really. How black can you get? How Fellini. How commedia del l'arte."

The musical's opening night party, originally planned for the Rainbow Room in Rockefeller Center, was moved to the Starlight Roof at the Waldorf-Astoria. The seven hundred guests invited to the affair included Mayor John Lindsay, Henry Ford (he flew in many of his friends), Jacqueline Kennedy, Angela Lansbury, Jerry Herman, Arthur Laurents,

Lena Horne, Milton Berle, Ed Sullivan, Sidney Poitier, Abe Burrows, Ethel Merman, and Marge Champion. The Nederlanders picked up the $15,000 tab for an event described by the *Times* as "one of the most elegant opening night parties ever held for a Broadway show."

Immediately following its premiere, Joseph E. Levine bought the film rights to the *Sweet Charity* for $2 million; the film industry was buzzing about who would play Charity. Earlier, Universal made an offer to finance a film version if Shirley MacLaine would play Charity. Verdon, who had lost the Tony that season to Angela Lansbury in *Mame* (though Fosse won the outstanding choreography award), was considered a dark horse, though Fosse rallied for her in the film role. Verdon's limited film appearances (her only starring role had been as Lola in *Damn Yankees*) and age—she was in her forties—eventually put her out of the running. In fact, by the time *Sweet Charity* closed on Broadway in July 1967 after 607 performances, Verdon had been replaced by Helen Gallagher. The physical demands of the role had taken their toll on her; despite a special vitamin developed at Cornell University to keep fat built up on nerve endings and increase stamina, Verdon began cutting numbers toward the end of her run in order to economize her energy, and left the show when the removal of a cyst forced her into the hospital.

When *Sweet Charity* began filming on January 29, 1967, the stage musical was still playing in London. But though Fosse had made great strides in his own career with the show and, concurrently, helped establish the director-choreographer on Broadway, the film musical was at its lowest point. Although Universal's *Sweet Charity* was Fosse's first fling with camera direction and illustrates his uncertainty at how to film dance, it also offers remarkably assured dance moments and foreshadows the direction his later, more ambitious films would take.

Fosse had a difficult time convincing film producers to trust him with the material or its star. Reflecting on his first directorial effort for the big screen, Fosse told *New York Times* reporter Chris Chase in April 1973, "I wanted Gwen to do it, and nobody would buy it. And then there was that offer from Universal for a half million but it was for Shirley MacLaine. So I went to Gwen and said, 'How do you feel about it?' and she said, 'Fine, it's your property, see it through.' "

MacLaine, who had not worked for Fosse since *The Pajama Game*, believes "Gwen didn't wish to play the part. Contrary to what a lot of people think, she couldn't have been more helpful. She showed me all kinds of things, secrets of how to balance steps with breaths, tricks with the hats, all kinds of different things like that. She brought me several photos of people she thought the screen character should look like.

"My progress in movies mirrored Bobby's progress as a director. I watched him turn into a magnificent director. [MCA's president] Lew Wasserman wanted me to do *Sweet Charity* [on film], but I said only if Bob could choreograph *and* direct. He said, 'I don't know about directing, he's never directed a picture before,' but I told him I thought Bobby would make a great Hollywood director. I called him a genius. Lou didn't know what I was talking about, but he hired Ross Hunter to produce and got Bobby to direct. Bob started me on Broadway, so I started him in Hollywood, and as soon as he got there, he took the camera apart and put it back together. He studied Fellini, who was his favorite director."

Lee Roy Reams, who Fosse used again in the film, recalls that during rehearsals Fosse would carry around with him a small Viewfinder, a toy which isolates images, and set up camera angles. "He used it to see all sorts of angles in the dance. The reason the movie didn't make it is because the camera couldn't stay still; it was always shifting to new moments. But every one of those moments was a gem. The thing I thought was so horrid was having to watch Gwen show Shirley the choreography. Shirley was wonderful, but seeing Gwen do it, anything else was an imitation."

Despite criticisms that MacLaine was an inferior dancer to Verdon, in the film MacLaine projects a quality in her interpretation of the character that is closer to Masina's than Verdon's. While Verdon infused Charity with Fosse's Chaplinesque choreography, MacLaine had more opportunity as an *actress* in the film to flesh out Fellini's tragic heroine. Because the camera could, through close-ups, reveal MacLaine's heart-breaking vulnerability and childlike euphoria, the film becomes a closer facsimile to *Nights of Cabiria* than to the Broadway production of *Sweet Charity*. Verdon's presence is missed most in the dance numbers, but fortunately Fosse cast two superb dancers—Chita Rivera and Paula Kelly—as Nicky and Helene, her wise-cracking sidekicks. Rivera had played Charity in the national tour of the show, and Kelly won praise as Helene in the London company that followed *Sweet Charity*'s Broadway run. This triumvirate is especially outstanding in "There's Got to Be Something Better Than This," which, set on a rooftop for the film, is far more persuasive than the stage version in underscoring the drab environ-

Shirley MacLaine rehearses for "If My Friends Could See Me Now" from the film *Sweet Charity*. *(Courtesy of MCA Publicity Rights, a division of MCA, Inc. Copyright © by Universal Pictures, a Division of Universe City Studios, Inc.)*

ment these women hope to escape. And while MacLaine is obviously the weakest of the three, both in her dancing and singing, her gamine screen presence translates the character vividly. When she falls to her knees in front of Oscar (John McMartin) at the end of the film, begging him to

marry her, her beseeching "Give a little girl a break" is almost too painful to watch.

When the $7.5 million film began shooting in early 1967, Fosse was unhappy with the suggestions of producer Ross Hunter, who did not appreciate Fosse's personal vision of how he wanted to change the look of the film musical. Despite some direct references to the stage production, the film was true to its promotional campaign blitz slogan, "the musical motion picture of the '70s." Robert Arthur replaced Hunter, and shooting went smoothly. *Sweet Charity* concluded filming in June 1968, a very different musical than that seen onstage.

What is most apparent when watching the film today is Fosse's understanding of two disparate mediums. Having done a significant body of work as a dancer and musical stager in film musicals of the Fifties— *Kiss Me Kate, My Sister Eileen, The Pajama Game,* and *Damn Yankees*— Fosse was familiar with dancing *for* the camera and how dances should be set up in film. His Broadway tenure as a choreographer allowed him to design dances for the proscenium stage, imposing different kinds of restrictions. Though *Sweet Charity* is a far-from-perfect film musical, its musical sequences rank as some of Fosse's best work.

Many numbers were dropped or replaced by new ones for the film. "I'm the Bravest Individual," which Charity and Oscar sing while stuck in an elevator in the theatrical production, is replaced by "It's a Nice Face," functioning almost as a monologue for Charity. The Fandango Ballroom in "Big Spender"—a great moment in dance cinema—begins with a seedy-looking man entering the dance hall. The camera focuses on details—a lit cigarette, a half-empty glass of beer—that establish both the atmosphere and clientele. The camera pans the line of fandango dancers soliciting the men on the other side of the partition with "Let's have some fun" and other come-ons before inching across the barre like a nest of vipers closing in on their prey. Fosse uses overhead and floor-level shots to create a near-claustrophobic, hothouse environment. The dancers' locked ankles, forward-thrust hips, cocked wrists, and inverted knees give them a frank sexuality. Fosse is clearly using dance as a metaphor for intercourse (he would explore this further in his next Broadway show, *Pippin*). Nervous studio executives found the original "Big Spender" too shocking and requested that Fosse film a second version, but when the number was screened for them, they, too, were impressed by the original's unconventionality, and the first version remains in the film. The pancake-faced hostesses of "Big Spender" recall the chorus dancers in Fellini's *I Vitonelli* and the prostitutes in his *Roma,* quintessential female grotesques Fosse would use again as *Cabaret*'s Kit Kat dancers.

Other stage-film alterations include the opening up of "I'm a Brass Band," Charity's reaffirmation of self-worth ("Somebody loves me!"). On stage, Charity is joined by a marching band parading against stark panels. The film's interpretation captures more effectively her dream world by setting the number on Wall Street at dawn. The juxtaposition of Charity's strangely dressed ensemble (costumer Edith Head attired the dancers in red drum-major jackets over black leotards with red rubber boots) with the corporate world is as jarring as Cabiria's excursions from the squalor of her home to downtown Rome.

"Rich Man's Frug," a choreographic extension of Fosse's "Rich Kid's Rag" in *Little Me*, also benefits from camera work that captures isolated movements such as the balled fists in "The Heavyweight" and the mincing goose steps in "The Aloof." The number, which reproduces through dance Fellini's scene between Cabiria and the Italian film star Mario in the Roman nightclub, is shortly followed by a scene between Charity and Vittorio Vidal (played by Ricardo Montalban, typecast perfectly as the Italian film star) that leads into "If My Friends Could See Me Now." Charity's props, the folding opera hat and cane, are direct references to Charlie Chaplin. The provocative use of the hat and the comedic pratfalls charmingly accentuate Charity's naïveté and playful sexuality.

Paula Kelly, Shirley MacLaine, and Chita Rivera in the rooftop dance "There's Got to Be Something Better Than This." *(Courtesy of MCA Publicity Rights, a division of MCA, Inc. Copyright © by Universal Pictures, a Division of Universe City Studios, Inc.)*

"Rhythm of Life," which parallels a scene in *Nights of Cabiria* in which Cabiria joins a religious pilgrimage, highlights the chief flaw in the film's dances. The Fellini film and Fosse's stage version good-naturedly satirize religions of the month and those swept up in their fervor. In the movie, however, Fosse over-directs. Cast as the religious leader Big Daddy Johann Sebastian Brubeck, Sammy Davis, Jr. (who received co-billing with MacLaine) sends up himself as a jive-talking, black huckster preacher. Reportedly, the number was filmed by five cameras in a continuous take and edited later. While the Broadway show used the scene to chastize genuflecting charlatans, the movie opted for a star turn for Davis.

If the dances in the film *Sweet Charity* complement or enhance Fosse's original choreography, Ralph Burns' orchestrations, with their brassy, sometimes truncated arrangements, are less effective. The omission of some of the Broadway score's ballads, including "You Should See Yourself," "Too Many Tomorrows," and the wistful "Baby Dream Your Dream" suggests Universal wanted a more upbeat soundtrack for its "musical-of-the-'70s" audience.

The studio also balked at Neil Simon's downbeat ending. Screenwriter Peter Stone fashioned two endings, one that retained the melancholy tone of the original, showing Charity alone in Central Park until she is approached by a group of flower children ("and she lived hopefully ever after"), and one in which Oscar regrets leaving her and rushes back to the park. In his haste to embrace her, he accidentally falls off a bridge, and Charity dives in the water to save him. But as he did in his editing of "Big Spender," Fosse won over wary executives; today the alternate "happy ending" is available only on the laser-disk release.

In reassessing the film, MacLaine recalls that working with Fosse "put you in touch with how devoted you are to the business. Sometimes it was as if that was all that mattered to him." If his obsession with detail and nuance brought his characters vividly to life, his analytical approach to directing also frequently removed him from the real world. During the filming, both Martin Luther King, Jr., and John F. Kennedy were shot. MacLaine and Paula Kelly, who continue to be outspoken political activists, were shocked when Fosse refused to cancel shooting those days.

"Bob couldn't understand that we didn't want to work—couldn't work—on those days," explains MacLaine. "People we were involved with socially and politically were gone. But to him, nothing was more important than the film. With Bob, that was his life. I remember how he actually used Kennedy's death to get a performance out of me. We were going to shoot another scene that day, but he switched it to one where

I'm supposed to be in this shattered state, crying on the telephone. He respected our private times, but, don't you know, he would take advantage of a good performance wherever he could find it."

Initially, *Sweet Charity*'s performance at the box office was lackluster. The film opened in Boston with a "reserved seats only" notice in its advertisements, indicating an expected ticket crunch. Audiences, however, were largely indifferent. Although over the years the film has earned more than $5 million on the basis of its cult status, it was considered a major disappointment when it opened, and a financial failure. While most

Shirley MacLaine, as Charity, rehearses "If My Friends Could See Me Now" with Fosse for the film *Sweet Charity*. (*AP/Wide World Photos*)

film critics praised Fosse's choreography, they found his direction choppy and the 148-minute film "labored." A *Morning Telegraph* review of *Sweet Charity* by Leo Mishkin exemplifies critics' reactions: "*Sweet Charity* is a more razzle-dazzle pyrotechnic display of fancy footwork in the dance numbers than the substantial musical-comedy drama it might have been expected to be. Indeed, even with Miss MacLaine going all-out in an effort to capture the ebullience, the charm, and the wistfulness of that tattered dance-hall girl seeking only true happiness (and a guy to go along with it), it is the director of the film who becomes the major figure in its transportation to the screen."

As Derek Elley has noted in his insightful *Films and Filming* examination of *Sweet Charity*'s newfound cult-film status: "Nothing builds a cult reputation faster than adversity, and despite a fascinating history of conception, *Sweet Charity* has had its full share in that department." Cult audiences continue to appreciate the film for Fosse's brilliant dance numbers, his "choreography" of the camera, the visual references to the flower-power Sixties, and Shirley MacLaine's winning portrayal of Charity. Although many Americans did not associate the film with *Nights of Cabiria*—few, in fact, had seen the film—in revival houses it is now often double-billed with Fellini's film, underlining Fosse's fidelity to the original screenplay.

Sweet Charity was a watershed for Fosse. In leaving behind the conventions of the Fifties musicals in which he had carved out his own distinctive niche as a choreographer, he catapulted into the Seventies with the experience of directing his first film, approaching future Broadway musicals with a cinematic perspective. As a time-capsule film, *Sweet Charity* epitomizes the where-am-I-going-what-will-I-find attitude of confused young people on the cusp of the Seventies. Thematically, *Sweet Charity* was Fosse's first direct influence by Fellini, who, along with Ingmar Bergman, became a wellspring of inspiration for him. Finally, the show's demanding choreography and strong central character provided many musical theater actresses with one of their most highly regarded roles. Verdon, Helen Gallagher, Chita Rivera, Juliet Prowse, Gretchen Wyler, Shirley MacLaine, Debbie Allen, Ann Reinking, and Donna McKechnie were given opportunities to expand their dramatic repertoire and prove to audiences once again that they could do more than dance. As much as Fellini and Fosse, they have made "the story of a girl who wanted to be loved" theater history.

V

THE THORNY TRIPLE CROWN

It was a good time
It was the best time
It was a party
Just to be near you
It was a good time
It was the best time
It seemed a short time
But such a good time

    —*"It Was a Good Time,"*
      by M. David, M. Curb, and M. Jarre,
      from Liza with a Z

CABARET

"I am a camera with its shutter open, quite passive, recording, not thinking. Recording the man shaving at the window opposite and the woman in the kimono washing her hair. Some day, all this will have to be developed, carefully printed, fixed."

—Christopher Isherwood,
Goodbye to Berlin, *1939*

When Christopher Isherwood wrote this introduction to his Brechtian tale of pre-Weimar Germany, little did he imagine his glimpses of Berlin decadence would presage no less than four different adaptations. By the Seventies, images from *Goodbye to Berlin* would be "fixed" in a play, two films, and a Broadway musical.

Cabaret, the 1972 hit film musical that is arguably Bob Fosse's most formidable achievement, was far from fresh material when he began preproduction on it in February 1971. Two decades before, John Van Drutten wrote the first adaptation of *Goodbye to Berlin,* a play called *I Am a Camera.* It focused primarily on one character from Isherwood's work, an American nightclub singer named Sally Bowles, and her assorted romantic entanglements in the face of Berlin's degenerating moral climate and the rise of the Third Reich. Julie Harris played Sally in both the stage play and the 1955 film version of *I Am a Camera.*

The Broadway production that eventually led to the Fosse film was directed by Harold Prince and starred Lotte Lenya, Jack Gilford, and Bert Convy, with Jill Hayworth as Sally Bowles. The most significant addition to the story was the inclusion of a character called the Master of Ceremonies, played by Joel Grey. Lyricist Fred Ebb provided the "emcee" with material that serves as a running commentary on life outside of the Kit Kat Club, where the Nazis are fast becoming an empowered political party. Ebb and librettist Joe Masteroff avoided a didactic tone by

As Sally Bowles, Liza Minnelli won an Oscar for her performance in *Cabaret. (Alan Pappé/Lee Gross Inc.)*

using the song-and-dance routines inside the cabaret to underscore the anarchy at hand. Many of the songs, such as the opening "Willkommen," are deceptively gay. "In here life is beautiful, the girls are beautiful, even the orchestra is beautiful!" boasts the pasty-faced emcee, but, as we examine the orchestra—transvestites and fat Fräuleins poised with their instruments—the mockery is made clear. Even before the opening number begins, the audience finds itself looking up into a mirror slanted over the stage that reflects—or mocks?—those who have come to see the spectacle.

Although some theatergoers and critics did not appreciate this kind of manipulation, *Cabaret* was an immediate hit, with its clean break from the genteel and formulaic musicals that had dominated Broadway in past decades. The contrast between the insular "life is a cabaret" stage and the warring anti-Semites outside its door created urgency and tension. But there was also humor. The comic vulgarity of the Kit Kat dancers who, in Ron Field's choreography, lay on their backs scissoring their legs menacingly/enticingly, is effectively burlesque. Equally startling is Sally Bowles, in a black silk slip, drinking Prairie Oysters (raw eggs and Worcestershire sauce), green fingernails glinting ("divine decadence, darling").

The film rights for *Cabaret* were optioned by Allied Artists Pictures in 1969 for $1.5 million. Billy Wilder, Gene Kelly, and a host of other prominent film directors turned it down, fearing it would not survive the delicate transplant to the screen. For a while it appeared *Cabaret*'s fate might become that of the thousands of plays, musicals, and novels optioned every year by production companies and left undeveloped.

Fosse, who was considered, in his own words, "virtually unemployable" after the film version of *Sweet Charity*'s initial box office disappointment, had kept a low profile, pondering several projects but committing to none. However, producer Cy Feuer, who had worked with Fosse on *How to Succeed in Business Without Really Trying* and *Little Me,* became involved with *Cabaret* and tagged Fosse as director.

Years later, Fosse would admit that Feuer had rescued him from the reject bin. But during Feuer's early negotiations with Allied Artists and ABC Pictures to retain Fosse as director, Fosse resented the compromises Feuer made to convince Hollywood's powerbrokers. "Cy Feuer *lied* to me," Fosse complained to *Penthouse* in 1973. "He told me he was fighting with the guys in Hollywood to get me the people and things I needed. Then I hear him on the telephone selling me out—promising not to give in to me. If he'd leveled with me, we could have worked it out together. But he told me first one thing, then another. I can't stand deception.

Because it shows. If you make a dishonest movie, it'll fail. If you make a dishonest relationship, it'll fall apart."

But nothing blemished Fosse's *Cabaret*. In fact, Fosse's film owes more to Isherwood than to its immediate source, Joe Masteroff's libretto in the Broadway musical, or to John Van Drutten's play. Jay Allen's screenplay, with assistance by Hugh Wheeler, eliminates the coyness that marred the Broadway show and emphasizes Sally Bowles (Liza Minnelli), from whom the film's dramatic action springs. Sally becomes the liaison between the song-and-dance illusions of the Kit Kat Club and life outside; no other character in the film inhabits both worlds.

Although Fosse himself did not cast Minnelli, he had known her and her mother, Judy Garland, for some years. Only in her early twenties when she was hired for the lead role in *Cabaret,* Minnelli was not new to either stage or screen. At nineteen she had won a Tony for her performance in the short-lived Broadway musical, *Flora, the Red Menace,* and a couple of years later, was nominated for an Oscar for her kooky performance in *The Sterile Cuckoo.* Explaining how he cast women in key roles, Fosse told *Penthouse,* "She has to be able to turn me on. I suppose that's sex appeal. She has to be someone I'd like to do it with, or if the part is an eighty-year-old washerwoman, then someone I'd like to have done it with when she was younger. She's got to have that turn-on quality."

Says Kathryn Doby, one of two American dancers used in the film, "One of the reasons I think [Fosse and Minnelli] hit it off so well is because they're both workaholics. She's as much a perfectionist as Bob is. I think their ethics made them work very closely. Liza had great admiration for Bob. She was willing to do absolutely anything he asked of her. They trusted each other."

That trust was not initially shared by Joel Grey, the only member of the Broadway company to reprise his role in the film. For Grey, who won a Tony for best supporting actor in a musical for *Cabaret,* his Master of Ceremonies marked the first time he had created an original role on Broadway, following years of replacing actors who had originated roles. When Grey was cast for the film version of *Cabaret,* understandably he did not feel comfortable with Fosse's overhauling of Masteroff's libretto. "First time before the camera," Fosse told the *Daily News,* "Joel went into his act. I stopped him, telling him he wasn't to play it as he did on the stage. He contended that that was the way he'd done it in the theater. I said, 'Joel, you're before the camera. Theater and film are two entirely different animals. In films, use restraint.' I would put my arms around him and say, 'Please do it again, and try it my way.' Took him about a week to get the hang of it. And he's great."

Fosse claimed to have fought tenaciously with studio executives in order to cast Michael York as the sexually unsure English tutor who is seduced by Sally. It was "that esthetic prizefighter look"—the slightly crooked nose and square jaw—that won Fosse over. "I could have photographed that face all day," he told the *Daily News*. He resisted hiring an actor who looked too effete or bookwormish. "It's so easy to fall into that limp-wristed fag stereotype," he told *After Dark* when asked about the treatment of homosexuals in some of his projects. "I like to startle the audience, make them rethink their perceptions of what a gay man looks like. People think that sexual experimentation was something exclusive to the Sixties. But, in *Cabaret,* you're talking about another sexual revolution that ended with Hitler. Men and women were trying *everything*. So you could have someone who looked like Michael York sleeping with a man. It was perfectly logical."

Preproduction of the film began in early 1971. Fosse and his assistant, Wolfgang Glattes, began scouting locations. Although most of the interior scenes would be shot at the Bavaria Studio near Munich, exterior locations figured importantly in the film as well. If the cabaret was to convey the "divine decadence" of a lurid fantasy, the real world must be depicted in vivid counterpoint. Fosse decided to shoot exteriors in the towns of Charlottenburg, Lübeck, Eutin, Dohlem, in the narrow alleyways near Savigny Platz, and in the Tiergarten. These locations evoked the startling contrast between the Kit Kat Club and the political upheaval occuring just outside its doors.

Fosse cast Michael York as Brian, *Cabaret*'s observant tutor, modeled after author Christopher Isherwood. *(Alan Pappé/Lee Gross, Inc.)*

Glattes recalls that Fosse "pored over the drawings of [German artist] George Grosz. He wanted to get that feeling of what it must have been like to have lived then. He didn't speak any German, so I also would serve as a translator when we went out. I spent a lot of time with him in certain neighborhoods, clubs, and bars just looking at all these German faces." Kathryn Doby, who is now married to Glattes, and Louise Quick were the only American dancers hired for the film. Quick says she and Doby sometimes accompanied the men because, "otherwise it would have looked kind of suspicious if one of the men walked up to some German woman in a bar and said, 'Hi, we're doing a big American movie and we want to hire you to be in it.' Some of these places were real dregs, very raunchy." In fact, aside from the drawings of Grosz and Otto Dix, and the forays to seedy bars and dingy nightclubs, Fosse had little else to draw upon for authenticity. After World War II, all vestiges of the Third Reich, or the era that brought it to power, had been destroyed or removed. Worse, the American cast and crew discovered that the Germans themselves were of little help. Most of them refused to acknowledge the period had even existed.

"You can't imagine the incredible scenes we've been through in Germany," Liza Minnelli told Rex Reed in a *Daily News* interview. "Like the clothes. I asked for some real '30s clothes, slinky, no bra. I said 'It should look like before the war' and the Germans all said, 'What war?' I mean, they don't want to know! So they came up with costumes that made me look like Joe Namath—wide Joan Crawford sleeves, padded shoulders, and pleats. I said, 'Forget it' and then Gwen Verdon, who helped me a lot, hunted around all the old antique shops in Paris and found a lot of old junk, and after we had everything settled, we discovered they had all the old costumes from the German films locked away in Munich, but they didn't want to get them out because it would look too much like the Nazi era all over again.

"I mean, you can't even find anyone who admits he is a German. They're all Austrians! . . . The first thing I did when I got to Munich was to try to find traces of that whole era. I wasn't there. I wasn't even born yet. I had nothing to do with it, so I wanted to know what happened. So I asked my driver, and he got very defensive. He said haughtily, 'Hitler killed more Germans than anyone else!' Even my dresser on the set was watching Joel Grey doing a Nazi number with swastikas, and she said, 'Why do we have to go through it all over again?' I had to explain it was very stylized and we didn't mean any harm by it. But they are very, very uptight. . . . People just will not talk."

If the Germans were reticent about the past, it only made Fosse more persistent in his efforts to reclaim it. He and Minnelli visited several places on the Reepersbahn, where they watched lesbians mud-wrestling and live pornographic sex shows. In Bavaria, they made a frightening discovery when they were told about a group of neo-Nazis. The strange juxtaposition of rampant sex and fascism was too tempting for Fosse to resist; it was, after all, the core of *Cabaret*. Hidden cameras were used to get authentic reaction shots from real people in real places. Some mistook his painstaking efforts to re-create history as Yankee intrusion. A few people involved in the production complained of anti-Semitic remarks from outsiders. "I really can't wait to get out of here and go home," Minnelli told the *News*.

Yet, within his company, which included more Germans than Americans, Fosse established a warm rapport. "I hung out with the crew a lot between the dances," says Louise Quick. "It was apparent everyone was sort of awed by Fosse and what he was doing with the film. Everyone knew this was not shaping up to be a traditional musical." According to John Sharpe, his choreographic assistant on the film, Fosse "inspired everyone else to work as hard [as he did]. In *Cabaret,* everyone was at full potential. It was an amazing thing to watch." Still, aside from Doby and Quick, the other dancers were all German, and Fosse's "thank-you-very-much" dismissals in auditions were quickly picked up even by those who did not speak English. Recalls Quick, "It was really amusing to hear the German sound men say it. If something did not go right, or if they were disappointed, they would say, 'stank you veddy much.' It got to be a running joke."

On the set, Fosse's *Cabaret* developed as something quite different from the stage version of *I Am a Camera*. In tone and substance, it more strongly resembles Isherwood's tale, though the emphasis has shifted somewhat to Sally Bowles, whose madcap exploits are constantly intercut with the rise of a power-hungry regime. During production of the film, it was learned that the real Sally, an expatriate American then in her sixties, was still living in Berlin. With all the publicity surrounding the making of *Cabaret,* it seems unlikely she would not have heard about the film, though she never showed up at the Bavaria Studio. No attempts were made by Fosse or Minnelli to contact her.

It was Fosse's intention to make the songs in *Cabaret* comment on the dramatic action, even more so than in the Broadway show. To do this, he jettisoned some numbers, such as "Pineapple," from the stage production altogether, modified others ("The Money Song" became "Money, Money"), and asked John Kander and Fred Ebb to create two

Joel Grey shows Liza Minnelli a styled haircut from a 1930's book while the makeup man looks on. *(Alan Pappé/Lee Gross Inc.)*

originals, the ballad "Maybe This Time" and the rollicking German barrel polka, "Mein Herr" ("You have to understand the way I am, mein herr/You'll never turn the vinegar to wine, mein herr . . ."). In keeping with Isherwood's original story, Fosse dropped some of the Broadway show's characters and whittled down others, such as Fräulein Schneider, the role played on the stage by Lotte Lenya. Orchestrations, under the direction of long-time Fosse associate Ralph Burns, minimized the lavish arrangements of the original; far more reliance was placed on the onstage six-woman band, occasionally supplemented on the soundtrack by another instrument or two.

The stage on which Minnelli, Grey, and the motley company performed was quite small by film standards, ten feet by fourteen feet, with a slight rake. It was so small, in fact, that Fosse refrained from placing more than six dancers on it at a time. The less-is-more approach offered the dancers more opportunities to develop their mostly nonspeak-

From left to right, Gitta Schmidt, Helen Vilkovorska, Inge Jaeger, Joel Grey, Angelika Koch, Louise Quick in "Willkommen" from *Cabaret*. (*Alan Pappé/Lee Gross Inc.*)

ing characters, and allowed Fosse, director of photography Geoffrey Unsworth, and camera operator Peter McDonald to experiment with odd camera angles seen earlier in the film *Sweet Charity*. Dancers bend over backwards on chairs and stools, are caught up in can-cans, thrust their hips forward in obscene affrontery to the audience—but it is the cinematography as much as the choreography that delivers the full impact. At times, the camera appears to be at eye level with the stage—where the Kit Kat audience is seated—leading our eyes up the dancers' fluffy petticoats; then, teasingly, it jerks away to rest on a crooked knee. Fosse fully explores the dramatic potential in his choreography, even before the dance scenes are spliced into those relating to Nazism.

"I tried to make the dances look like the period," Fosse explained to *After Dark*, "not as if they were done by me, Bob Fosse, but by some guy who is down and out. I tried to keep this in mind, but it's so difficult. You think, 'Oh, I can't really have them do *that*. That's embarrassing; it's so bad, so cheap.' But you think, 'But if I *were* the kind of guy who only works with cheap cabarets and clubs, what else would I do? So I worked from that, always trying to keep it lively, entertaining."

In his dancers, too, Fosse sought to recapture the look of well-fed, buxom German women as they might have appeared in the early Thirties. He wanted them all a little overweight, and requested that they eat a hearty breakfast every morning. "It was the only time I remember he tried to make his dancers *gain* weight," says Louise Quick, a Kit Kat dancer who also performed in *Sweet Charity* and *Pippin,* and assisted Fosse on *Liza with a Z.* "I had lost all this weight before we began rehearsals and was very pleased with the way I looked. Then I met the producers, who frowned at me. One said, 'Oh, you're much too thin!' "

Fosse also asked the women to stop shaving under their arms. According to Minnelli, this caused considerable protest. ". . . [T]he girls hated it," she told the *Daily News,* "because they had to grow hair under their arms. So when we finished the musical numbers, we had a party and everybody gave them razors and soap and they all shaved under their arms again."

Fosse called upon the assistance of Gwen Verdon as well, who flew from New York to Germany with a Gorilla-head mask in her lap for one of the musical numbers when a suitable costume could not be located in Germany. She also helped redesign Minnelli's costumes, since Fosse hated the heavy brocade on many of Sally's dresses created by the film's original designers. One of Verdon's most stunning creations was a purple embroidered chemise with a black fringed sash belt. John Sharpe believes Verdon even came up with the helmetlike Louise Brooks bob that will forever be associated with Liza Minnelli.

"Gwen was her usual invaluable self," says Louise Quick, who applied her makeup under Verdon's supervision. "She was always there, always working. Bob liked for his dancers to do their own makeup. He kept these George Grosz books in the makeup room for us to look at for inspiration. The look I came up with for my character was achieved through a combination of drawing and this idea Gwen gave me where you put melted crayon on your eyelashes. We used to melt wax in a spoon over a candle. Then, you dipped a little mascara brush in it and put it on your eyelashes. They got awfully thick that way, but the thicker they were, the more Bob liked them. So, on top of the two or three pairs of eyelashes I was already wearing, Gwen and I melted green crayon and dripped the beads on the tips of the lashes. The effect was rather startling."

"Natural" armpits, pudgy thighs, and bizarre mascara only added to the look of decadence Fosse was after in *Cabaret*. Like Fellini, his approach to filming a musical relied less on traditional American conventions than it did on the more European notion of creating a link between reality and illusion. The dances, then, are only deceptively "so bad, so cheap." The vulgarity of certain numbers accentuates the sometimes-violent scenes they abut. During an Austrian slap dance, for example, the funny and familiar picture of dancers in shorts and suspenders merrily slapping their thighs turns vicious when the camera suddenly veers from inside the club to a narrow alley outside, where the club's proprietor—who had earlier ejected a Nazi youth—is brutally beaten by the brownshirts. Later, a routine kick line abruptly changes into a goose-step routine. In yet another number (later cut from the film), the flying skirts in a can-can are pierced by Sally's agonized screams during her abortion. Rarely has choreography been used to such a dramatic effect in a mainstream film.

Perhaps most disturbing is the number "Tomorrow Belongs to Me," the only song performed outside the Kit Kat Club, in a lush Biergarten. The scene begins with a conversation between Maximilian (Helmut Griem) and Brian (Michael York), who are physically attracted to one another, though each is also sleeping with Sally. They are interrupted by a seraphic blond, blue-eyed German boy, who sings a lilting anthem. It is only when the camera moves down the sleeve of his military uniform and rests on the red swastika armband that we realize he is one of the Hitler Youth, and that the deceptively beautiful song is a call for the nationalism of the Nazi party. He is soon joined by other young Aryan men and women, who rise and sing; one old, possibly Jewish, man in the crowd remains seated alone.

So subtly choreographed are these scenes that the audience is rarely conscious of the camera's manipulation. Each time we re-enter the cabaret for another music-hall routine, the restless camera pans around the audience and stage before moving outside to capture some image of political anarchy. It would be a mistake, however, to think that *Cabaret* concerns itself only with grandiose themes, since what really propells the story is the romance between Brian and Sally. They are both expatriates— Brian from England, Sally from the U.S.—who provide the link between life in the cabaret and outside it. And as we watch their love affair blossom and inevitably deteriorate, so has Fosse presented, in very brief film time, the rise of the Nazis.

The subtlety with which Fosse reveals so many ongoing dramas—

In his quest for absolute authenticity, Fosse asked his Kit Kat dancers not to shave under their arms and to gain weight. (*Alan Pappé/Lee Gross Inc.*)

the cabaret, Brian and Sally, the Nazis—is particularly impressive in the musical format. In the Broadway version of *Cabaret,* even the most acid numbers seemed tempered with showbiz fussiness, as though the producers feared too little razzle dazzle would not make for good box office. The late choreographer Ron Field's brilliant "Telephone Dance" is, perhaps, more spectacular than any of the dances in Fosse's *Cabaret*; but its sheer virtuosity calls more attention to itself than to the plot. The stage show lacks the seamlessness between on- and off-stage scenes found in the film.

This is particularly apparent in the final, explosive number, "Cabaret." The success of the Broadway show has spurred countless renditions of this song; while they have, no doubt, earned substantial royalties for Kander and Ebb, many place it entirely out of context. In the Broadway version, and even more so in the film, "Cabaret" is far more than an invitation to escape to a cozy little boîte with a glass of champagne. The song is placed near the end of the show, after Sally has aborted Brian's baby and the two have decided to part—a separation which also indicates Sally's conscious decision to stay in a country abounding with terrorism and oppression, while Brian's conscience cannot allow him to remain. When Minnelli launches into the song she borrows heavily from Judy Garland's stage mannerisms, gesticulating wildly, throwing out her arms to the audience in a desperate "love me!" gesture, eyes popping, mouth quivering. "Cabaret" was not written as the pleasant piano-bar sing-along it has become: "Life is a cabaret, old chum/Come to the cabaret" is Sally's proclamation to pursue stardom at all costs, even her own happiness. "Old chum" is not a term of endearment. As in Fosse's *Chicago,* in which Chita Rivera opens Act II with "Welcome back, suckers!" Sally baits the audience. We buy her hokey Lulu-in-Berlin image, which is, perhaps, Fosse's greatest feat as master of the musical form. The selfish, cynical antiheroes at the center of some of his best and most controversial projects—Sally Bowles in *Cabaret,* the Leading Player in *Pippin,* Roxie Hart in *Chicago,* Paul Snider in *Star 80*—have become these shows' biggest selling points. In Fosse films and stage musicals, nothing wins over audiences like a loser.

A few years after *Cabaret* was released, Fosse told *New York Magazine,* "I had to break away from movie musicals that just copy the Broadway show. Or movie musicals that copy conventions of the stage. *Singin' in the Rain, An American in Paris,* all the Gene Kelly, Fred Astaire musicals— they're classics. But they represent another era. Today I get very antsy watching musicals in which people are singing as they walk down the street or hang out the laundry. . . . In fact, I think it looks a little silly.

You can do it on the stage. The theater has its own personality—it conveys a removed reality. The movies bring that closer."

To achieve that reality, Fosse often resorted to drastic measures. To a degree, he could depend on the cosmetic conceits of heavy makeup and period costumes to convince the audience. Location shots also added authenticity to the film. But the acting was, of course, most important to Fosse, who used every means to provoke honest portrayals from his actors. Marisa Berenson, who played a beautiful Jewish heiress in the film, followed Fosse from Paris to Germany, so intent was she on getting the part in *Cabaret*. Although he finally cast her, it was not without reservations; she had few film credits and he wasn't sure she had had enough experience for the role. When he failed to get a realistic reaction shot from her in a scene where she opens her front door and sees that her beloved dog has been killed by a group of Nazis, Fosse went to a butcher and got a package of bloody intestines. The next day shooting on the scene resumed, and when Berenson opened the door and saw the carnage, she nearly swooned. "I think that's fair game," Fosse told the *Los Angeles Times*. "Anything to get the horrified, repulsed expression."

Not everyone involved with the film was pleased with Fosse's direction. Set designer Tony Walton, who worked with Fosse on *Pippin, Chicago, All That Jazz,* and *Star 80,* recalls how Fosse feared he would be fired halfway through production. "Fosse always had this mischievous little boy reaction to management that stemmed back to his being fired from a show [*The Conquering Hero*] early in his career. In *Cabaret,* there was a thin wall between his office and the producers'. One day he overheard them discussing bringing in another director because they weren't totally satisfied with what they were seeing. I don't think they understood how it was all going to fit together in the end. Fosse was upset but it didn't surprise him; he believed money people were only concerned that the show was a hit, and *Cabaret* was hardly a routine musical. I think the only time he ever connected with a producer was with Stuart Ostrow in *Pippin,* and that was because Stuart was also a director."

However distrustful the producers may have been during filming, once Fosse began postproduction on *Cabaret* in late 1971, they began to see he had created something unlike any other movie musical before it. It had been financed at a frugal $3 million but had gone over budget by $1 million, though Fosse held the reins tight. "There was no free hand in the cookie jar," says Louise Quick.

A heavy promotional blitz for the film began after editors from *Time, Life,* and *Newsweek* saw color slides taken during production. Ultimately, Minnelli graced the covers of *Newsweek* and *Time* (which called the movie "mostly slack and sour" but loved Minnelli), and *Life* ran a six-page spread. Word was building; *Cabaret* was going to be a smash.

In New York, *Cabaret* opened in early 1972 at the Zeigfeld Theater, at one time known for featuring first-run, big-budget musicals. In its first week there, it pulled in an impressive $2,000. Most critics responded euphorically, and even those that demurred grudgingly admitted that Minnelli and Grey were splendid. For Fosse, the long-coveted respect from the serious press had finally arrived. Publications that catered to the movie industry, such as *Films and Filming,* wrote lengthy articles about Fosse's accomplishments with *Cabaret.* One writer spoke of the old Broadway adage that making a film out of a stage play is like cutting up a sofa to make a chair. But, in *Cabaret,* "the balls have been grafted back on the bull."

The late Ron Field, who won a Tony for best choreography for the Broadway production of *Cabaret,* recalled talking to Fosse at the Zeigfeld premiere of the film in early 1972. "It was a very glittery affair. Cameras popping, lots of limos. Everyone was there: Misha [Baryshnikov], Liza, Hal [Prince]. The anticipation in the audience was almost tangible. I thought the film was an incredible achievement, and I said, 'Bob, it's *wonderful!*' Whether he appreciated that or whether he thought it was just bullshit, I don't know. He was so damn shy, and really did not have a lot of confidence in himself. He sort of mumbled 'thanks' and disappeared in the crowd."

Fosse, who had grown a beard in Germany, took on the air of a bemused, if somewhat weary, auteur. After *Variety* reported that the film stood to earn over $20 million in the first few months of its release—five times its investment—Fosse quipped, "Do you think that now we'll have a raft of Hollywood musicals about Nazism, with homosexual leading men?" The statement was as much an acknowledgment of his own achievements with the film's controversial subject matter as it was an indictment of Hollywood's tendency to sanitize or exploit sexuality in the movies. And though it was true that Fosse had succeeded in dealing straightforwardly with homosexuality for the first time in a mainstream musical, *Goodbye to Berlin*'s author, Christopher Isherwood, believed the film still fell short of being convincing in its depiction of Brian, a character inspired by Isherwood himself. "I didn't like the treatment of homosexuality in *Cabaret,*" Isherwood told members of the Modern Language Association in December 1974. "The movie reduced it to a kind of amusing but harmless weakness—like bed-wetting. The boy is treated as a kind of heterosexual manqué."

Neither did television censors approve of Fosse's straightforward approach to the sexual entanglements of Sally and Brian. When ABC broadcast *Cabaret* in September 1975, network censors objected to some of the dialogue and promptly had it edited. This included a pivotal scene between Sally and Brian in which both learn they have been sleeping with the same man:

BRIAN: Oh, screw Maximilian!
SALLY: I do!
BRIAN: (pause) So do I.
SALLY: (pause) You two bastards!
BRIAN: Don't you mean you *three* bastards?

Editing this exchange from the film leaves the romantic relationships between the three lovers ambiguous. When the wealthy Maximilian finally writes Sally and Brian a note indicating that he will be away for some time, television audiences are left with the impression that business commitments have hastened his departure, rather than that the ménage à trois has run its course, and that he is bored. Film critics were incensed over the "butchering" of *Cabaret*. Rex Reed decreed that "ABC castrated the sense out of *Cabaret*," and swore never to review theatrical films on television again.

Such indignities seem especially unjust for a film that won eight Academy Awards in 1973, including one each for Fosse (best director), Minnelli (best actress), and Grey (best supporting actor). *Cabaret* was an enormous hit in the United States—more in the cities than the hinterlands—and, surprisingly, in Germany as well. In West Berlin, where it was filmed, *Cabaret* was especially popular, though, again, its foreign release did not escape the censors. "Tomorrow Belongs to Me," dubbed a "Nazi anthem," was excised because it was believed the song would rekindle resentment toward the Germans. Some months later, though, the scene was reinstated, and the film continued to do brisk business.

Cabaret's triumph affected Fosse profoundly. For the first time, he was embraced by Hollywood as a heavyweight film director, giving him a heretofore unclaimed cachet. After winning his Oscar, Fosse allegedly received twenty scripts to consider in one week, and admitted to disconnecting his home phones. Tony Walton believes that had Fosse not directed *Cabaret* out of the United States, the film might have received the same Hollywoodizing as *Sweet Charity*. "There is an amazing leap between the film *Sweet Charity* and *Cabaret*," he notes. "It shows, I think, that you don't take for granted the parts [of a movie] you're not familiar with. *Sweet Charity* was produced in a very conventional Hollywood way; when Bob was able to do *Cabaret* elsewhere, he was able to make a much more personal attack."

Just as his stardom was ascending, Fosse's home life had begun deteriorating. Verdon was tired of her husband's much-publicized infidelities with chorus dancers, which had begun before the days of *Sweet Charity,* and which *Cabaret*'s cast members claim were hardly kept secret in Germany. In 1971, he and Verdon were legally separated. "I was living like a wife and mother, which is really what I wanted to be," Verdon told the *New York Times*. "But I was the wrong kind of wife for him. I think Bob outgrew me. Bob started writing and he was involved in all kinds of things, and I was so involved with Nicole I didn't really care if I worked or not. I guess the hardest thing was I was honest with Bob and I admired him. I got sick of not being able to admire him. He began to think, 'Oh, you're my wife.' I hated that. . . . See, I don't know what he wanted. That's where I'm really stupid. But I know I wanted to be able to admire him and be part of everything and be recognized as someone who had a right to an opinion. . . . He's a fabulous father to Nicole. We just don't live together. That's all. But he's the best friend I've got."

"Most people have dreams of doing something special with their lives," Fosse told *Penthouse*. "Worrying about the washing machine or the diapers—well, that's just not very special to me. . . . Look, marriage is pleasant, but it isn't very exciting."

Because he had been out of the country so long making *Cabaret,* Fosse felt he had neglected his role as a father. Fearing his wife and daughter were slipping away from him, he looked to *Cabaret*'s Oscar sweep to help him regain his stature as a family man.

The night he won his first Oscar, Fosse claims to have been "full of tranquilizers and ready for failure." In the *Los Angeles Times,* he recounted a conversation he had with his ten-year-old daughter, Nicole, when he called her from Los Angeles after being named best director. "She said, 'hi,' and I said, 'What did you think of the show?' and she said, 'Nice.' So then I said, 'Well, how's your new bicycle?' and when she got off and Gwen got on, I said, 'I'm so disappointed. I thought she'd say something about my beard or tease me about my baldness, and she hardly said anything.' And Gwen said, 'You should have been here. When you won it, she screamed so loud she said, ' "I broke something in my throat." ' "

As Fosse showed seven years later in the autobiographical *All That Jazz,* Nicole was his link to that part of him that constantly needed reaffirmation as a good father. Already, his pretty blonde daughter showed promise as a dancer, thanks to religiously taken ballet classes. Fosse was determined Nicole would have the *formal* training in dance he believed he'd missed out on as a hoofer. They communicated well through dance steps and combinations, but as a father Fosse felt he was foundering. He told the *New York Times* that year, "She seems to like me, and to have accepted the separation. But you see, she goes to this school where half the parents are divorced." If he separated from Verdon in order to explore his own sexual curiosity, it was Nicole who returned him to a home life away from rehearsal studios and opening night parties. Fosse also continued to remain close to Verdon, and their divorce was never finalized. Fosse-dancer-turned-director Gene Foote claims Fosse directed Verdon in 1975's *Chicago* because, "he owed her one," but Fosse also knew that she brought out the best work in him.

"I think it's my fault that the marriage failed," he admitted to *Penthouse* two years after the separation. "It has to do with when I work, I shut everything out. Gwen's one of the most incredible people I've ever met, and we have this beautiful daughter . . . some of the happiest times we've ever had were when we

were working. We work well together. I admire her, and she has . . . well, respect for me. Look, I don't know if any marriage could work for me. I certainly tried harder with Gwen than the other two. Marriage is a disaster for me. It's been one big closing in New Haven."

Clutching his best director Oscar for *Cabaret,* 1973, it was Fosse's first nomination. *(AP/Wide World Photos)*

PIPPIN

Immediately after *Cabaret* went into postproduction, Fosse began work on his next Broadway musical, *Pippin,* about the son of King Charlemagne of the Holy Roman Empire. The musical had a rocky preproduction period, stormy rehearsals, and a financially disappointing early run, but it went on to become Fosse's longest-running show on Broadway, playing 1,944 performances—long enough to be still running during the arrival of Fosse's next stage musical, 1975's *Chicago.*

Stylistically, Pippin is a complete integration of book, music, and dance; from Tony Walton's mobile set to the dancers, or "Players," themselves, everything in *Pippin* moves. As for the dances, *Pippin's* erotically charged choreography revealed a man fascinated by the creative possibilities of sex on stage. In fact, one of *Pippin's* Players, Ann Reinking, became Fosse's girlfriend and muse.

To appreciate Fosse's accomplishments with *Pippin,* it is helpful not to be too familiar with the actual story itself. In Fosse's treatment of the tale, using a libretto by Roger O. Hirson, Pippin bears faint resemblance to the original Pepin—who lived around AD 780 and, in dying, denied his father, King Charlemagne, an heir to the throne.

In large part, Pippin's life and his search for fulfillment reflect Fosse's own unending curiosity. He is described as "a child who showed a thirst for knowledge," and who says in the show "the knowledge I'm looking for can't be found in books. . . . I promise not to waste my life on common ordinary pursuits." But it is really Pippin's journey through a

Ben Vereen flanked by two Players in *Pippin. (Martha Swope)*

series of hard-knock experiences that calls the most attention to Fosse. As Pippin struggles to get his father's attention and find something authentic in his own life, he embarks on a series of adventures. He tries to be a soldier, but discovers he is not bloodthirsty enough. On the advice of his grandmother, he explores the bucolic pleasures of country living. After a series of kinky sexual exploits—involving everything from lesbians to sadomasochists—Pippin decides sex is ultimately a selfish act, which leaves him totally unfulfilled. Briefly, he becomes a revolutionary, pitted against his own father, whom in Fosse's version he kills on moral grounds. Disillusioned, Pippin renounces the throne and, addressing the audience, says: "I know this is a musical comedy, but I want my life to mean something."

That "something" comes to be a young woman named Catherine, a widow who claims to be "conservative with a budget, liberal with a meal." She takes Pippin into her home, where he befriends her young son. Catherine and Pippin fall in love, but Pippin begins to miss the high

Leland Palmer as Pippin's licentious stepmother Fastrada. *(Martha Swope)*

life and leaves her, only to be tempted by "the grand finale": suicide. In the end, he chooses life over death, a conclusion that, while pat, keeps the show upbeat and life affirming. *Pippin*'s ending, in fact, is the only part of the show that seems to duck from the Fosse philosophy of life.

Pippin belongs to a genre of musicals originating in the Sixties— *Hair, Jesus Christ Superstar, Godspell,* and *Dude*—rock musicals that capture the anti-establishment tone of the era. All of them shunned the escapist storylines of earlier musicals, choosing to conjure medieval and Biblical subjects and ally them with concerns of the day—war, oppression, drugs, sexual experimentation. Ben Vereen, whose career was launched after winning Tonys for Judas in *Jesus Christ Superstar* and The Leading Player in *Pippin,* today believes that "The message itself [in these musicals] was very important; we could use parts of *Hair* in our world today. The part of the show that is still relevant is that we need to come together again as people and learn to love each other.

"But there was a lot of dishonesty built into that philosophy, too. Excuses to self-destruct because it was easier than facing reality. A lot of people who were caught up in the trendiness of the Sixties missed the spirit of these shows. In many ways, my experiences during [*Hair*] crippled me. I got seduced by the belief that drugs could heal; that sex and love were the same thing." So when I look back on *Hair, Superstar,* and *Pippin,* my feelings are very mixed. Today, Vereen says his former life-style is a thing of the past. "I cleaned myself out, gave up drinking, and started loving me again."

Arguably, *Pippin* remains the most topical of these early rock operas today. Certainly, in its day, it matched one of the oddest couples on Broadway: a Broadway veteran, Fosse, with twenty-five-year-old composer Stephen Schwartz, who already had a Broadway hit to his credit, *Godspell.* If *Pippin* is, in part, concerned with the generation gap between Pippin and his father, so were the show's rehearsals plagued by angry confrontations between the young composer and a director-choreographer old enough to be his father.

"Bob and Stephen Schwartz had different concepts of the musical," says Kathryn Doby, who was one of the Players in the show as well as Fosse's dance assistant. "If you read the original concept of *Pippin,* it was more like a fairy tale. Bob made the show relevant to 1972 by bringing in current political comments, comments on his own celebrity. Stephen had such a big ego for one so young. He was the young genius, and he wanted to have his show, and only his show." Midway through rehearsals, Fosse told *After Dark,* "[Stephen's] only twenty-five years old, and some days he's only twelve. But he's a very talented person. I like his score very much."

When approached to be interviewed for this book, Schwartz wrote back: "[I]t is no secret that Bob and I did not enjoy a particularly happy working relationship, and in the spirit of *de mortuis nil nisi bonum,* I would prefer not to be interviewed about it." Still, the tempestuous exchanges between Fosse and Schwartz are worth some examination, if only for the unusual piece of theater that ultimately developed.

The score for *Pippin* was written while Schwartz was a student at Carnegie Tech, and he had been working on it off and on during the seven years it took for the music to come to the attention of producer Stuart Ostrow. With the phenomenal success of *Godspell,* Schwartz had considerable bargaining power on Broadway, but his pop songs did not always meet with critical approval; the *New York Times* described *Pippin*'s score as "characterless."

With Schwartz's songs and Roger O. Hirson's slight book, Fosse saw an opportunity for the first time in his career to put the score and book at the service of his choreography. However mediocre he felt the music and the libretto were, his grand scheme was to present his own ideas in the guise of his dancers, the Players, on which the book and songs would comment, *not* the other way around. Because Fosse kept the dancers close to him as the show began to take shape, Schwartz quickly found himself without allies when Fosse had him barred from the Imperial Theatre during rehearsals.

"Bob Fosse is not interested in writers," Schwartz told the *Daily News,* seemingly unaware that some of Fosse's best friends included writers Paddy Chayefsky, Herb Gardner, Peter Maas, and E. L. Doctorow. "You cannot do content with staging. I knew he was wrong for the show when we were ready to go out of town. The tension kept getting worse and worse. The showdown came when he was called in to make a final choice on dancers. I picked the ones who could sing, and he vetoed all of them. When I complained, he demanded that I leave the theater. And I did. For two days. Today I fight back. The cast rallied around Bob and they can't stand me. I don't speak to him or to Stuart Ostrow. . . . I'd worked on that show for seven years. I know I'm tactless. I just wanted somebody to ask what I think, and if they give me a good reason I'll back down."

In a court ruling that recalled Fosse's arbitration award for his choreography in *The Conquering Hero,* the American Arbitration Association ruled in a two-to-one decision in November 1973—over a year after *Pippin* opened on Broadway—that Schwartz had the right to lease the Australian rights to the show to his own chosen producer, and to revise the script. Schwartz was deeply dissatisfied with Fosse's version of *Pippin,* even after it proved to be a hit on Broadway. When the London production did not fare well with critics, Schwartz saw an opportunity to rally for a production of *Pippin* as he had envisioned it. Thus, there are two versions of *Pippin:* Fosse's, which appeared on Broadway, in London, Vienna, and a national tour; and Schwartz' Australian production.

"I don't think Stephen ever fully understood what Fosse was trying to do with the show," says Tony Walton, who won a Tony for his commedia del l'arte sets. "When he asked me to do the sets for *his* version, I told him that I couldn't because I had conceived the show for Fosse, and I had to adhere to his vision of it. *Pippin* was unusual. Fosse was saying, 'Ignore what you read and hear, because the animal I'm after is something else.' He was burrowing his way into it."

While Fosse pushed and probed his way through rehearsals, he demanded only that his cast and collaborators trust his instincts. For the most part, they did—how could anyone question the man responsible for *Cabaret*?—but not implicitly. "My agent at the time read the script and advised me not to do it," recalls Vereen of *Pippin* after Fosse cast him in the then-amorphous role of the Leading Player, who leads Pippin down a thorny garden path to self-discovery/self-destruction. "I had my reservations, too, but I said, 'If Bob's doing it, I want it.' Then I went down to Philadelphia to do the Joey Bishop Tennis Tournament. I was reading the script on the way down and I wept; man, it was *terrible!* I hardly had a part.

"At the first rehearsal, the cast gathered around this big table to read the script. Everyone was there: Jill Clayburgh, Irene Ryan, John Ruben-

Costume designer Patricia Zipprodt invented a special fabric to "sculpt" *Pippin*'s provocative armor. *(Martha Swope)*

stein, Eric Berry, Leland Palmer, Chris Chadman, Kathy Doby, Kandy Brown, Pam Sousa, Gene Foote, just to name a few. I remember sitting there, turning pages and reading, 'enter Charlemagne,' 'enter Pippin,' 'enter Fastrada.' Bob kept looking at me during the reading, and when it was over he came over to me and said, 'Don't worry about it. Just trust me on this one.' "

To inspire this trust, Fosse kept Vereen and the band of strolling mummers, the Players, close to him on and off the stage. During auditions, where over 5,000 dancers were seen and "thank-you'ed," Fosse requested only that the eager faces in front of him "surprise me." "If you could understand what he was talking about," says Gene Foote, another Player, "that this was a show about magic, then you understood what he was after. He really wanted that feedback. This was not a show for

Pippin's Tony-winning Leading Player, Ben Vereen, in a sea of flexed fingers. (*Martha Swope*)

dancers who expected to get spoon-fed. That's how he got such a good group of players." After rehearsals, they would go to dinner with him or join him for his favorite cocktail, a daiquiri. He told them how necessary it was that they believe in the entire concept of the musical. "It made all of us feel close and important," says Kathryn Doby.

Because much of the show was concerned with sexual expression as a means to finding individual identity, Fosse encouraged the Players to seduce the audiences with their physical presence. He told the *New York Times,* "Always before if I found a male dancer that I knew was homosexual, I would keep saying no, you can't do that, don't be so minty there. This time, I used the kind of people they were to give the show individuality, and they were so happy about it. I think it helped the show. . . . Sure there are lots of homosexuals in dance. And I think there are lots of homosexuals in sports, and in muscle building, and in any field where people pay a lot of attention to their bodies."

It would be wrong, however, to think *Pippin* was the musical equivalent to *The Boys in the Band.* Pippin, it is assumed in the libretto, is heterosexual, though it is sexuality itself—neither gay nor straight—that Fosse explores in the show. But because so many of the partnerships involve men and women, some reviewers took this as a sign that Fosse was single-handedly returning the American musical back to "normal" sexuality. "Our musical theater is dominated by homosexuals," lamented Martin Gottfried in a now-famous *New York Post* column that is quoted today by dancers and press agents for the ire it elicited from gays at the time. ". . . Fosse's heterosexuality is obvious in his shows, . . ." continued Gottfried, "it is great to see the women in *Chicago* and *Pippin* costumed, choreographed, and treated to celebrate their physical, sexual grandeur."

Fosse's curiosity about male homosexuality and lesbianism manifests itself in frequent pas de deux and pas de trois in his choreography and, in the film *Lenny,* in a ménage à trois. Although not always sexual, there is usually a provocative edge to these groupings. In *Pippin,* the young hero's numerous sexual entanglements result in an extended ballet, "With You," which leaves Pippin exhausted and disillusioned. Although sexuality prevails in post-*Pippin* Fosse choreography, as well as in his nondance work, it is often presented as an ultimately crippling desire—by the time Fosse began *Star 80,* it had become associated with spiritual *and* physical death.

Because *Pippin* is in effect an elaborate charade involving assorted magical illusions, the audience is tricked into believing that the strolling minstrellike Players are an affable lot intent on protecting the hapless Pippin. In effect, Fosse uses the entire chorus in the place of the Joel Grey

Master of Ceremonies, in *Cabaret*. In both cases, these seemingly benign characters threaten to corrupt, even murder, the "good" Players. Falling back once again on his knowledge of old-time music-hall entertainments, Fosse, along with Tony Walton and costume designer Patricia Zipprodt, create a Romanesque canvas that, in an instant, can change from fraudulently jocular ("Magic to Do") to brooding and sinister ("War Is a Science").

Tapping into Roger O. Hirson's thematic notion that there is no separation between Church and State in times of war, "War Is a Science" begins with a tamborine tarantella while King Charlemagne prays, "Give us the strength to butcher evil." As light pours through stained glass windows, modeled after those in Chartres, Vereen as the Leading Player slinks onto the stage dressed in black and wearing a straw hat, flanked by two women in breastplates. Suddenly the stage is bathed in Jules Fisher's blood-red lighting while assorted body parts are seen scattered about the stage or impaled on rapiers. "You ain't seen nothin' yet, folks," Vereen grins. Finally, there is only one soldier left alive on stage. Near death, he gasps, "We won!" as though there were anyone left to celebrate the victory, or any reason to celebrate.

As dark as "War Is a Science" and several other numbers from *Pippin* are, those who worked with Fosse are quick to point out that his use of sex and violence is never gratuitous, and is frequently redeemed by humor, admittedly black. "Bob looked for the humor in violence," says Gene Foote. "Like Charity being pushed in the lake twice, or the feeling he establishes in *Pippin* and *All That Jazz*. I know that Bob had considered suicide several times. I know he went into therapy and sought help. It's difficult to explain what goes on in the creative mind. Look at a great painter like Van Gogh, whose life was clouded by darkness; yet, look at the light that he painted. There is that same quality in Bob's work. Really nice people create really *nice* work. I don't know anyone who would say Bob was a *nice* guy."

Fosse admitted he saw himself as the Mephistophelian Leading Player. (In fact, Patricia Zipprodt's all-black costume for Vereen seems to be modeled after the basic black wardrobe Fosse acquired during the early Seventies.)

In "The Finale," the Leading Player and the Players attempt to get Pippin to step into a box that he is instructed to set on fire, thus committing suicide. "The goal, as Bob saw it," says Gene Foote, "was to get Pippin into that box so we could all have an orgasm." The Players simulated acts of masturbation with startling conviction. "The finale *was* our orgasm," says Foote; "I remember Jennifer Narin-Smith was

mortgaged his house. Motown Records, the largest investor, came up with the balance. Still, the production was short of money when it went to Washington. Roger L. Stevens, director of the Kennedy Center's Opera House, where *Pippin* was slated to open, put in $100,000 and guaranteed a $50,000 per week gross during its run. Because the Kennedy Center is subsidized by the federal government, Stevens' additional bankrolling of the show meant that the United States government essentially was functioning as a producer. By guaranteeing the show against a loss during its four-week run, Fosse and the rest of the creative staff could concentrate on tightening the show before it went to Broadway.

One suggestion that was made to Fosse during rehearsals by his close friend, writer Paddy Chayefsky (*Marty, Network*), was to eliminate the intermission. The reasoning was that there was no logical cutoff point for an Act I finale, and that the musical's impact on the audience during

Ann Reinking *(Martha Swope)*

"The Finale" was determined by the dramatic momentum built up during the previous two hours. The Shubert Organization, which managed the Imperial, objected to removing the intermission, which meant losing a considerable profit from the bar crowd. Nonetheless, *Pippin* played as a one-act, two-hours-and-fifteen-minutes musical, and audiences didn't seem to mind.

Pippin's opening night party in Washington was as much a show of loyalty to Fosse as it was the culmination of months rehearsing. Because the producers had done everything next to selling the shirts off their backs to finance *Pippin,* there was no money left for a cast party. But the players were unfazed. They made their own party, carted in food, beer, and tapes, and, according to Tony Walton, "really made a celebration. All the dancers came up to Bob to have him dance with them, but he wouldn't. About two or three in the morning, he got my wife, Gen, up on the floor to dance. She went to put her arms around him, but Bobby said, 'No, don't touch. Just put your hands up to mine and hold them about five inches away. Feel the heat and follow.' She sort of followed him around as everyone else fell back and watched. It was the most extraordinary thing, and amazingly erotic."

For a show that ran nearly five years and returned a net profit of $3,318,415, *Pippin* fared poorly at the box-office during its wobbly early weeks on Broadway. It opened in October 1972 to strong word of mouth and generally good reviews. The critical consensus was that Fosse had found magic in a mediocre book and score, or, as Clive Barnes wrote in the *New York Times:* "What will certainly be memorable is the staging by Bob Fosse. This is fantastic. It takes a painfully ordinary little show and launches it into space." Yet, *Pippin*'s advance, which was a mere $350,000 before it arrived on Broadway, did not look promising. After the show opened, *Pippin*'s weekly gross receipts started out strong, then ebbed to just over $72,000; it required $60,000 just to break even.

Peter Le Donne, the advertising executive for *Pippin,* suggested to Stuart Ostrow that he do a television commercial for the show, something that had never been attempted before for a Broadway musical. "One day Bob called me at home and said, 'I'm thinking about doing a commercial for the show,' " remembers Ben Vereen. " 'Can you meet me at the studio?' " The result was a thirty-second commercial featuring Vereen, Pamela Sousa, and Kandy Brown performing a dance from the war sequence. As they danced, the voiceover told viewers they could see the other 119 minutes of *Pippin* live at the Imperial without commercial interruption. The spots ran on popular night-time television shows such as *Maude, Columbo,* and *Sanford and Son,* and cost Ostrow about $16,000 a month. The results were staggering. Before the *Pippin* commercial, the show's weekly box-office average was down to $18,000; after it aired, *Variety* reported its weekly take at around $113,000—"the highest for any show on Broadway." His contract gave Fosse 10 percent of the profits in addition to his 5 percent royalty of the gross receipts; by August 1974, he had made $148,802 in profit and $550,546 in royalties. Not surprisingly, Fosse went back to Le Donne when he wanted to make a television commercial for 1975's *Chicago* and the revival of *Sweet Charity* in 1986.

Although *Pippin* did not win the Tony Award for best musical for the 1972–73 Broadway season (that went to Stephen Sondheim's *A Little Night Music*), the show did receive five Tonys. Fosse won for best direction and choreography; Vereen, for best male performance in a musical; Tony Walton, for best scenic design; and Jules Fisher, for best lighting. With an Oscar and a Tony under his belt in one year, Fosse's triple crown year would be complete with an Emmy.

John Rubenstein, Jill Clayburgh, and eight-year-old Shane Nickerson contemplate the simple pleasures of country living in 1972's *Pippin,* directed and choreographed by Fosse. (*Martha Swope*)

LIZA WITH A Z

Before Fosse began rehearsals on *Pippin,* he staged and choreographed a landmark variety special for NBC starring Liza Minnelli. *Liza with a Z* was filmed May 31, 1972 at the Lyceum Theater before a hand-picked live audience. With *Cabaret,* Minnelli finally had established herself as a singular talent, not simply July Garland's daughter—a hard-won achievement. *Cabaret* and *Liza with a Z* display Fosse's earnest efforts to capture the "it" quality about Minnelli. The "concert for television," sponsored by Singer, was broadcast in November 1972, only a month after *Pippin*'s debut on Broadway, and completed Fosse's triple-crown with an Emmy.

Having performed on television variety shows hosted by Sid Caesar and Ed Sullivan in his dancing days, Fosse was not unfamiliar with the television medium, though it was one he believed held little attraction for dancers or choreographers. Dance on television before *Liza with a Z* tended to look flat and uninteresting, with chorus dancers cluttering up the screen like confetti. Dance patterns were usually shot straight-on for television or, when overhead camera angles were used, looked gimmicky.

Because Fosse was scheduled to begin rehearsals for *Pippin* in July 1972, only five weeks of rehearsals were alloted for *Liza with a Z.* Louise Quick, who assisted Fosse on the choreography, notated the dances and had to learn all of them in case she had to step in for one of the dancers. "It was nonstop work," she remembers. "We shot with two live audiences, and after that there was a seventeen-hour call for pick-up shots.

After *Cabaret,* Fosse and Minnelli reteamed for the television special *Liza with a Z.* Fosse won an Emmy for direction and choreography. *(Courtesy of Dance Magazine)*

Bob had hired extras whom he matched up to people who had been in the audience those nights. Even though television audiences rarely saw the audience at the Lyceum during the show, it was important to Bob to get an authentic look of a crowd, even if only for a split second.

The entire production was shot on film, not videotape. Most television variety shows use videotape because it is less expensive when shooting numerous scenes, but it also has a grainy quality that is distracting when the camera cuts in for a close-up or pulls away for a long shot. Although the 35-millimeter film used for *Liza with a Z* resulted in a far more costly production, it remains a hallmark for television standards.

Liza with a Z featured trademark Fosse dances and costumes, but it was, of course, Minnelli who illuminated the stage. Fred Ebb, who wrote the show, provided her with just enough stage patter to segue from song to song without slackening the momentum of Fosse's staging. An impressive program of songs—covering blues ("God Save the Child"), rhythm ("Ring Them Bells"), character ballads ("It Was a Good Time," "You've Let Yourself Go"), and Tin Pan Alley ("Bye Bye Blackbird," "My Mammy")—was, of course, concluded by a medley from *Cabaret*. For both Fosse and Minnelli, 1972 and 1973 are remembered as zenith years of shared victories. Success was never sweeter for either again.

With success comes temptation. After Fosse won the Tony, Oscar, and Emmy in 1973, suddenly everyone was his best friend. He became the Great White Hope for Broadway, cinema, and television. Every major star who'd ever had the ambition to be in a musical wanted to work with him—Gene Kelly, Streisand, Sinatra, and later, even Michael Jackson and Madonna. But as expectations increased, allusions to his "genius" made him profoundly uncomfortable. His shy and retiring personality was at odds with the media's portrayal of him as a cross between Harold Prince and Otto Preminger.

The pressure to produce more work on the level of *Cabaret, Pippin,* and *Liza with a Z* meant long nights holed up at his rehearsal studio adjacent to the Edison Hotel. He was also fond of the now-gone Broadway Arts studios at Broadway and Fifty-sixth Street. "His best creative time began at 11 P.M. or midnight and went into the early morning hours," says Gene Foote. "He adored Broadway Arts—that room with the smell of sweat and the griminess. He knew those mirrors, those windows. He felt private in there. . . . I don't think he cared so much about making money. Well, sure he did—we all do—but his biggest

problem was like that of Woody Allen, Fellini, and Truffaut: he had to say what he had to say. And he wouldn't stop working until he felt he'd said it."

With opportunities calling from every direction, Fosse rarely found time to sleep. Sleep meant missing parties, losing deals, cutting back on his own work. So, he began experimenting with stimulants to cheat time. He snorted cocaine and popped Dexadrine in the morning, another at lunch, one or two more at dinner washed down with a few daiquiris or a Scotch. When he felt his heart racing too fast, he reached for a barbiturate to calm down, a Valium to get to sleep for a few hours. Then there was the always-present cigarette dangling from his mouth. As humorously depicted in *All That Jazz,* it was not uncommon for him to step into the shower with the butt still clenched between his teeth.

"There was a certain romanticism about that stuff," Fosse told *Rolling Stone* in 1984. "There was Bob drinking and smoking and turning out good work. Still popping pills and screwing around with the girls. 'Isn't it terrific macho behavior?' they said. I probably thought I was indestructable. . . . I see so many cokeheads in the industry. Right up to the projectionist. It starts to affect their work and how they think. But I love cocaine, so I really have to stay away from it."

Fosse seemed at a loss how to balance his former identity as a rarely seen choreographer with his new-found celebrity. In spite of the 1973 media blitz, Fosse remained his own best press agent. Swen Swenson, who had danced for Fosse in *Little Me,* says he detected a noticeable change in Fosse after he'd won the triple crown in 1973. That year, Shirley MacLaine was performing at the Palace Theatre, attracting a glamourous crowd of stars. Swenson recalls seeing Fosse after the show on opening night. "There was a mass of people crowded in the basement of the Palace trying to congratulate Shirley," says Swenson. "Suddenly I saw Bob, still in his casual rehearsal clothes, cigarette dangling, running around with Liza and getting his picture taken. I managed to squeeze up next to him, and asked how he'd liked the show. 'Uh, I didn't see it,' he said. I got this picture of him at home sleeping with his alarm clock set, knowing when the show was going to close and dashing down to the

Minnelli and Fosse at the Shubert Theatre after receiving Tony Awards in 1978. Minnelli won for *The Act,* Fosse, for *Dancin'. (AP/Wide World Photos)*

Palace just in time for the photographers. He was still promoting himself. I wanted to say, 'Oh, Bobby, just *relax!*' "

Unfortunately, Fosse did not know how to relax. "Fosse had a dark side," says Kathryn Doby. "He played with suicide so many times. It was always in the back of his mind. There were always these little remarks that you didn't know whether to take as jokes or if he was serious. . . ."

"[A]fter the awards, I had a really serious depression," Fosse confessed to *Penthouse* in 1973. "Like, you know, that this was it. I was pleased with the attention—I needed it, I really needed it badly. But at the same time there was something of a downer about it. I knew it shouldn't be like that. I mean, if *I* were to write my life I'd say that when I was forty-five—which is just the right time to enjoy it, not when you're too young, but after you've been up and down—while I'm still young enough to enjoy the success and recognition, that's when I would like it. And that's when I got it. I couldn't understand why I wasn't happy. Instead of jumping down the street and being all smiles, I'd find I was badly depressed. And then, eventually, I had to say fuck it, it's over, and get back to work. That's the important thing, to *work*. . . . Consider suicide? Yes, I've flirted with it. It's like a girl, you know? An attractive woman. You can only fool around with her so long."

By 1973, Fosse had finally arrived after over thirty-five years of paying his dues. The thirteen-year-old Bobby Fosse and his "Le Petit Cabaret" had matured into a *Cabaret* colored by his own experiences on the vaudeville circuit. By dint of his films, Fosse had become one of the first to define "choreographer" to lay audiences. But there was a price to pay for the triple crown, which rested uncomfortably on Fosse's head. Drugs, booze, cigarettes, and sex contributed to his feelings of insecurity. He separated from Gwen Verdon, perhaps the only woman who truly understood his complexities and accepted them, and worried about becoming estranged from his daughter Nicole.

Always, it was the work that mattered, the fear that if he took a breather, the phone would stop ringing. "I'm really basically lazy," he told the *Chicago Sun-Times*. "The only way I can combat it is to remind myself that if I ever stop I'll never get started again." But the relentless pace he kept in the early Seventies was bound to catch up with him. By 1974, it did. While editing his next film, *Lenny,* and rehearsing the Broadway-bound *Chicago,* Fosse's heart did a time step, and missed a beat. Exit to hospital, stage right.

VI

ALL THAT GLITTERS

Give 'em the old razzle dazzle
Razzle dazzle 'em
Give 'em an act with lots of flash in it
And the reaction will be passionate
Give 'em the old hocus pocus
Bead and feather 'em
How can they see with sequins in their eyes?
What if your hinges all are rusting?
What if, in fact, you're just disgusting?
Razzle dazzle 'em
And they'll never catch wise

> —*"Razzle Dazzle,"*
> *by Fred Ebb and John Kander*

LENNY

o be on the wire is life. The rest is waiting."

A Flying Wallenda high-wire artist provided this preface to Bob Fosse's much-debated 1979 film *All That Jazz,* a reflection of the director's life and career. But the statement is equally germane to all of Fosse's projects following his banner triple crown year in 1973. From his vantage point high atop Broadway in an office suite he shared with Paddy Chayefsky, Fosse contemplated a future of infinite possibilities.

"You know, I've been hot and cold in this business so many times," he said in an interview with *Filmmakers Newsletter* in 1975. "For example, after the film *Sweet Charity,* I couldn't get arrested. But after *Cabaret* and all those awards, I was really hot and had my choice of material. There were a lot of properties floating around in different stages: novels, screenplays, adaptations. And *Lenny* was among them."

Lenny was Fosse's first nonmusical project, a stark film biography of Lenny Bruce based on the 1971 Broadway show *Lenny,* written by Julian Barry and directed by Tom O'Horgan. It would be the first of four projects between 1973 and 1979 that mulled over Fosse's own life. *Lenny, Chicago, Dancin',* and *All That Jazz* are Fosse's multimillion-dollar sessions with his analysts: the stage and screen. Although all of Fosse's endeavors from *Sweet Charity* forward are in some way related to his own experiences as a dancer-choreographer-director-writer, these four Seventies efforts speak as much about Fosse himself as of his continued evolution as a filmmaker and choreographer.

Mr. and Mrs. Lenny Bruce (Dustin Hoffman and Valerie Perrine) during their Catskills gigs at the start of their careers. *(Copyright © 1974 United Artists Corporation. All Rights Reserved)*

On first appraisal, there does not appear to be much in common between the word-oriented *Lenny* and the all-dance musical *Dancin'*. And what does the life of star murderess Roxie Hart in *Chicago* have to do with that of renowned director-choreographer Joe Gideon in *All That Jazz*? Even the time frames of these shows—from Chicago in the Twenties to Las Vegas in the Fifties and New York City in the Seventies—are so far apart that comparisons seem almost futile. Each work, however, is relevant to Fosse's life. All are concerned with the livelihood of itinerant performers—according to Lenny Bruce, "just trying to make a buck"— the myth of the superstar, and the reconciliation between the performance artist and his offstage life.

Even a revue such as *Dancin'* reveals a man exploring his identity as a choreographer. A Bojangles routine (Fosse as a young, aspiring Chicago dancer) shares the bill with a ballet (Fosse the frustrated concert-stage choreographer). *Lenny, Chicago,* and *All That Jazz* incorporate text, and can therefore examine more profoundly the schism between genuine talent and hype, and the inevitable mutation that results when the two are married by the media. *Chicago* exorcises the demons of Fosse's performing past, the ghosts of talentless vaudeville players who must resort to extremes—in this case, murder—to win elusive celebrity. The lyrics of one song from the show, "Razzle Dazzle," speak for old-time Tinseltown/Tin Pan Alley's style-over-substance: "Give 'em an act with lots of flash in it/And the reaction will be passionate."

Fosse was not merely interested in all that glitters. Rhinestones, sequins, and ostrich feathers were, of course, almost synonymous with his profession, and we see a profusion of them in his Seventies work. But they are merely props to lure the audience into his work's dark heart. Whether it was his newfound status as a star director and the attendant financial clout it gave him, drug-induced artistic "visions," or a combination of the two, by the time Fosse began work on *Lenny* it was apparent that the movie was as much about him as it was about Lenny Bruce.

It's easy to understand why Fosse chose to follow up his *Cabaret* Oscar with *Lenny*. Despite the plethora of film projects offered to him after *Cabaret,* Fosse decided to keep his next film on a relatively small scale—*Lenny* was budgeted at only $2 million, and filmed for nearly $3 million. He had seen the 1971 Broadway production *Lenny,* and envisioned the rather elaborate, expressionistic stage treatment of Bruce's life captured more directly through a camera's lens. Although *Lenny*'s format, with its quick cuts between stage performances and off-stage scenes, is by no means linear, Fosse dispensed with the theatrics of the Broadway production and opted for a mannered, almost Spartan, black-and-white presention—a colorless film whose main characters live in a world of encroaching darkness.

"As soon as I knew I wanted to do *Lenny,*" Fosse told *Filmmakers Newsletter,* "my first decision was to do it in black and white. Why I made that decision I do not know except there seems to be something more realistic about black and white. That's an odd thing, because, of course, we see everything in color. And yet in film, black and white always seems more realistic."

Of course, the subject matter was familiar to Fosse, but, for the first time, rather than dress it up in the guise of a musical, he relinquished song and dance. The film does not use dance per se, but the camera has been choreographed with Fosse's signature obsession with detail. Director of photography Bruce Surtees, whose father, Bob, helmed the camera for *Sweet Charity,* and English cameraman Jeff Unsworth ferret out seemingly inconsequential "moments" in crowd scenes or at parties, rounding out every locale and creating a sense of authenticity. In his approach to filmmaking, Fosse worked much like Bruce, whose monologues sounded improvised but were actually put together following months of preparation from former gigs. Both men realized the impact of the *illusion* of spontaneity. And, like Bruce, Fosse did not wish to mince the truth. Many critics of the film (and the Broadway show, both of which were written by Julian Barry) believe *Lenny* diluted Bruce's involvement with drugs and "freak" sex, and complained that Dustin Hoffman's performance was too "nice." Nonetheless, Fosse effectively conveys an obsessed performer's attempts to express himself to a morally inhibited public.

Throughout Fosse's career, his own attempts to break free of mindless entertainment are similar to Bruce's thwarted efforts to liberate language from categories of "good" and "bad" words. If Lenny Bruce was considered a "dirtymouth" comedian, Fosse's Broadway dances from shows such as *New Girl in Town* ("The Red Light Ballet"), *Little Me* ("Real Live Girl"), *Sweet Charity* ("Big Spender"), and *Dancin'* ("The Dream Barre"), among others, pushed the limits of good taste as defined by ever-shifting standards of obscenity. Bruce, however, was penalized far more severely than Fosse. From 1961 to 1964, he was repeatedly arrested for obscenity and/or possession of narcotics. He declared bankruptcy in 1965, and was dead the next year from a drug overdose, which some claim was intentional. Bruce fulfilled Fosse's own death wish to succumb at an early age; he was only forty.

Fosse and his collaborators came into the film with first-hand knowledge of Bruce's work and his personality. Tom O'Horgan, Julian Barry, and Fosse all worked with Bruce early in his career. At the time,

Fosse did not consider him a very good stand-up comic. Bruce, like Fosse, was trying to establish his credibility onstage, to present himself as a new kind of performer. Marvin Worth, the film's producer, was Bruce's first manager. When Worth, Barry, and O'Horgan banded together to bring *Lenny* to Broadway in 1971, it was only after their attempts to make his story into a film had failed. Originally to have been called *The Lenny Bruce Story,* Columbia Pictures commissioned the script, then indefinitely shelved it. After the Broadway show became a critical and popular hit, along with Albert Goldman and Lawrence Schiller's biography *Ladies and Gentlemen, Lenny Bruce!!,* film interests stirred again. United Artists producer David Picker offered the project to Fosse, and nearly seven years after Bruce's death, *Lenny* became his motion picture obituary.

Casting the film was obviously crucial, since, as Fosse envisioned the picture, it was to be as much a film about Harriet "Hot Honey Harlow" Bruce as it would be about her husband Lenny. The "behind-every-good-man . . ." axiom intrigued Fosse, no doubt because, with his marriages to Mary Ann Niles, Joan McCracken, and Gwen Verdon, it had proved to be true. Honey and Bruce at one time performed as an act, as did Fosse and Niles, and Fosse valued the contributions of the wife-sidekick, even though it ultimately put stress on the marriage itself. Bruce's marriage to Honey was far more punishing than were any of Fosse's with his wives, resulting in a near death pact between two substance and sex junkies.

On Broadway, Cliff Gorman was a mesmerizing Lenny, and his tour de force performance won him a Tony. Although Fosse considered Gorman for the lead role, United Artists wanted a bigger name. Finally, the candidates were narrowed to include Gorman, Ron Liebman, Al Pacino, and Dustin Hoffman. At the urging of writers and Fosse friends Shel Silverstein and Herb Gardner, Hoffman—who had never seen Bruce perform and was not a fan—was persuaded to take the lead part.

"I didn't want to do the film," Hoffman told the late Arthur Bell of the *Village Voice.* "It was too hairy, too tender ground, too soon. People I'd talk to would suddenly start crying. It was important, they'd tell me, to catch the dichotomy that was Lenny. On stage, he was a tiger. In real life, he was agreeable, generous to a fault; people loved being with him, until just before his death when he got demonical. With such strong emotions at stake, I didn't want to jump into it."

Valerie Perrine was nominated for a best actress Oscar as Hot Honey Harlow, a stripper, in *Lenny. (Copyright © 1974 United Artists Corporation. All Rights Reserved)*

Casting for Honey was no less competitive. "Every major actress in Hollywood with a full bust and a convincing foul mouth is up for the role," gossiped the *Hollywood Reporter,* but ultimately the list was winnowed down to Tuesday Weld, Joey Heatherton, Ann-Margret, and Valerie Perrine. Fosse's first choice was Ann-Margret, but she reportedly objected to the excessive nudity, which Fosse declared was absolutely necessary in the role. Fosse balked, Ann-Margret walked, and Valerie Perrine, a former Las Vegas showgirl, won the role of Honey. At five-foot-eight-inches and boasting ample measurements of 37-24-36, the twenty-eight-year-old Texas blonde had the right mix of innocence and seductive physicality to play a woman who is, by turns, a stripper, junkie, lesbian, and whore.

"I was introduced to Bobby [Fosse] through my agent," Perrine recalled to the *New York Times* in 1974. "I did a screen test, and then worked on a few scenes with Bobby, and then I got the part. I guess it was something he saw, some special qualities. . . . Oh, I know this is going to sound horrible, but I may as well be frank—he thought I was the best actress he tested."

Fosse agreed: "I feel Valerie Perrine . . . is a real discovery," he told *Filmmaker's Newsletter,* "probably the best actress I've ever worked with. She has an ear for truth that I haven't seen in an actress in a long time."

Admittedly, Perrine had not had a lot of experience prior to *Lenny,* certainly nothing that demanded the stretch required for Honey. Undoubtedly, there was a bit of typecasting involved, since Perrine formerly had been the ultimate Vegas showgirl, performing for $800 a week—". . . a helluva lot more money than a secretary makes"—as a lead dancer in the Lido de Paris revue at the Stardust Hotel. At a friend's birthday party in Hollywood, she met agent Robert Walker, who, she says, told her, "You'd be perfect for the part of Montana Wildhack" in the screen version of Kurt Vonnegut's *Slaughterhouse Five.* She went on to play the bed-hopping groupie of drag-car racers in *The Last American Hero* before Fosse cast her in *Lenny.* All three films afforded Perrine opportunities to disrobe provocatively, but only the latter film gave her a full-blooded character as well.

Honey Bruce, like Charity Hope Valentine, Sally Bowles, and, later, Roxie Hart and Dorothy Stratten, lives to perform. Her absolute power to rouse an audience is strangely at odds with her identity offstage. All five women come alive under the glare of stage and camera lights, their image refracted and distorted by the man—Fosse or the men in the scripts—directing them. In character and outside of it, Valerie Perrine is the quintessential Fosse actress, and it's not surprising that he considered her one of his best. She was completely malleable.

She almost proudly admitted to the *New York Times,* "I've never had any acting lessons. I don't know anything about Chavanasky, or whatever you call him. I really don't know what I do. I don't think about anything until I get on the set, I think of something that has happened to me in the past—like in that crying scene with Dustin in *Lenny,* I thought of an old boyfriend who had hurt me, and that really did it."

Although Perrine declared she had little in common with the real Honey Bruce, whom she met during the film's production (Honey and Kitty Bruce, her daughter with Lenny, were consultants on the set), Fosse intuitively sensed that her outspoken, dizzy, uninhibited personality was right for the role, just as Minnelli, the daughter of a torch song legend, was perfect for *Cabaret,* and Verdon, an aging musical-comedy dancer, was well-suited for jaded hoofer Roxie Hart in *Chicago.* Perrine, Hoffman, and Fosse, in fact, were extremely close during production, which helped give the movie its feeling of intimacy. Fosse loved Perrine's sense of humor.

During a scene in which Lenny pulls the bedsheet off a tantalizingly naked Honey, Perrine confessed she had a little surprise for her co-star. "[Dustin] couldn't believe his eyes," she told *Viva* in 1975. "I had gotten a big springy rubber cock from the prop department and tucked it right between my legs—and the minute the sheet was off, it sprang up and started going *boing! boing! boing!* That really cracked Dustin up." In preparation for one of her strip numbers, Perrine was asked to shave down her pubic hair so that it wouldn't show through her G-string. She shaved it in the shape of a small heart and, on Valentine's Day, presented the results to Fosse, joking, "I have a heart on for you, Bobby."

Her rapport with the press was no less immodest. When Rex Reed interviewed her for the *Daily News* in 1975, she lit a marijuana joint and then extracted a hash brownie from aluminum foil and ate it. By her own account, she had an affair with at least one man in each of her first three films, including *Lenny,* and was only upset when the press got them mixed up. "I wasn't fucking Dustin Hoffman," she told *Viva,* setting the record straight, "I was fucking the camera operator." Of her much-publicized substance abuse, she admitted to the *New York Times,* "I've experimented with almost every drug known to man—acid, mescaline, peyote, cocaine, and opium." And when reporter Guy Flately asked her what she looked for in a man, Perrine replied, "Oh . . . about ten inches," and burst into laughter.

Outrageous, hip party-girl Val was Perrine's public image, but Fosse also exploited her vulnerability. By exposing herself so completely, Perrine had no defenses. During a scene that called for Perrine to break down on camera, Fosse told her moments before the film was rolling that

her then-boyfriend had been in a severe motorcycle accident and was not expected to live. The grueling twelve-hour-a-day, four-month shooting schedule reached a breaking point for Perrine during a pivotal, graphic lesbian scene, which begins Honey's and Lenny's descent into a inferno of sex binges and heroin-sniffing marathons.

"I went through *hell,*" she told the *New York Times.* "The night before [the lesbian scene], I fantasized about women, figuring it would put me in a more liberal attitude about touching a woman, and not be disgusted by it. But when we finally got to it, it was so technical it was like a dance. Bobby acted it all out for me before we shot it, and he kept saying, 'Don't worry about it, Valerie.'

"He was so right. Once we started, I kept thinking about camera angles and things. I had no sexual feelings at all while we were doing it. We were both shaking a little bit. The other actress was very young, and in her first role with a big director, so I kind of adopted a sisterly attitude towards her."

Fosse requested that both Hoffman and Perrine learn as much as possible about their characters during preproduction of *Lenny.* He himself had sifted through stacks of interviews conducted by Lawrence Schiller—with Bruce's attorneys, girlfriends, competing comics—for his book with Albert Goldman, *Ladies and Gentlemen, Lenny Bruce!!* The results were expectedly mixed. Fosse discovered that no two people had the same impressions of Bruce as a comic, lover, father, or rabble-rouser. He remained an enigma. "A party would say to me, 'Lenny said this.' Then another would say he didn't," Fosse told the *Los Angeles Times.* "It was hard to piece together the character." To keep the tone of the film as true-to-life as possible, Fosse set up a simple interview structure, a variation on the *Citizen Kane* format in which characters are questioned about the protagonist.

Fosse's own quixotic, Hitchcockian presence is felt in *Lenny.* Though we never see his face, the hands operating the reel-to-reel tape used to interview Honey, Bruce's mother Sally Marr, his agent Artie Silver, and others, belong to Fosse. So does the voice asking the questions. And though the questions and answers have an air of spontaneity, Fosse claimed there was minimal improvisation. Another typical Fosse quirk was casting actors who were in some way related to the film's subject. In *Star 80,* for example, he hired *Playboy* publisher Hugh Hefner's brother

Lenny (played by Dustin Hoffman) busted again for obscenity. Fosse hoped *Lenny* would make a statement about freedom of expression and hypocrisy. *(Copyright © 1974 United Artists Corporation. All Rights Reserved)*

to play a photographer who shoots the first nude pictures of Dorothy Stratten, pictures that launched her career as a nude model. For *Lenny,* Fosse considered casting Bruce's real mother, Sally Marr, herself a comedienne, to play Sally Marr.

"Sally Marr is probably one of the most unique women you'll ever meet," he told *Filmmaker's Newsletter.* "She does jokes, bits, all the time; she's a real performer—always 'on.' I knew there was no one I could get exactly like her. But I thought that casting her would somehow cheapen the picture; it would seem like an attempt to cash in on a kind of maudlin feeling about Bruce's death. So I decided against it." Instead, he cast actress Jan Miner, perhaps best known as Madge in the commercials for Palmolive dish washing detergent.

Hoffman, Perrine, and Miner inundated themselves with material on Bruce. Hoffman estimated that in six months he had spoken to fifty people who knew Bruce well. When Perrine met the real Honey Bruce while filming in Miami she ". . . didn't identify with her," she told the *Daily News.* Conversely, Hoffman related enormously to Lenny. "He was a man who loved his country and believed in the Constitution, in the right to freedom of speech," he told *Time,* but bristled when asked if the comic was a social reformer or a pornographer. "The words weren't used to make the audience horny," he quipped. Hoffman, who stayed in character between shots, was overheard by a *New York Post* reporter bargaining with some Brooklyn Heights school children requesting his autograph. Taking on the guise of Lenny, he told them, "If you swear at me—show me your real feelings—maybe I'll do it." "Immoral is not that which is crude or obscene," he told Arthur Bell. "Immoral is what is deceitful, dishonest. Lenny preached that. It was his downfall."

During the film's sixteen-week shooting schedule in Miami, Las Vegas, Los Angeles, and New York, Fosse overshot excessively for the onstage nightclub scenes. Nearly 500,000 feet of film was spent, often with two or three cameras operating at the same time. Fosse's reputation for overshooting was widely known after *Cabaret,* but in *Lenny,* where Hoffman was required to perform his Bruce routines in front of live audiences, it was imperative that cameras were running when Hoffman "warmed up" the audience, even though most of the performance scenes capture only glimpses of routines after Hoffman has settled into the character.

"I've spent so many years of my life as a choreographer," Fosse told *Filmmakers Newsletter,* "that pictures and composition are very important to me. As a choreographer you see everything with a frame. So my mind just seems to work in terms of framing, and the movement comes from dancing. . . . I was very cold when I made the film. I had neither a great love nor a dislike of Lenny Bruce. I think some of that coldness shows in the film—and I rather like it."

Lenny was eagerly awaited by film critics and moviegoers curious to see how Fosse would follow up *Cabaret*. When it was released in November 1974, the film encountered many of the same problems that beset the stage treatments of Bruce's life and, of course, Bruce himself—how to market "dirty" language. Fosse himself had begun filming *Lenny* uncertain how to present words that might be interpreted as ethnic slurs. "He was afraid of offending," says Ben Vereen, whom Fosse called to discuss a scene in which Bruce, during his act, addresses a black man sitting in the audience as "nigger, nigger, nigger." "He asked me, 'Do you think it's too much?' I said, 'Bob, you're telling a man's story. You've got to tell the truth.' "

Twelve radio commercials, each thirty seconds long, had been prepared to promote the film. United Artists, correctly believing that the unusually explicit language in the film (it was, at one point, given an X rating, which was later rescinded) and the black and white film would prohibit a television sale of *Lenny,* chose to concentrate its publicity campaign on radio. But many of the radio stations that received the ad tapes refused to run them on the basis that references to blacks, Jews, gays, and the disabled were considered offensive. Commercials deemed especially controversial included a now-famous clip of a Bruce monologue that involved the words "kill Christ"—referring to the comedian's belief that he would rather have his child see a pornographic movie than the violent "Christian" film *King of Kings*—and another about desegregation with a punch line that had Ray Charles and Stevie Wonder bumping into each other. Legal dilemmas and accusations of "obscene" had followed Lenny Bruce beyond his grave.

It was a situation with which fans of Bruce's work were all too familiar. Unable to see the forest for the trees, critics of Bruce's material were frequently so disturbed by his scatological references that the jokes' larger social implications went unheard. The irony reverberated years later in Fosse's career as well. When, at one point in the film Bruce tells a judge trying him for obscenity, "I don't wanna do tits and ass!" it is hard not to think of *Star 80*'s disastrous critical reception, when many reviewers accused Fosse of exploiting sex in a film allegedly about sex and exploitation. It is unlikely that either Bruce or Fosse set out to become social reformers and, in the end, it is debatable how effectively they actually reformed their audiences. But clearly they sought to move past the facile titilation of "tits and ass" entertainment, whether in the form of scantily clad chorines or four-letter words. For both men, the most devastating criticism was not that they were prurient; rather, that their methods to entertain were considered ineffective.

Although *Lenny* opened to generally enthusiastic reviews, one of the longest and more insightful notices—and one that Fosse claimed caused him to re-examine the film—appeared in the *New Yorker*. Pauline Kael, who admitted the film was "very well made" and that Fosse "is a true prodigy," faulted *Lenny* for misrepresenting Bruce as a social reformer.

Dustin Hoffman as Lenny Bruce in Fosse's 1974 film *Lenny. (Copyright © 1974 United Artists Corporation. All Rights Reserved)*

"This Lenny, with his flower child's moral precepts, is a drag," complained Kael. ". . . When he assaults his nightclub audience, singling out individuals as niggers, kikes, and greaseballs, he expounds on how much better the world would be if those words were freely shouted. Apart from the idiocy of the picture's endorsing this dubious theory and trying to wring applause for it, there's the gross misunderstanding of Bruce's methods. . . . He did heartlessly cynical bits because there [were] only two possible audience reactions—to be outraged or to laugh. And either way he was a winner. . . . There was a good reason for him to become a counter-culture hero; his scabrous realism never seemed a matter of choice."

However much Fosse may have rejected critics' assessments of his work, he claimed to have found Kael's comments valid; but directing for the stage and screen is always interpretive, and thus subjective. Fosse was attracted to Lenny Bruce because he stood for things important to him. "What I was interested in," he explained to *Filmmakers Newsletter,* "was a man who stood against hypocrisy and for the use of free speech. And also the man who helped change the style of comedy."

Lenny had its naysayers, but its exclusive engagement at Cinema I in New York City broke the house record previously set by *The Exorcist.* In March 1975, United Artists announced that the film had grossed nearly $11.5 million, a significant profit considering that its budget was a fraction of that. At the Cannes Film Festival, *Lenny* was hugely popular, and Perrine won the Best Actress award. Months later, the New York Film Critics voted her Best Supporting Actress. She, Hoffman, and Fosse were all nominated for Academy Awards in 1974, though the film lost in all of its categories.

Lenny is another Fosse film best remembered for the value of its participants in a successful collaborative effort. It boosted the careers of all its contributors, though, of the cast principals, only Hoffman would go on to attain comparable fame with other projects. Like Gwen Verdon and Liza Minnelli, Valerie Perrine never matched her performance in a Fosse project with subsequent roles. After a string of disasters *(W. C. Fields and Me, The Electric Horseman, Can't Stop the Music),* she has appeared infrequently and, most recently, in supporting roles. "I'm not career aggressive," she told Rex Reed shortly after *Lenny*'s release. "I'm not fighting for roles, I have no career structure or motivation, I just go where I want to go and do what I want to do." Hot Honey Harlow may have typecast Perrine, but it offered her a rare opportunity to cast her bid for stardom. Like so many of Fosse's actors and dancers, she is recognized best for one film bearing his signature—and hers.

CHICAGO
• LATE 1920's •

CHICAGO

W hile *Lenny* went into postproduction, Fosse returned to the stage and began work on *Chicago,* a "musical vaudeville" that was as much a tribute to his wife as it was an exorcism of his days performing on the burlesque club circuit.

Verdon had wanted to do the show ever since she had seen *Roxie Hart,* a 1942 film starring Ginger Rogers that had evolved from a 1926 stage play and a 1927 silent film, both titled *Chicago.* But to Verdon's dismay, the author, Maurine Dallas Watkins, said the rights weren't for sale; in her later years, she had become a born-again Christian and believed the play glamorized a scandalous way of living. Verdon was only one of many parties interested in acquiring *Chicago*; luckily enough, when Watkins died in 1969, her estate awarded the rights to producer Richard Fryer, Fosse, and Verdon.

Watkins's *Chicago* was based on an actual murder case she covered as a cub reporter for the *Chicago Tribune.* On April 3, 1924, a tall, red-headed woman named Beulah Annan shot her lover in the back as the Hawaiian foxtrot "Hula Lou" ("She's got more men than a dog has fleas . . .") played on her Victrola in the background. Later, she telephoned her husband, Al, a mechanic, and confessed to murdering "the man who tried to make love to me."

When the police arrived, a very tipsy Beulah admitted she had been having an affair with the man, but killed him after he threatened to walk

Tony Walton's dazzling art deco curtain and set design for 1975's *Chicago. (Martha Swope)*

out on her. During the next few weeks, Chicago natives followed with interest her sensational trial. Beulah's attorneys painted her as a naïve, not-too-bright, lonely woman whose original confession was made under the influence of alcohol. Hers was only one of seven jealous-lover murder trials currently in the news, but Watkins found it the most illuminating. The media's presentation of Beulah as Chicago's "prettiest prisoner" and her willingness to do or say anything to be acquitted struck Watkins as a reflection of Chicago's rapidly degenerating morality.

During her imprisonment, Beulah claimed she was pregnant (Illinois law denies execution of an expectant mother), and her trial was delayed. In the interim, she capitalized on more attention from the adoring newspapers. At her trial, her lawyer described Beulah as "a frail little girl struggling with a drunken brute," and the twelve-member jury (including four bachelors) returned the verdict "not guilty." Of Beulah's exoneration, Watkins wrote: "So Beulah Annan, whose pursuit of wine, men, and jazz music was interrupted by her glibness with the trigger finger, was given freedom by her beauty-proof jury." Four years later, Beulah died in a sanitarium under an assumed name.

Although the rights to *Chicago* became available in 1969, Fosse did not really begin working on it until 1973, during *Liza with a Z,* when he approached the composer-lyricist team of John Kander and Fred Ebb to write the score. They had written the music for *Cabaret* and some songs for *Liza with a Z,* and were anxious to work with Fosse again. Verdon, who had not performed in a musical since *Sweet Charity,* had separated from Fosse in 1971, but, as she told the press, she and Fosse had always kept their professional and personal lives independent on the stage.

"It's terrific working with him again," Verdon responded to a *Daily News* query regarding the nature of their unusual relationship. "I know everyone's wondering, now that we're separated, what it's going to be like working together. It was never husband and wife when we worked together before, it was always as actress and director. He always said I'm the best Fosse dancer, and I believe I am. Why, I'd set my hair on fire if he asked me to."

When Fosse finally got around to doing *Chicago* in 1974, he was still finishing *Lenny,* but already had made up his mind about casting decisions. In addition to Verdon, who was to receive 10 percent of the box-office grosses, playing star lonely-heart killer Roxie Hart, Verdon and Fosse decided her fellow murderess-hoofer Velma (based on a real character from Watkins' account named Belva Gaertner, who was herself acquitted) would be played by Chita Rivera. Verdon and Rivera had been long-time friends, but had never worked together, though both had auditioned for the role of Claudine in 1953's *Can-Can* (the part that eventually went to Verdon).

"Actually," Fosse told *Dance Magazine* in 1975, "having Gwen and Chita to work with is what made this basically a movement kind of show—*especially* when you have two people like that who want to do movement. They're both such *ideal* dancers—in other words, ideal instruments, like there's almost nothing you can't ask them to do that they can't come damn close to doing! They're very valuable, as well, for their judgments and opinions."

Chita Rivera (left) and Gwen Verdon as gun molls Velma Kelly and Roxie Hart in *Chicago. (Martha Swope)*

Rivera, who had had surgery on her right knee before undertaking the role, humorously recounts how Fosse fostered a feeling of complete devotion among the cast. "I remember one day in rehearsal, Bobby said, 'Now, Chita, I want you to jump into this spot,' which, I think, was something like eight feet *upstage!* Without thinking, I jumped. I must have looked like a *giraffe!* So I did it—unbelievably—and he sort of looked at me like I had three eyes and said, 'Chita, I didn't mean *that* spot.' Then, he points to one that had been just a few inches from me. That's what I mean when I say I would've done anything for him."

Graciela Daniele, who, in the showstopping "Cellblock Tango," played a Hungarian prisoner named Hunyak, also fell under the Fosse spell. Daniele, the dance captain of the show, says, "It's hard to avoid falling in love with a master. I mean, we were all in love with him—not just a sexual love. It was this total idolization, plus the fact that he was very good with us. It wasn't like in *All That Jazz,* where he screams at one of the dancers until she breaks down. I never saw that in *Chicago.* I don't think he ever forgot how hard it is to be a dancer."

But it was Verdon whom Fosse worked with most closely. Tony Stevens, one of Fosse's dance assistants in the show, says that there was an almost palpable kinesis between them. "When he watched her work," Stevens recalls, "you could see he was totally in love. Their love existed on that artistic level. The way he touched her, you could tell she was still his favorite body. You didn't have to know them to see they had a history. But I don't think Gwen shared Bob's darkness, or, if she did, it was her experience with Bob that had created a darkness in her."

Long-time Fosse assistant Kathryn Doby contends, "I think Gwen was Bob's closest friend and vice versa. Initially, they didn't want to get a divorce because of Nicole, but, just as importantly, they were so good for each other. No one choreographed for Gwen like Bob, and Gwen was perfect for Bob's choreography."

From the beginning, things went smoothly with preproduction for *Chicago.* Because Fosse had been "sitting on" the show for so many years, some of the numbers, including the sizzling opening, "All That Jazz," and the requisite Latin variation, "The Cellblock Tango," were almost fully formed before he brought the dancers in. "I would say Bob knew ninety percent of what he was going to do when his dancers came into rehearsal," estimates Tony Stevens. "He really prepared."

Tony Walton, who designed the sleek black-and-chrome deco set—complete with an elevator and rotating stairs—recalls that in his first meeting with Fosse, the director told him that he considered Verdon the best dancer alive, and that he didn't want audiences to think otherwise because of her age, even though the script itself (co-written by Fosse) has

Gwen Verdon performs "Whatever Lola Wants" in the 1955 stage version of *Damn Yankees*. Stephen Douglass co-starred. *(Photofest)*

Shirley MacLaine as Charity Hope Valentine in the 1969 film *Sweet Charity*. (Copyright © Universal Pictures, a Division of Universal City Studios, Inc. Courtesy of MCA Publicity Rights, a division of MCA, Inc.)

Ben Vereen, flanked by two "Players," won a Tony Award for his mesmerizing Leading Player, a Mephistophelian figure who attempts to woo Pippin with riches, women, power, and, finally, suicide. *(Martha Swope)*

A bosomy member of the Kit Kat Club's onstage, all-female band mugs with Joel Grey between sets. *(Alan Pappé/Lee Gross Inc.)*

Fosse cast Michael York as Brian, a role modeled after author Christopher Isherwood (who wrote the story upon which *Cabaret* was based). According to Fosse, York had the right mix of a school teacher's intelligence and a pugilist's streetwise intuition. *(Alan Pappé/Lee Gross Inc.)*

Tony Walton's evoca-
tive illustration of
1920s burlesque
dancers (top) was
transformed by
Fosse into provocative
choreography for a
scene in *Chicago* (left).
(Martha Swope)

Fosse discovered Ann Reinking in the early Seventies, cast her
in his *Pippin* chorus, and made her a star in 1978's *Dancin'*.
Here she performs her famed "thunderbolt battements."
(Martha Swope)

Set designer Tony Walton won an Oscar for his fantasy sequences in *All That Jazz*. Ben Vereen and Roy Scheider are in the film's climactic finale. *(Alan Pappé/Lee Gross Inc.)*

Fosse demonstrates a port de bras to Ann Reinking in *All That Jazz*'s knock-'em-dead (literally) finale, "Bye, Bye, Life." *(Alan Pappé/Lee Gross Inc.)*

Fosse's last Broadway musical, 1986's *Big Deal*, featured the showstopping number "Beat Me Daddy Eight to the Bar." *(Martha Swope)*

Perhaps Fosse's most well-remembered choreography is found in *Sweet Charity*, especially in the notorious "Big Spender," seen here in the 1986 Tony Award–winning revival. *(Alan Pappé/Lee Gross Inc.)*

(Alan Pappé/Lee Gross Inc.)

Roxie saying at one point, "I'm older than I ever intended to be." Verdon was in her fifties. "I want to plan the dance area in a way that suits her and is logical for the rest of the show," Walton says Fosse told him.

"I was very proud of the first scaled model of *Chicago* that I did for him," says Walton, who won a Tony Award for his *Pippin* set. "I snuck it into his house in Quogue, Long Island, through a window he'd left unlocked. It was the kind of thing that would tickle him, I thought, and I left it on top of the piano. At that time, I'd created the set so that the bandstand was an enormous top hat, and the brim of the top hat was on a spiral around it, so that when you turned the set, the brim either became high or low. When the brim was turned high, it became a straw hat, and when it was turned low, it became a top hat. I was sure it was going to knock him out; it seemed so in his court."

But Fosse did not take to the design. "When he found it," remembers Walton, "the first thing he said was, 'I was only gone half an hour. How the fuck did this get here?' I had been waiting for a 'Wow!' Finally he said, 'I would really like to see a show on a set like that, but I sure as hell ain't gonna stage *my* show on it.' "

Fosse was most outspoken when he said the least, and it was his silences that most intimidated and perplexed those around him. Graciela Daniele's character, Hunyak, was a Hungarian prisoner who spoke only two words of English, "not guilty," and would utter them any time she had an opportunity to speak. She was one of six "prisoners" waiting trial for the murders of their boyfriends/husbands, and had the least dialogue. After several weeks of rehearsal, she grew anxious when Fosse failed to respond to her interpretation.

"He hadn't said *anything* to me in five or six weeks," recalls Daniele, "so one day I went up to him and said, 'Bob, I'm sorry. I guess I just need a little pat on the back. But am I doing okay?' He looked at me and said, 'I don't understand what you're saying.' And I said, 'You don't understand? You want me to translate?' He was walking away from me, but he spun around and said, 'No, because I think you're guilty!' Then he turned and left me standing there."

Years later, she and Fosse talked about his "direction" of her that day. "I just wanted you to feel totally isolated," he told her. Daniele says his (non)reaction to her character forced her to plunge further into the world of Hunyak, a woman segregated from the other prisoners because she could not speak English. "In my mind, I would relive the murder and how it happened. Bob made me understand what it's like to capture a moment as an actor if you play a true character, even in a small role."

Jerry Orbach played Billy Flynn, a shyster lawyer renowned for getting his comely female clients exonerated for their murder raps. Fosse,

who wanted the entire production to convey a sinister atmosphere, had read that Orbach knew some gangsters and a lot of detectives. "The stories were partially true," Orbach admits. "And Fosse used to razz me about it. But it was because he considered me a guy of the streets that he liked me. [Streetlife] was something he aspired to know more about, rather than something he was familiar with. Growing up as he did in vaudeville, he was sort of exposed to one side of it, but I think he wished he'd been out in the street more. It held an allure for him."

Jerry Orbach and Ann Reinking, who replaced Gwen Verdon as Roxie Hart, in *Chicago. (Martha Swope)*

Tony Stevens believes Fosse's fascination with his own dark side was cathartic. "He *was* the emcee in *Cabaret*," Stevens says, "always the orchestrator of the Big Event. Bob was a flagrant manipulator—anything to get out the truth. Because, as a creator, you always struggle with how much you want to tell the audience—a group of strangers—about yourself. Do I really want them to know I go in a back room and rip off someone's clothes, or do I hold back? Bob was trying to come to terms with the reality of his life."

Fosse's "reality of life" almost became his grand finale in 1974 when a massive heart attack nearly killed him right between editing *Lenny* and early rehearsals on *Chicago*. For weeks, he had experienced numbness in his left hand and was short of breath. He had attended a screening of *Lenny*, and, deciding it still needed to be cut more, he took the film back to the editing room, and removed between three and four minutes of it. During a lunch break at *Chicago* rehearsals the day after the screening, he stopped by New York Hospital, claiming he was having trouble breathing. Cardiologists examined him and told Fosse if he went back to rehearsals, he would die.

"He was in emergency and they called me," Verdon told the *New York Times* in 1981. "I went there and he said, 'Please don't let them keep me in this place.' Well, I got to the doctors and I said, 'He's staying. I'm his wife. We're not legally divorced,' and I took advantage of it and signed the papers. He hated me for it, but the man was obviously very ill."

For three days he remained in intensive care. Only Verdon was allowed to see him. After a week of tests, he underwent bypass surgery to remove a clogged artery. Just when he thought the worst was over, another heart attack hit him after surgery.

Ann Reinking, herself hospitalized with a cracked bone in her spine, a dance-related injury, was visiting Fosse at the time of the second seizure. "I got over there as soon as I could," Reinking told the *New York Times* in 1980, "and one day, while I was sitting with him, he had another, more serious attack. That part was just like in [*All That Jazz*]. There really *was* a nurse who wouldn't believe he was in agony because he had just had a shot."

"I had heart attacks I didn't even realize were heart attacks," Fosse admitted in a 1979 *Life* profile. "I had one after the bypass operation. They didn't tell me you could have one after the operation. I thought, 'I've got through this. I'm on easy street, all patched up.' And then, whack!"

"It was such a shock," says Daniele. "I went to see him in the hospital, expecting him to be near death, and there he was carrying on like a fool, pestering the nurses and giggling like a little boy. Here we all were, so concerned about him."

An air of ironic solemnity hovered in Fosse's hospital room the first few days after his surgery. At Fosse's memorial twelve years later, long-time friend Herb Gardner humorously recounted the night before the morning of his bypass surgery, when Fosse had requested that Gardner and Paddy Chayefsky witness his will.

"It's around midnight, very grim room, just me and Paddy and two solemn lawyers and Bobby, semiconscious and weighing about a pound, hooked up to all kinds of tubes and wires and a heart monitor with its tiny blipping screen. I immediately sign the will on the back where it says 'Witness.' Not Paddy. He has never put his signature on *any* document without studying it carefully. He goes to a chair in the corner of this tense room and reads the *entire* will, twenty or thirty pages of it. He gets to the last page of the bequests; he mumbles quietly to himself, 'Hey, I'm not in here. . . .' He checks the page again; then he looks up and shouts across the room to Bobby, 'Fuck you, *live!*'

"Bobby starts to laugh, his laughter building, fully awake now, rolling around in the bed, pulling the tubes and wires with him, the heart-monitor screen looks like it's showing reruns of *Jeopardy*. The lawyers remain solemn and embarrassed, Paddy signs the will. Bobby appears to have fallen back to sleep, smiling. Then one of the lawyers, referring to a clause in the will stipulating a sum of money to be left for a party in Bobby's honor to be hosted by Paddy and me, comments that another famous director has put a similar party clause in *his* will. 'For how much,' Bobby says, opening one eye. The lawyer tells him the figure. 'Make mine ten grand more,' says Bobby, and falls back to sleep."

Not everyone, including some of Fosse's physicians, expected him to recover; his behavior in the hospital did not indicate he was slowing down. When a *New York Magazine* reporter visited him to do an inteview promoting *Lenny,* Fosse told him, "You could go bananas in here; I'm the Harpo Marx of the floor, goosing the nurses." His antiseptic little cubicle was cluttered with his treasured possessions: books (he was reading André Gide at the time), posters from his shows, flowers from Dustin Hoffman, a nude poster of Valerie Perrine ("the doctors pay more attention to it than to me," Fosse muttered). The interview, the reporter noted, was constantly interrupted by phone calls from wellwishers and folks who had vested interests in *Lenny* and *Chicago.* The shows must go on.

Fosse was especially worried about the future of *Chicago.* Three numbers were nearly finished, and he was reluctant to lose his cast. He gave some of the dancers personal loans and told the producers to find as many cast members as possible other jobs until *Chicago* could resume rehearsals. "When I heard Fosse had his heart attack," says Jerry Orbach, "I think I was furious because we were gonna be out of work. The producers called me and told me what had happened and that the company would start again in a couple of months. They were very good about offering everyone in the cast work until the show got on its feet again. They offered me a production of *Macbeth* with Charlton Heston in Los Angeles. I said, 'No, thank you; I'll wait for *Chicago*.'"

In fact, most of the cast waited for Fosse. For many of them who had worked with him in the past, he was something of a father figure. Others were equally devoted to Verdon. There was a sense among the performers that the show was going to be a hit, if only Fosse could get better. When he finally returned to the production some months later, everyone noticed a marked difference in his directing approach. "He was much more willing to let the dancers improvise and input," says Tony Stevens. "He'd take a nap every day at lunch. It was a tense time. When he got up to dance, we'd all get worried."

By the time *Chicago* was ready for its out-of-town run in Philadelphia in late 1974, it was apparent Fosse had half a show finished. Fortunately, despite dismal reviews, his health was returning. Perhaps it was simply the determination *not* to fail that was responsible for the enormous changes *Chicago* made before its Broadway debut—60 percent of it was reconceived after Philadelphia—fueled by rumors that director-choreographer Michael Bennett was working on an innovative musical about the lives of struggling chorus dancers, scheduled to open around the same time as *Chicago*. Was it any good? Fosse wanted to know. Should I be worried?

Chicago opened to generally favorable reviews, though its presiding bleakness and cynicism nearly negated its impressive achievements in staging and choreography. In his efforts to depict the circus sideshow that results when law and journalism buckle to the allure of show business, Fosse had imbued the entire production with an angst that cast a shadow on his homage to burlesque and vaudeville, married brilliantly with stylized realism. A number called "Mr. Cellophane"—a close facsimile of the song "Nobody"—featured a jilted husband dressed up like a clown. In "We Both Reached for the Gun," the entire number was staged as a ventriloquist act; lawyer Billy Flynn sits his client Roxie Hart on his lap like a dummy as she lip-syncs responses to his questions. In the finale, when Roxie (Verdon) and Velma (Rivera) launch a song-and-dance act, capitalizing on the fleeting sensationalism of their murder trials, they walk toward the audience with bouquets of roses, tossed to their adoring fans. Though audiences heard them saying, "thank you, thank you," according to Gene Foote, a dancer in the show, Fosse had told his leading ladies to throw out the roses *thinking* "fuck you, fuck you."

But some critics believed Fosse's sardonic foray into crime and punishment was mean-spirited and excessive. "[I]t's really an overstaged show," remarked *New Yorker* dance critic Arlene Croce, "the height of theatrical decadence; everything that we're meant to react to is in the staging. It's strange to think of Fosse as the last German Expressionist—strange that his own decadence as an artist should take such a visually corny and alien form."

It was not the specter of critics that cast a pall over *Chicago,* which enjoyed a large advance sale before its opening and, despite a few shaky weeks, continued to build even after Verdon left and was replaced first by Liza Minnelli, and then Ann Reinking, Fosse's girlfriend at the time. *Chicago*'s nemesis proved to be *A Chorus Line,* the most phenomenally successful musical of the Seventies. The wash of publicity surrounding its *théâtre vérité* tales of beleaguered chorus dancers all but eclipsed *Chicago*'s own considerable achievements. At the Tony Awards that season, *A Chorus Line* shut out *Chicago* from all of its nominated categories—direction, choreography, score, actor and actress in a musical, and best musical—cementing the long-time rivalry between Bennett and Fosse.

Tony Stevens, who had left the workshops of *A Chorus Line* to assist Fosse on *Chicago,* says he felt torn during the awards ceremony. "I was thrilled for Michael and *A Chorus Line*. It was my first love, because of what it did for dancers, what it did for me. But I still wanted *Chicago* to be acknowledged for something." Chita Rivera believes *"A Chorus Line* did quite a number on Bobby. I didn't think it was quite kosher that it ran away with all the awards. Bobby never fully appreciated the show for what it was until he saw it out of town *after* Broadway."

Sandahl Bergman, who danced for Fosse in *Dancin'* and *All That Jazz* and Bennett in *Coco, Follies,* and *A Chorus Line,* claims Bennett and Fosse had a "friendly competition between them. I never saw any kind of hostility between them or heard nasty innuendos. Whenever there was a cast change in one of their shows, four or five dancers would leave at one time and either go to the new Fosse show or the new Bennett show. It got to be a joke. Bobby would say, 'Well, I guess Michael's really mad at me now that I've pulled all of you out of *A Chorus Line*.' "

A Chorus Line catapulted a cast of relative unknowns into the limelight. Two blocks away, at the 46th Street Theatre, *Chicago* was struggling at the box office. Donna McKechnie, who had previously danced for Fosse in the chorus of *How to Succeed in Business Without Really*

Trying, won a Tony over Verdon and Rivera for her portrayal of an aging chorus dancer named Cassie in *A Chorus Line.* McKechnie says she "heard Fosse was enraged that I was even nominated. He thought I should have been in the best supporting actress category, but Michael [Bennett] had demanded to the nominating committee that I be put in the best actress category. Suddenly, I realized how political it all was. Bob was the 'older' director-choreographer; he believed his show should be recognized more [than Bennett's]." Eleven years later, Fosse would cast McKechnie as Charity Hope Valentine in a national tour of *Sweet Charity.* Apparently, all had been forgiven.

Chicago's problems did not stop with the Tonys that year. Three years later, in a Los Angeles Civic Light Opera production, general managers Cy Feuer and Ernest Martin, who had helped produce Fosse's *Cabaret,* requested the show's script be revised to eliminate any references to which the CLO's audiences might object. Censorship and controversy had plagued Fosse since "Whatever Lola Wants" from *Damn Yankees;* after the freedom-of-speech-oriented *Lenny,* he was hardly in the mood to be chastized as a "dirtymouth." Red-circled objections to the script included changing "I gotta pee" to "I gotta tinkle," abbreviating "son-of-a-bitch" to "S.O.B.," and "God damn you" to "damn you." The phrase "screwin' around" had been highlighted with an "O.K. if necessary" written next to it. It had even been suggested that one entire number, "Class," be removed.

Fosse and Verdon were livid, and *Chicago*'s cast immediately petitioned against any changes. "[I] feel if you give a little, you're opening yourself to giving a lot," Fosse told the *Los Angeles Times.* "This isn't Mary Poppins at lunch in county jail. . . . It's a tough milieu. I learned that when I filmed *Lenny.* This is particularly odd coming from Cy Feuer and Ernest Martin, whose *Can-Can* is one of the most vulgar things I've ever seen."

"I'm on [New York] Governor Carey's Board for Commissioners of Libraries," huffed an indignant Verdon. "I've seen libraries take the works of André Gide off the shelves. They're destroying *Catcher in the Rye.* We can't have this. I can hear the matinee ladies over the squawk box in the dressing room: 'Want an orange juice?' one will say. 'No, I'm going to pee,' will be the answer, with a laugh, as though they were liberated."

Ultimately, minimal changes were made in the score and libretto. With the help of a one-minute, $100,000 television commercial and different Fosse-associated women in the Roxie Hart role, *Chicago* played for over three years on Broadway. It was still around, in fact, when Fosse's riskiest show to date—*Dancin'*—opened at the Broadhurst Theatre, only two blocks away.

DANCIN'

I t's like playing Monday night football eight times a week. It's a bruising show. The injuries, I can't tell you—wrists, ankles, backs, pulled muscles. It's really tough on the dancers. We have a cast of sixteen with about eight backup people. That's an extraordinary number of backups, and we need them all."

Fosse was talking about *Dancin'* to the *Bulletin*. The show, budgeted at $600,000 (all of it raised in twenty-four hours), has often been compared with Bennett's *A Chorus Line,* because of its emphasis on dancers dancing. But, in fact, *Dancin'* had very little to do with *A Chorus Line.* True, both featured a chorus of dancers at the heart of the show, but *Dancin'* was the first Broadway show to jettison the other elements of a traditional musical: the libretto and score. *Dancin',* unlike *A Chorus Line,* was more of a revue that, in fractured movement vignettes, presented the strengths and weaknesses of Fosse's choreography.

For years, Fosse had been working toward choreographing a full ballet, first for the now-defunct Harkness Ballet in New York, and, later, for the Joffrey. He wanted to have the cachet of Jerome Robbins and Agnes de Mille, Broadway choreographers who had used musical theater dances as springboards to the concert stage. Ballet, he believed, would legitimize him as a choreographer, since it was a "serious" art form. But even beyond the insecurities Fosse felt about his limitations as a jazz choreographer, there was the ever-present desire to venture into new

Ann Reinking in *Dancin',* in 1978. She and Fosse had a much-publicized, stormy five-year relationship. *(Martha Swope)*

territories, as he had done in film. If Fosse had no turnout, bad posture, and inarticulate hands, how could he choreograph a ballet? Yet, his physical "handicaps" hadn't hindered him from Broadway.

"He was always intimidated because he never studied ballet," says Kathryn Doby, his assistant in *Dancin'*. "The Joffrey asked him I don't know how many times to do a ballet. Yet he was exact in his own style. In his later years he was working on something that might have been for the Joffrey. If he would have done it, I think it would have been brilliant."

But Richard Englund, a board member and director of the Joffrey II company, believes that even after ten years of negotiations with Robert Joffrey, the late artistic director of the dance company, the much-discussed ballet "never came to much. [Fosse] wanted very much to be a 'legit' choreographer—to do a *ballet* ballet. He may have done some work on it, but the ballet always stayed in the idea stage."

Instead, Fosse did *Dancin'*, which came as close to approximating a full ballet as anything he ever created, with the notable exception of a ballet modeled after Michelle Fokine's *The Firebird* called *Magic Bird of Fire*, which he choreographed and daughter Nicole performed at the Fashion Institute of Technology in 1982.

Dancin' had accumulated over the years. In fact, some of the numbers in it were dances he'd had to cut from previous musicals. At fifty, Fosse had acquired an almost paternal affection for them; he also realized his days as a demonstrater *and* choreographer were numbered.

Originally, *Dancin'* was to have had a slight story, a series of connected vaudeville numbers. Fosse approached Frank Loesser about writing a script, then Fred Ebb. But, as it became increasingly clear that the show, like Fosse's past stage efforts, was to be an exercise in style over substance, the idea of a libretto became less and less important. Finally, Fosse brought in Herb Gardner and Paddy Chayefsky to write the few spoken words, the introduction and prefaces to some of the numbers, for *Dancin'*.

"With a heart attack behind me, I just didn't feel I could spend time on a book musical," Fosse told the *Bulletin*. "That kind of show takes about three years to do. I didn't have those years to sit with a composer and to evolve a book. So I went with music that was already published and forgot about story. Most stories in musicals are only long cues to the next number anyway." On opening night of *Dancin'*, the librettist Alan Jay Lerner (*My Fair Lady, Camelot*) sent Fosse a telegram reading, "You finally did it. You got rid of the author."

Auditions for the show were rigorous. For the eight women's roles, Fosse auditioned over eight hundred dancers. Rene Ceballos, whose solo "Rally Round the Flag" was one of the highlights of *Dancin'*, remembers that "every dancer in New York was talking about this show, you have no idea. It was only my second show on Broadway after *A Chorus Line,* and I didn't know if I had half a chance, but I figured I'd give it a try. It was a long audition. There was Fosse's 'Tea for Two' combination, a jazz combination, and then each dancer had to sing a song for him. Surprisingly, I didn't feel nervous at all. He had a quality about him that put you at ease. He was standing by the piano, and I stood a little ways away from him and sang. He had a pleasant look on his face, nothing menacing at all about him. He even walked up to the people he rejected and thanked each one for coming."

The dancers eventually cast in *Dancin'* were among the best Broadway had to offer; many, of course, were former Fosse gypsies. Assisting him was former Fosse dancer Kathryn Doby, heir apparent to Gwen Verdon in terms of her knowledge of Fosse's dances. The cast eventually

Willa Kim's Latin-inspired costumes for "Percussion" earned her a Tony nomination for 1978's *Dancin'. (Martha Swope)*

came to include Wayne Cilento, Christopher Chadman, Vicki Fredericks, Sandahl Bergman, Charles Ward (recruited from American Ballet Theatre), John Mineo, Gregory B. Drotar, Richard Korthaze, Gail Benedict, Karen Burke, Blane Savage, Ross Miles, Linda Haberman, Jill Cook, Edward Love, and Rene Ceballos. In retrospect, it was an amazing ensemble of dancers. Although they are not household words today, nearly all of them—with the exception of Charles Ward who died of AIDS in 1986—have gone on to achieve success in entertainment-related fields: acting, choreographing, directing, and dancing. And, for most of them, *Dancin'* opened the door.

If there was a "star" in the *Dancin'* chorus, it was Ann Reinking, whose five-year relationship with Fosse was coming to an end at the point when he was about to launch her film career (the next year she would star in *All That Jazz*). Since *Pippin,* Reinking had won plaudits as

Karen G. Burke, Wayne Cilento, and Jill Cook point the way in *Dancin'*. *(Martha Swope)*

well as Tony and Drama Desk nominations for her non-Fosse stage work, including the musicals *Over Here, Goodtime Charley,* and *A Chorus Line,* in which she replaced the original Cassie, Donna McKechnie. For years, Fosse had wanted to give Reinking a vehicle in which to showcase her strengths as a dancer. "I choreographed the 'Trumpet Solo' in ['Sing, Sing, Sing'] for her, just to use her extensions, her legs, which are so beautiful," Fosse told the *New York Times* in 1978.

This solo remains one of the most breathtaking dance performances on the Broadway stage. Reinking's sweeping layouts, in which one of her legs shoots toward the ceiling as her back bends and her long, silky hair grazes the floor, were reminiscent of Suzanne Farrell's famed "thunderbolt battements"—a phrase coined by dance writer Arlene Croce.

"Sing, Sing, Sing" had been choreographed by Jack Cole in the Fifties, when Gwen Verdon was his assistant, and Fosse's two-part restaging, complete with requisite Cole knee drops, was dedicated "For Gwen and Jack. The latter would have hated it"—alluding to Fosse's belief that Cole never liked him after he married Verdon and made her a Fosse dancer.

But Fosse had recently become enamored of Jessica Lange, a pretty blonde starlet whose biggest film role at that point was starring opposite a giant ape in Dino de Laurentiis's sprawling big-budget remake of *King Kong.* After five years with Reinking, it appeared Fosse's relationship with her was about to end, and not painlessly. "Breakups are difficult enough," says Rene Ceballos, "never mind the pressure of opening a Broadway show in the midst of having personal problems. Annie had a lot to do in the show, and she was also breaking up with the director-choreographer, the man she loved. It was like Cassie and Zach in *A Chorus Line.*"

Dancin' made Reinking a Broadway star and earned her another Tony nomination, but the rewards did not come without punishments. One of these was "The Dream Barre," in which a young man (Charles Ward) and woman (Reinking) fall in love at the ballet barre. Many dancers in *Dancin'* believe the embarrassing sexual innuendos (including variations on intercourse positions and cunnilingus) came about through Fosse's antagonism towards Reinking, who would later share an apartment as roommates with Ward. Fosse, some dancers believed, imagined Reinking and Ward were lovers. The Shubert Organization's Bernard Jacobs, one of the show's producers along with Columbia Pictures, says he and Fosse "strongly disagreed on that cunnilingus number, which [The Shuberts] thought was particularly distasteful." New York City Ballet principal Robert La Fosse (no relation to Fosse), who, in 1979, took over Ward's roles in the show, believes "The Dream Barre" "sort of demeaned ballet.

What can you say about a number in a ballet class where a girl is rubbing her pussy against some guy's leg? It certainly has never happened to *me* in a ballet class. In *Dancin'*, I think Fosse couldn't decide between becoming a ballet choreographer or sticking to the old bump-and-grind.''

In general, critics were not kind to *Dancin'*. " 'Dream Barre,' the pantomime of inept lust, becomes rather tasteless," decreed *Time,* while the *New York Times* believed, "At its strongest, *Dancin'* has the qualities of a spectacular recital rather than an integrated musical show." And the *Village Voice* simply spat, "*Dancin'* is appallin'." The reviews notwithstanding, in *Dancin'* Fosse's choreography undeniably connected with the audience in those numbers most closely aligned with his experiences as a performer. "Sing, Sing, Sing," "Percussion," "Big Noise from Winettka," and the amusing "Fourteen Feet," in which seven performers "dance" in shoes nailed to the floor, were commentaries on Fosse's experience with nightclub hoofing, vaudeville, and jazz dance. Even unusual character pieces, such as "A Manic Depressive's Lament," a blues number, succeeded because most audiences knew how glibly morose Fosse could be. It was part of his signature.

But when Fosse extended himself beyond his reach, the results were telling. Attempts to homogenize ballet and jazz dance in numbers like the opening "Crunchy Granola Suite," with words and music by Neil Diamond, or the *faux* ballet combinations in the drug-inspired "Joint Endeavor," with words and music by Carole Bayer Sager and Melissa Manchester, ended up falsifying both dance techniques. "*Dancin'* was

Bob's fantasy of 'If I had my own little company, here's what I'd create,' " believes Robert La Fosse. "He created unusual steps and defined a style, but I don't think he was a genius as a choreographer. His films were brilliant, but to create a ballet, you have to have been a ballet dancer and worked in a company. You have to have a sense of the history behind it; the knowledge behind the dance."

Offstage, the cast found the show to be more physically debilitating than anyone, including Fosse, might have guessed. "This show is about the sheer joy of dancing," Fosse told the *New York Times* in 1978, though, paradoxically, the roster of injured dancers seemed to make it about anything but "joy." "It was to be a very strenuous show," he remarked to *New York Theatre Review*. "So the first prerequisite was to choose all young strong people who really love to dance, because they were going to be asked to do more than has ever been asked of dancers on Broadway."

"It was a grueling show," recalls Sandahl Bergman, "I used to run offstage screaming, 'All I do is sweat and change! Sweat and change!' I would literally run offstage, grab a hairdryer in one hand and a pair of tights in the other and get ready for the next number. There wasn't even time to smoke a cigarette. Everybody did everything. It was a heavy dance show."

Phil Friedman, Fosse's stage manager for the show, said, "It was terrible. Every night there was a crisis. So many injuries we never knew if the curtain was going to go up that night. I've always said the better the dancer, the less injuries. Well, we had the best dancers, and everyone was having trouble with the show, so I guess that says something about Bobby's choreography." Friedman estimates that during the show's four-year run, there were "hundreds" of torn ligaments and hamstrings, thrown backs, twisted ankles, dislocated shoulders, torn groin muscles, and "assorted broken fingers and toes."

So many injuries put to test the dancers' devotion to their mentor. It brought to the surface personality conflicts and unresolved sexual tensions. "If you drink too much, do too many drugs," Sandahl Bergman says of Fosse's behavior at the time, "it effects the way you act and think. You start to bounce off the walls. Bob was at his worst when he was working." During the show's out-of-town run in Boston, Fosse fought bitterly with some of his dancers. One was Ross Miles, who, reportedly, was so frequently injured in *Dancin'* that he later left the show. Jill Cook

Fosse staged the inventive "Fourteen Feet" number with clog shoes nailed to the floor. *(Martha Swope)*

was another dancer Fosse battled with, although other dancers believed he was sexually attracted to her. More importantly, he argued with his devoted assistant, Kathryn Doby, who was singularly responsible for "whipping into shape" many of Fosse's dances. "He treated her very poorly," says Bergman. "It was hard for some of us to watch, because we knew how lucky Bob was to have her. Without Kathryn, I'm not sure many of Bob's shows could have happened. Not only did she help him fine-tune the dances, she was responsible for keeping them sharp after his shows had been running for awhile. And she had an amazing memory, which he did not. But in *Dancin'* he was at her constantly. He turned on her, and one day she was gone."

Tony Walton, set designer of *Pippin, Chicago,* and *All That Jazz* says "[Fosse thought] that whatever that tenuous thing is in a dancer that keeps them working at their peak and delivers their expression artfully

George M. Cohan's "Yankee Doodle Dandy" received the Fosse razzle dazzle in the "America" suite of *Dancin'. (Martha Swope)*

must be dealt with carefully. Cruelty was implicit. It was part of what you had to put them through to achieve the nuts and bolts of their work."

As demanding as Fosse could be, *Dancin'* proved to be a milestone musical for dancers, financially as well as artistically. Up until the show opened at the Broadhurst Theatre in 1978 there was no Equity contract that fulfilled the requirements for performers in the sort of roles Fosse had created for his cast. Before, there were principal performers, who received higher salaries, and then there were chorus players, who received less. But the show's unusual format, in which all sixteen of its performers had principal roles *and* also understudied other roles, forced Actors Equity to reconsider its standard contract. Ultimately, every dancer in *Dancin'* was given a contract as a principal. The large salaries *almost* made up for the nightly injuries. But the dancers weren't the only ones who cleaned up at the box office. At one point in the show's run, *Life* reported Fosse was rumored to be making $28,000 a *day* from *Dancin'*.

Its success on Broadway was, in part, due to its inherent weaknesses as an evening of dance. As critical as one may be about its oil-and-water mix of dance forms, there was something for everyone in the show's brash concoction of movement and music. The score ran the gamut from Johann Sebastian Bach to Oscar Hammerstein II and Cat Stevens. If matinee ladies blushed at "The Dream Barre," there was always the flag-waving George M. Cohan anthem "Yankee Doodle Dandy" to offset the flesh and fantasy.

"Bob used to tell us before we opened, 'If this show isn't a success, it's not your fault,' " remembers Rene Ceballos, who was in *Dancin'* for two and a half years. "He was afraid it might not work without a book, and he wanted us to know he appreciated the fact that we were all working so hard. I also think he knew the reviewers were going to be hard on him, that they might not accept an evening of dance as a Broadway show. After all, it was three acts of dancing. But, to our surprise, *Dancin'* was a smash hit. Audiences didn't have to speak English to love it. Bob proved that dancing really is a universal language."

Dancin' won Tonys for Fosse (outstanding choreography) and Jules Fisher (lighting), and ran nearly four years, with 1,774 performances. Of Fosse's shows, only *Pippin* had had a longer run. At his death, he was, in fact, working on *Dancin' Too,* his proposed follow-up. On the heels of his first Broadway flop, *Big Deal,* he might have been worried about finding financial backing for it, but the Shubert Organization claims to have expressed interest in the sequel. As long as Fosse stuck to dancing, no one doubted that he was bankable.

ALL THAT JAZZ

Bob's ideas come from something within him that is not the everyday man," Gwen Verdon told the *New York Times* in 1979. "The creative person is an absolute monster who tries to destroy Bob Fosse. His face changes. He gets ropey looking. His eyes sink into his head and it looks like a death mask. I've worked in insane asylums and the inmates don't look as weird as Bob. He's driven, jumpy, crazed and psyched up. Raw. He's like those safe-crackers in old movies who file their fingertips down to keep them sensitive."

Sensitive fingertips is an accurate metaphor for *All That Jazz*, Bob Fosse's twitching *cinéma á clef*. *Times* film critic Vincent Canby once heralded it as "an uproarious display of brilliance, nerve, dance, maudlin confessions, inside jokes, and, especially, ego," while *New York Magazine*'s reviewer David Denby dismissed it as "a characteristic product of our confessional age. . . . It's as if the film had been put together by an editing machine free-associating wildly on a psychoanalyst's couch."

Like it or hate it, *All That Jazz* was exactly what Fosse intended it to be: a haltingly autobiographic, expensive, studio-produced home movie about the travails of a sought-after Broadway and film director-choreographer named Joe Gideon who chases pills, liquor, and skirts. Between bouts of self-destruction and self-degradation, Gideon attempts to finish an elaborate new Broadway musical that sort of resembles *Chicago* in creative process, and a film that very much resembles *Lenny* in content.

Fosse standing behind director's chair of alter ego Joe Gideon in *All That Jazz*. Life imitates art. *(Copyright © 1979 Columbia Pictures Industry. All Rights Reserved)*

Then there are the three "leading ladies" in Gideon's life vying for attention between his rehearsals and heart attacks: Audrey (Leland Palmer) and Michelle (Erzsebet Foldi), who in look and/or attitude bear uncanny likenesses to Gwen Verdon and Nicole Fosse; and Kate, who is played by Ann Reinking herself.

But *was All That Jazz* about Bob Fosse? Fosse vacillated wildly in admitting and denying that it was—though resemblances to Bob Fosse were not purely coincidental. "I'm afraid of saying, yes, there is a lot of me in Joe Gideon," Fosse grudgingly confided to the *New York Times,* "because people have used the word 'self-indulgent' about the film. But critics are constantly saying that an artist should draw more from himself and less from others. This is what I've done. So why do I get this reaction? It frightens me. That is why I keep disclaiming."

While Fosse was recuperating from his multiple heart attacks in New York Hospital in 1975, he read Hilma Wolitzer's novel *Ending,* about a woman whose husband is dying of cancer, and bought the film rights. The book's personal relevance to his own precarious existence hit a nerve. Fosse's brush with death had, of course, been his own doing—popping Dexadrine, smoking five packs of cigarettes a day, and drinking Scotch sloshed down with Valium to offset the Dexadrine had finally taken its toll. Although Fosse had toyed with the idea of suicide as a young man, the birth of his daughter in the early Sixties gave him a new perspective on life. If his films and stage musicals continued to explore the dark side of humanity and freely associate sex and death, Nicole Fosse—a beautiful blonde, blue-eyed child who, by the late Seventies, had matured into an attractive and talented dancer, thanks to obligatory dance classes, North Carolina School of the Arts, and, of course, those genes—was her father's escape from his own cynicism.

"It was hard for me to lecture her about pot when I was standing there holding a glass of booze," Fosse admitted to *Life* in 1979. "I'm saying, 'You know it's bad for you, better not smoke that stuff.' And I've got the worst drug in the world in my hand. The worst."

The do-as-I-say-not-as-I-do routine Fosse used to warn Nicole may well have sounded half-hearted; by 1979, only four years after his near-fatal heart attack, he had already regressed to former bad habits. "When I thought I was going to die," he told *Life,* "I made a lot of resolutions. I promised, 'I'll be a good boy. I'll cut out smoking. I won't drink so much. I'll try to be fair, think of the other person's side of a situation. I won't be selfish.' That lasted about four months. I'm not very good at keeping promises—even to God."

And so he made *All That Jazz,* Fosse's reminder to himself that life is not a dress rehearsal. With his friend Robert Alan Arthur (who died midway through production), he wrote a script that, in tone, may bear passing comparison to the confessional films of Federico Fellini, Ingmar Bergman, and Woody Allen, but in style is distinctly Fosse. In fact, rather than trying to copy the work of these three contemporaries—directors he admired greatly—he claimed the greatest *visual* influence on *All That Jazz* was John Huston's *Moulin Rouge,* one of the first film musicals to break away from full-body shots and capture glimpses of legs or fractured sequences of a dance. The jagged, almost abstract, presentation of movement, Fosse believed, conveyed the energy and vitality of dance far more effectively than head-on shots of bodies whose choreography was so literal as to be predictable.

"Sometimes the razzle dazzle doesn't mean very much," Fosse once said to the *New York Times;* but in *All That Jazz,* razzle dazzle takes on a weightier role. He told the *Times,* "I wanted music and dancing in it. I wanted to try and move people in different directions. I wanted to show the fear and anxiety a person goes through in the hospital, and the stress of someone under business pressure. Many people are under this stress. They are trying to do something with their lives but instead become self-destructive with pills, alcohol or in psychological ways."

As cinema, *All That Jazz* has often been compared to Fellini's *8½* and Woody Allen's *Love and Death.* Like *All That Jazz, 8½* is Fellini's summation of his life and work. Fosse even used Giuseppe Rotunno, Fellini's director of photography, to film the picture. And Allen's *Love and Death,* like Fosse's film, finds obvious connections between falling in love and dying. But *All That Jazz* might be better contrasted to the many ballets in which the mythic figure of the ballerina is seen as a mystery to be solved, the fantasy of the soul. As poorly as Joe Gideon treats women, the movie is most sympathetic to them. Gideon's ex-wife Audrey becomes his confidante, the only one who will tell him the truth about how good (or bad) his latest dance really is. Michelle, his pubescent daughter, confronts him with his ineptitude as a father in such a loving, forgiving way that perhaps her utter devotion to him is the only thing stronger than his guilt from putting work over family. His girlfriend Katie has an equally incisive insight into Gideon. Part of her power over him stems from her mesmerizing gifts as a dancer. As Ann Reinking, who played Katie, put it in a 1979 *Playboy* interview, "He's in love with talent."

The most disturbing figure in the film is Angelique, an ethereal blonde cloaked in a diaphanous white shroud. Played by Jessica Lange, Fosse's girlfriend at the time she was cast, Angelique is Gideon's apotheosis, a death figure whose allure threatens to bring him closer and closer to relinquishing his own life. Like the Dark Angel in George Balanchine's ballet *Serenade,* who covers the male dancer's eyes and points over his shoulder to a direction impossible for him to follow, Angelique hopes to lead Gideon to a place he cannot ascertain—the afterlife. And to a hedonist/death-monger like Joe Gideon, the sexual appeal of Angelique is ultimately irresistible.

"Casting Jessica Lange as the Angel of Death comes from a personal fantasy," Fosse told *Playboy*. "For me, many times, Death has been a beautiful woman. When you think something's about to happen to you in a car or on an airplane, coming close to The End, this is a flash I'll get—a woman dressed in various outfits, sometimes a nun's habit, that whole hallucinatory thing. It's like the Final Fuck."

For Fosse and Lange, *All That Jazz* proved to be exactly that. However frequently Fosse may have committed indiscretions with his numerous wives and girlfriends, he could not condone the same treatment from them. When Lange began seeing American Ballet Theatre's superstar dancer Mikhail Baryshnikov in 1978, it

was a double blow for Fosse; not only was his competition a younger, attractive man, he was also a ballet dancer.

"Jessica, well, I mean, she's so damned smart," Fosse told the *Boston Globe*'s Kevin Kelly. "After she made *King Kong,* she couldn't get arrested [Fosse was fond of that expression]. They said she was just the usual dumb blonde, that she couldn't act, all that stuff. Well, I wish I was dumb like Jessica Lange! When she and I were going together—there was a time when we saw each other a couple nights a week—I always had this feeling there was Someone Else. Had the feeling I wasn't her Number One Man. And, see, I got this idea: I thought if I could just get her into the studio . . . get on my little dance shoes . . . strut around, then she'd just, y'know, fall.

"Well, I couldn't figure out who these other people were she was seeing. Then I started hearing names like Misha. Misha this. Misha that.

Above, at the opening-night party for Fosse's 1978 *Dancin',* he and girlfriend Jessica Lange share a slow dance at Tavern on the Green *(AP/Wide World Photo).* Left, Roy Scheider with beautiful angel of death Angelique (Jessica Lange) before his grand finale in *All That Jazz. (Alan Pappé/Lee Gross Inc.)*

She'd say it a lot. Misha. So I put it together, and, sure enough, found out that it was Baryshnikov. Here I had been inviting her to watch *me* dance! Then she finally said, 'You at the studio, how about tonight?' I yelled, 'Forget it!' "

Casting his estranged girlfriends was only one indication of the film's cinema verité quality. Fosse dancers, tech crew, friends, colleagues, even family appeared in *All That Jazz*. Longtime stage manager Phil Friedman played himself, as did Kathryn Doby, as Joe Gideon's dance assistant. In leading or cameo roles, Leland Palmer, who played Fastrada in *Pippin,* was cast as Gideon's estranged wife Audrey, and Ben Vereen

Fosse demonstrates for Leland Palmer during filming of 1979's *All That Jazz,* an allegedly autobiographical treatment of Fosse's life. *(Courtesy of L. Palmer)*

cannibalized his own image as an obsequious, mugging nightclub singer named O'Connor Flood. Although Cliff Gorman, who starred as Lenny Bruce in the Broadway show, lost out to Dustin Hoffman in Fosse's *Lenny,* Gorman played a Bruce look-alike in *All That Jazz*'s film-within-a-film, *The Standup*.

Alumni dancers Sandahl Bergman, Jennifer Narin-Smith, Vicki Fredericks, and Gene Foote either danced or assisted Fosse with his choreography. Jules Fisher, Fosse's lighting designer and sometime-producer, played himself, as did music supervisor Stanley Lebowsky. One of Fosse's favorite celebrity reporters and critics, Chris Chase, appeared as television movie critic Leslie Perry (who, using her "four-balloon rating system," gave Gideon's film *The Standup* "half a balloon"). Even Nicole Fosse, then sixteen, put in a brief appearance as a dancer stretching against a Coke vending machine. But Gwen Verdon was conspicuously absent.

"I think it's a magnificent film," Verdon said judiciously in a 1981 *New York Times* interview. "I think it has nothing to do with our life or his life. I guess the way I truly acted was not theatrically right for the story that Bob was telling." Ann Reinking, who auditioned for the role of Katie along with several other actresses, also took exception to Fosse's presentation of their relationship. "Bob had me dating other guys while he was in the hospital," she told the *Times* in 1979. "I never did that."

But Tony Walton, who won an Oscar as *All That's Jazz*'s "fantasy designer," says, "It was very precisely scripted, and much of the dialogue was based on interviews he had done with those of us he'd worked with. The events depicted in the movie actually occurred while we were rehearsing *Chicago,* when he had his heart attack. Everyone around him at that time was intensely interviewed and tape recorded. He made no secret about why he was doing the tapes. . . . It usually took about two years for me to recharge my batteries after working with Fosse. He was a very intense and demanding man."

Others found the art-imitates-life film troubling. Kathryn Doby, who admits that "playing myself was the most logical thing for me to do," also says that shooting the scene in which Audrey informs the cast of Gideon's latest musical that he's had a heart attack was "spooky, having already gone through it [in *Chicago*]. Stan Lebowsky, Phil [Fried-man], and me . . . there was something eerie about all of us being in a movie about us. What makes an artist put his personal life on the screen?"

Sandahl Bergman was hired as the lead dancer in the explosive "Airotica" dance in the film after another woman previously cast in the role refused to shuck her bra at the number's climax. Bergman was on vacation from *Dancin'* when Fosse called her about his dilemma. "He was in a pinch and asked me to do this nude scene. I told him, 'You know I trust you, Bobby, but I'm from Kansas. I'm not sure my mom and dad can handle it.'" But Fosse persuaded her and, after three days, Bergman made her film debut in the controversial number. Today she acknowledges the part has been a mixed blessing. "That movie changed my life, for better and for worse. Because of *All That Jazz,* I was immediately thought of as just another beautiful blonde dancer and a so-so actor. I've been trying for years now to live it down." But the role also brought her

Sandahl Bergman (standing) leads dancers through the controversial "Airotica" ballet from *All That Jazz. (Copyright © 1979 Columbia Pictures Industry. All Rights Reserved)*

instant attention, and shortly thereafter Bergman was starring opposite Arnold Schwarzenegger in the first of his successful *Conan* films.

In another key supporting role, John Lithgow was cast as Lucus Sergeant, whom producers of the musical in *All That Jazz* ask to replace Gideon after his heart attack. Sidney Lumet was originally to have played the part, but Fosse lost the esteemed director when *All That Jazz* went over schedule and conflicted with Lumet's own filming schedule. Lithgow, who says he "auditioned [his] heart out" for the role of Billy Flynn in *Chicago,* had met with Fosse to discuss early drafts of *All That Jazz,* then called *Dying.*

"I don't know if the character was based on someone who intervened during his heart attack in *Chicago,*" says Lithgow, "or if he had a specific individual in mind. But he used to make little jokes about the character; once, he told me, 'Just imagine Harold Prince and Mike Nichols shaking hands.' I didn't even know these people, but it was inferred Lucas was modeled variously on Nichols, Michael Bennet, and Gower Champion. I realized the character was the embodiment of every rival for a top-dog position in America. Bobby's view of anyone up against him was that they were a snake," Lithgow laughs. "It was my function to embody all the jackals nipping at Bobby's feet."

In the role of Audrey, fashioned unmistakably after Gwen Verdon, Fosse had two women in mind. "For a long time, Bobby wanted me to play Gwen in *All That Jazz,*" says Shirley MacLaine. "I got the famous Fosse pressure to do it: 'Oh, I really want you to do this *for me,* it's my *life.* It's really true. I'm trying to be so honest with myself.' I said, 'But Bob, the man dies in the end. How can it be true?' And he replied, 'I promise I'll die at the first preview.' "

But MacLaine didn't think she was in good enough shape to undertake the dance requirements of the picture, and she also realized playing Audrey would mean heavy "tell–all" confessions with Fosse about her own life. "He always wanted to know if I'd been to bed with Castro," she laughs. "Bob was interested in personal things, and I didn't feel like I could tell him everything he wanted to know. . . . Our relationship was him using me at certain times in his life to help him figure out who he was. But I was not one of the people he would call up and ask to tell him why he was terrible so he could tape record it and use it for some in-development project."

"He called me on the road several times, . . ." recalls Leland Palmer, whom Fosse also pleaded with to accept the role. "Once he called me late at night because he was lonely. I don't remember the conversation. I think he just needed to talk to a friend." In years past, Fosse had tried to persuade Palmer to take over Verdon's roles in *Sweet Charity* and *Chicago*. But Palmer was fighting showbiz burnout. After sporadic film work, including dancing opposite Rudolph Nureyev in Ken Russell's *Valentino,* she unofficially retired in 1977. "I was tired," she says. "I didn't like Hollywood. I went to a lot of auditions and wasn't successful. The things I was doing seemed degrading to someone who wanted to act and dance. I just needed to explore and teach a little, do different things." But, after much coaxing from Fosse, she read for the part of Audrey and was hired. "During rehearsals [for *All That Jazz*]," she says, "I became good friends with writer Robert Alan Arthur, and he told me that Bob was disconcerted I'd turned down *Chicago* because he'd wanted me to do Gwen's role to see if I could do her in the movie." After three years, Fosse's attempts to cast Palmer as Verdon finally paid off.

In the lead role of Joe Gideon, Fosse first had cast Richard Dreyfuss, but "artistic differences," along with Fosse's belated misgivings *after* Dreyfuss was cast, led to Dreyfuss leaving the project. "He wasn't built for [the part] physically," Fosse told *Life* in 1979, "but he had such drive, such recklessness, I thought, 'Well, somehow I'll fake around the dancing. There are choreographers that sit on chairs, maybe that's the kind I'll make him.'"

Fosse, of course, was not the kind to sit around on chairs. "Bob was always riding the camera like this wonderful horse," says Palmer. "He hung around the dancers' necks, under their armpits, crawled between their legs. He *was* the dancers; he *was* the audience, loving it and working hard, standing back and judging it." When Fosse realized he could not envision Joe Gideon as a sedentary choreographer, problems began between him and Dreyfuss. Other actors considered to replace him included Jack Nicholson and Keith Carradine. Fosse even contemplated playing himself, but discovered he was uninsurable after his heart attacks. Finally, he cast Roy Scheider, then forty-six, best-known for his tough-guys roles in films such as *The French Connection, Klute,* and *Supercops.*

Scheider was not a dancer, but he had an athletic, wiry body and, after he grew a goatee, bore more than a passing resemblance to the gaunt choreographer in black everyone knew as Bob Fosse. "Going through the script before we began to shoot," Scheider told *Playboy,* "Bob would tell me what stuff was true and what wasn't true. But the stuff that was factual was the first stuff that went out of the script . . . the Joe Gideon we created is a combination of Fosse and myself and any other guys we knew who were like that. . . . When the girl played by Ann Reinking says to him, 'I wish you weren't so generous with your cock,' he immediately thinks, Hey, y'know, that's pretty good . . . I can use that later. He's a guy who has removed himself several times, to

watch his life unfold. So it becomes tough for him to see reality, to *feel.*
. . . An expression Bob uses a lot [is] *flop sweat.* That's what you get
when you think you're bombing out. That's the real autobiographical
link between Fosse and this film—that doubt, which I think all great
artists have."

Fosse was especially sensitive to management intervention in his
picture. From the beginning, *All That Jazz* was a hard sell. Even with the
critical and popular successes of *Cabaret* and *Lenny* behind him, it took
him over a year to convince Columbia Pictures to take the risk on his
dance with death. Originally budgeted at $6 million, the film quickly
consumed every penny as Fosse overshot production numbers in the
Astoria Studios in Queens, New York. When the money was gone and
the picture was only halfway finished, Columbia threatened to pull the
plug and close down the picture. Executive producer Dan Melnick took
forty minutes of the film, put the reel in his suitcase, and, one weekend,
met with producers at other studios to try to convince them to bankroll
All That Jazz. The following Monday, he'd shaken hands on a deal with
20th Century–Fox to finance the other half of the picture. Estimates are
that *All That Jazz* cost between $12 million and $20 million between the
two studios—one of the most expensive funerals ever.

Fosse's mistrust of producers, lawyers, and doctors did not go
unnoticed in the film. Part of *All That Jazz*'s comic appeal is its ruthless

Fosse and Scheider promoting *All That Jazz* on "The Today Show," 1980. *(AP/Wide
World Photo)*

ribbing of "legitimate" professions, contrasted with the carnivorous milieu of show business. "There was a moment in my first scene where Lucus is sitting in the auditorium with his feet up on the back of another seat," recalls Lithgow, "and he asks, 'How much *is* Joe getting [to do the show]?' And Bill [William LeMassena, who played producer Jonesy Hecht] reads these staggering figures. Well, I had this idea to cross my legs while he's reading the numbers, as if the thought of all that money was giving me a hard-on. Bob, who saw a sexual dimension in everything, thought that was just fantastic. He believed people were driven by sex, greed, and the fear of death. That was his gritty, streetwise view of the world."

This point was conveyed emphatically in a scene where the producers, meeting with insurance executives and lawyers for Joe Gideon's postponed Broadway musical, learn that because the $480,000 show has been insured for $1 million, they could earn a profit on it of $519,000 *without* opening. This revelation is intercut with graphic scenes of a real open-heart surgery operation (supposedly Gideon's), performed by Dr. John E. Hutchinson III, who gets his own credit at the end of the picture. Hutchinson consulted with a male patient scheduled to undergo the surgery, and got permission from him to have the operation filmed for *All That Jazz.* Although some reviewers cried "snuff!" Fosse effectively showed how Gideon's producers (and his own?) were literally bleeding him dry. The sardonic tone is maintained throughout the film, as Gideon nears his call to receive death. In one scene, where he flees his hospital bed and cavorts around the hospital in his nightgown, Gideon is seen running barefoot in about five inches of water in the hospital's boiler room. Suddenly he looks up at the camera and addresses the audience and/or God: "Whatsa matter? Don't you like musical comedy?"

"What is death with dignity?" the standup comedian in Gideon's film asks his audience. "You don't drool." As *All That Jazz* builds to its climactic grand finale—Gideon's death—there is little doubt that Fosse is using all of his music-hall hocus pocus to trump up death as the biggest showstopper of them all. The five stages of death recounted in the film—anger, denial, bargaining, depression, and acceptance—are made manifest in distinctly theatrical ways. As in *Pippin,* which also associates sex and death, the audience is wowed into expecting nothing less spectacular than a twenty-one–gun farewell salute to Gideon. His surrealistic hospital production number, in which Ann Reinking, Leland Palmer, and Erzsebet Foldi pay their respective tributes to him, is staged to vintage songs with ironic titles: "After You've Gone," "There'll Be Some Changes Made," and "Some of These Days."

At Fosse's 1987 memorial at the Palace Theatre, where the brilliant "cattle-call" auditions were filmed for the opening of *All That Jazz* ten years before, Roy Scheider spoke of Fosse's own reactions to his fictitious death scene in the picture. "While staging *All That Jazz,* Bobby would sometimes say inadvertently something very profound and moving about himself. I remember when we were filming the finale to the movie. . . . We had gotten to that section where Joe Gideon, whom I suppose represented the best and the worst of both of us, was running into the audience saying goodbye to all of his friends and getting all that love back. We did it a couple of times and then I came down to Bobby and he said, 'You know, that must be kind of exhilarating,' and I said, 'Yes, Bobby, it is.' I smiled and said, 'Why don't you try it,' and he said, 'Naaaah . . .' in that way he always said naaah. . . . But finally he agreed. The band started playing and off he went into the audience, hugging and kissing all his associates and co-workers, lovers, and friends. When he got back he was puffing, and he said, 'Jesus Christ, that's terrific!' And I said, 'Yeah, Bobby, it is.' And then he said softly, with tears welling, 'And you know, Roy, the best part of it is that they forgive me, too.' And I said, 'Yeah, Bobby, we do.' "

Fosse's leading ladies in *All That Jazz*. From left, Leland Palmer, Erzebet Foldi, and Ann Reinking. *(Copyright © 1979 Columbia Pictures Industry. All Rights Reserved)*

Shirley MacLaine was stunned after seeing a screening of *All That Jazz*. "It was like Ibsen, the ultimate American musical tragedy. I thought it was the work of a complete genius, someone who had truly mastered his craft. Later, the projectionist rewound the film, put it in the can, and left the theater. I saw him on the street, around Forty-seventh and Broadway, with *All That Jazz* in his hand, and I thought everything that's gone into this genial, tyrannical, vulnerable artist is in that man's hands."

Not surprisingly, *All That Jazz* fared better with European audiences and critics than it did in America. Before it was released in the States, the film was shown at the 1979 Cannes Film Festival, where it shared the Golden Palm award for the best picture with Akira Kurosawa's *Kagemusha*. Although it was nominated for nine Academy Awards, including best picture, best actor (Roy Scheider), and best direction, *Kramer vs. Kramer* swept the major awards that year. For its technical achievements, *All That Jazz* won four Oscars, including costume design, art direction, editing, and music. When it opened, it was an extremely popular film, especially in urban areas, and has gone on to attain cult status for its unorthodox subject matter and superb cinematizing of dance. As Fosse's last film musical, it remains unchallenged ten years later in its magical blend of old-fashioned song and dance with state-of-the-art technology—and, of course, Fosse's own distinct ironic humor. Despite moments of film-dance brilliance in *Saturday Night Fever, Flashdance,* and *A Chorus Line,* the definitive film sequence of struggling dance hopefuls remains the opening five minutes of *All That Jazz,* in which hundreds of Broadway gypsies are winnowed down to the ten chosen for Gideon's show as George Benson's "On Broadway" is heard in the background.

After *All That Jazz* had wrapped, Fosse confessed he was suffering postproduction depression. "I guess I'm very tired," he told *Life*. "I sit there like some brainless thing watching game shows. People win prizes and jump on each other and kiss, and it makes me sad that they're so happy. I get all weepy. I don't know what the hell's going on. It suddenly breaks my heart, like there's something I'm missing out on."

"I hate show business," Joe Gideon tells his girlfriend Katie from his hospital room in *All That Jazz*. "But, Joe, you *love* show business," she counters. Gideon pauses a beat. "That's right," he says. "I can go either way."

VII

FOSSE'S FINALE

Life is just a bowl of cherries
Don't take it serious
Life's too mysterious
You work
You save
You worry so
But you can't take the dough
When you go go go
So keep repeating
It's the berries
The strongest oak must fall
The sweet things in life
To you were just loaned
So how can you save
What you never owned?
Oh, life is just a bowl of cherries
So live and laugh at it all

> —*"Life Is Just a Bowl of Cherries"*
>   *by Lew Brown and Ray Henderson*

STAR 80

crew everybody. I'm gonna write and produce and direct and do everything myself, and if it fails, what have I got to lose? I mean, it's either a rave from the *Times* or it's a funeral."

That's how Fosse replied when asked by former *New York Times* reporter and friend Chris Chase in 1973 what kind of project he would do if he had only a year to live. By the Eighties, Fosse had fulfilled his "screw everybody" prophecy. He would do almost everything himself. But the close-gripped control of *Star 80* and *Big Deal*, Fosse's final two completed projects, was not the only thing they had in common. Dissimilar as they appear on first examination, both the film and the musical are representative of Fosse's thematic concerns as a film and stage director. Each was based on works from another medium: *Star 80*, on Teresa Carpenter's compelling, Pulitzer Prize–winning *Village Voice* cover story, "Death of a Playmate"; *Big Deal*, on the 1959 Italian *Rififi* spoof, *Big Deal On Madonna Street*, whose stage rights were optioned by Fosse in 1967. Central characters in both projects are prototypes of the Fosse antihero: the unlucky, unwanted Paul Snider in *Star 80*; the incompetent band of black thieves conniving to pull off a big-time heist in *Big Deal*.

More importantly, both works reflect Fosse's world-weary cynicism. At the point in Fosse's career when he had mastered the pyrotechnics of creating a film or stage musical, his thematic concerns all but subverted his accomplishments as a technician. As Vincent Canby noted in his *New*

Paul (Eric Roberts) begs Dorothy (Mariel Hemingway) to come back to him in *Star 80*. (Copyright © 1983 The Ladd Company. All Rights Reserved)

York Times review of *Star 80*: "Watching *Star 80* is like witnessing a huge sound-and-light show, one designed not to call up the history of the pyramids, the Parthenon or even the Brooklyn Bridge but a contemporary world where sleaziness has triumphed." And for all its apparent minimalism, *Big Deal* was Fosse's most technically ambitious Broadway effort, a $5 million musical requiring over 200 lighting cues to accommodate the show's 43 scenes.

Like Michael Bennett, Fosse had become increasingly disenchanted with the traditional musical-comedy structure of song-dance-narrative, preferring to integrate these traditionally separate elements into one. The "choreography" in *Big Deal* that went unnoticed by most theatergoers was demonstrated in the orchestration of every component—music, libretto, lights, sound, set, and choreography. The show's numerous crosscuts and fade-outs attest to Fosse's understanding of film technique and of how to cinematize the Broadway stage. One could justifiably carp that Fosse gave short shrift to some of *Big Deal*'s twenty-three songs— sometimes truncating them to splintered verses—but, as long as the orchestra played, there was rarely a moment on stage that did not *move*.

Similarly, Fosse's approach to filming *Star 80,* especially its pacing and perspective, indicates that he was continuing to follow his own instincts as a choreographer. The film has an edgy, nervous quality to it due to the restlessness of the camera. Its hyperactivity and the abruptness of the editing captures the manic energy of Snider. As in *Lenny,* Fosse attempts a docudrama effect, though, in *Star 80,* the end result is less gritty and more repellent. Despite an electrifying performance by Eric Roberts, Snider was not a celebrity of the magnitude of Lenny Bruce, and audiences simply were not interested in sitting through a brutalizing film about a lowlife talent scavenger who murders a beautiful starlet.

In reality, Fosse's own star-making system had temporarily stalled with his final productions. *Star 80* made neither Mariel Hemingway, who played Stratten, nor Eric Roberts the superstars their performances indicated they might become. Some suspected that Roberts, whose sycophantic portrayal of Snider is the heart of the film, should have received an Academy Award nomination that year but was cheated out of it by Hollywood politics: *Star 80*'s indictment of Tinseltown flesh-peddling cut too close to the bone for many Academy voters, culled almost exclusively from the film community. Fosse, who had received best director nominations for his previous three films, *Cabaret, Lenny,* and *All That Jazz,* was overlooked as well.

Neither did *Big Deal* establish its principals as superstars. Although Cleavant Derricks received a Tony nomination, he did not win. *Big Deal*'s only award was to Fosse, a Tony for outstanding choreography—an accolade that did nothing to keep the show from closing the day after the award. Being in a Fosse production was still a boon to any actor's career, and both Devine and Roberts concur that it gave them subsequent opportunities; yet their work with him, however outstanding, has not yet resulted in the sort of careers Fosse made possible for Gwen Verdon in *Damn Yankees,* Ben Vereen in *Pippin,* Liza Minelli in *Cabaret,* and Ann Reinking in *Dancin'.*

As many company members of *Big Deal* have indicated, Fosse believed he had disappointed them. Always the first to take the blame, Fosse was undoubtedly hit hard by the back-to-back failures of *Star 80* in 1983 and *Big Deal* three years later. Though his revival of *Sweet Charity,* also in 1986, was a Broadway hit, that production was supervised with a curatorial eye by Verdon, while Fosse devoted most of his attention to his *new* musical. Box-office figures indicated audiences wanted the old Fosse back and the reactions to his new work frustrated and perplexed a man obsessed with forging new turf on stage and in cinema. The pressure to produce a hit and satisfy his own need to create films and stage musicals that were more than knee-jerk entertainment took its toll on his health. Painful sciatica—all but immobilizing his hips and the tops of his thighs— ongoing heart ailments, and respiratory problems resulting from his heavy smoking habit sidelined him temporarily from *Big Deal* rehearsals. "If I fail, what have I got to lose?" he had told the *New York Times* thirteen years earlier. But, in fact, he had much to lose. The failures of *Star 80* and *Big Deal* had put his career, and his life, in jeopardy.

The grisly murder of Dorothy Stratten provided an oddly appropriate code to Fosse's film career. Paul Snider's final act of retribution against his wife in many ways epitomized all that Fosse believed was wrong with show business. Fosse drew immediate parallels between his career aspirations and Snider's snuffed-out dreams of immortality. Discussing his interest in the Paul Snider–Dorothy Stratten story, he told the *Chicago Tribune*'s Gene Siskel, "His was a milieu that I'm interested in. I've read *Playboy* for years like a lot of people. I thought the guy's background in sleazy nightclubs was something I (as a former nightclub entertainer) had some familiarity with; so I felt I could deal with that portion of the story. It was about Hollywood, and I suppose there is a bit of anger in me about Hollywood that I have to get out."

Star 80 focuses on the Pygmalion transformation of Stratten, but it is also a prism refracting Fosse's own romantic entanglements, the women he made stars and lovers, not always in that order. In a 1979 *Life* profile, Fosse discussed his elusive quest for happiness, often sacrificed in order to give his girlfriends freedom to develop as actresses. At that time his newest flame was model Julie Hagerty.

"I met Julie, and she didn't seem interested in acting at all," Fosse recalled. "Hooray, I thought. She was a model. Fine. Let her go model. And suddenly she said she was appearing in a little show off-off-Broadway for a friend of hers. I went down and saw it, and she was a natural. I mean a natural comedienne. So I got my agent [ICM's Sam Cohn] to come, and he grabbed her up; pretty soon she was gone. I think she's going to be a movie star. . . . You always think, this one will be the one—the one who'll alter your life. With her, I tried harder than I used to. I miss her. I miss her a lot."

The similarities between Snider and Fosse do not extend beyond an affinity for street life and relationship histories. Although Fosse told Gene Siskel he believed Snider was "seemingly innocuous, sleazy but not [a] dangerous character," Snider comes across in both Teresa Carpenter's *Village Voice* article and Peter Bogdanovich's 1984 biography of Stratten, *The Killing of the Unicorn,* as a self-interested, parasitic lowlife. His entrepreneurial pursuits, according to Bogdanovich, ranged from drug trafficking to wet T-shirt contests in Vancouver and Los Angeles night-clubs. Besides discovering Stratten, his primary claim to fame was the production of the first male strip act, which would later become known (under different management) as the Chippendales. "If he hadn't committed murder," says Eric Roberts, "he probably would have made a lot of money, which was what really mattered to him." As Carpenter points out in her *Village Voice* piece, "The two things it seemed he could never get enough of were women and money."

Snider discovered Dorothy Ruth Hoogstraten working at a Dairy Queen in Vancouver. She was uncommonly pretty, eighteen years old, and rangy at about five-foot-eight. It was, by all accounts, a whirlwind courtship between a teenager who didn't know what she wanted to do with her life and an avowed pimp who did. Despite protestations from Stratten's mother (her Dutch father had long ago left the family), Snider arranged a photo session for Dorothy with a local photographer that resulted in her first nudes. Another photographer who had worked for *Playboy* took subsequent shots; those landed on *Playboy* publisher Hugh Hefner's desk, and Stratten was promptly flown to Los Angeles for test shots.

Hefner took to her with unbridled enthusiasm, attempting to get her into numerous compromising positions that, according to Bogdanovich, culminated in a Jacuzzi seduction. Allegedly, the overwrought young woman broke down in tears at the prospect of having to sleep with

Hefner if she was to become the magazine's twenty-fifth anniversary Playmate (she wound up Playmate of the Month for the August 1979 issue).

With her splashy *Playboy* debut, Stratten was pressured by Snider to marry him. Although her own fledgling career had surpassed Snider's modest—and usually illegal—means of income, and despite her own misgivings that he did not fit in with her new circle of "friends" at the Playboy mansion, she had an overriding sense of loyalty to this man who vaulted her out of Vancouver and into the public eye. They married in Las Vegas and, while Stratten was filming her first film, the low-budget *Autumn Born,* Snider secured a two-story Spanish stucco house near the Santa Monica freeway in West L.A., which he and Dorothy would share with a young internist. Spending Stratten's money faster than it was earned, Snider withdrew enough from her savings account to put a down payment on a new Mercedes, pinning on a "Star 80" license plate as a tribute to his wife.

"I somehow identified with him," Fosse told *Rolling Stone* in 1984, "because he was trying to get in. It's not that I've been excluded that much, but I know that sense of them all knowing something I don't know. And that makes me very angry. I'd like to be offered all of Hollywood's perks, just so I could refuse them. To this day, I get nervous when I have to see the big shots at the studios. Even though they're pretty schmucky guys, it's like being called to the principal's office."

Film director Peter Bogdanovich's intervention in Stratten's life sealed her fate. Although many of *Playboy*'s models had gone on to do film and television, none had Stratten's meteoric rise, or, arguably, the raw talent. By 1980, she had starred in two low-budget exploitation pictures and appeared on television. Sensing that Bogdanovich was more capable of making Stratten a "legitimate" star than he was, Hefner gradually relinquished his control over her career. In 1980, the year Dorothy became Playmate of the Year, Bogdanovich cast her in his film *They All Laughed* and became her lover.

The dissolution of her marriage with Snider began when Stratten moved into Bogdanovich's hotel room while the film was on location in New York City. Neither Stratten nor Bogdanovich wanted Snider around during the shooting because of his obnoxious behavior (Hefner had already banned him from the *Playboy* mansion), and because his presence would have distracted Stratten from her work. Suspicious, Snider hired a private detective. He believed a divorce was impending and was concerned about his financial stakes should Dorothy leave him.

When filming for *They All Laughed* wrapped in mid-July, 1980, Stratten returned to Los Angeles and moved in with Bogdanovich. She

met Snider twice more, once to discuss the separation, once to decide on the exact sum Paul would receive as settlement from Dorothy's earnings. Between their first and second meetings, Paul had acquired a twelve-gauge Mossberg pump shotgun "for security," apparently with the help of their housemate.

Dorothy arrived at Paul's house Thursday, August 14, 1980 at around 12:30 P.M.; she would never be seen alive again.

Paul, who had some experience making weight-training benches, forcibly strapped her into a bondage bench he had made expressly for the occasion. Amid the grotesquely overblown images of Stratten on the walls of Snider's bedroom shrine to her, he raped and sodomized her so brutally she was, according to Bogdanovich's account, disfigured. The shell from the 12-gauge entered her left eye point-blank. Her last act was to raise her left hand to her face, causing the tip of her left forefinger to be blasted away. After she was dead, Snider moved the body to the bed and, again, had intercourse with it. When detectives found Stratten early that evening after the murder had been reported by Snider's housemate, bloody fingerprints marred her buttocks and one shoulder. Both knees were on the carpet, and her torso was draped over a bottom corner of the bed, fully rigid. Her hair hung limply over her face, hiding the black ants and other insects crawling on it.

Snider was found with the gun in his hands. He had been on his knees, perhaps in supplication to the woman he had created and destroyed, when he put the barrel to his head and pulled the trigger. The jolt pitched him forward, blasting his brains and blood in an arc across the ceiling and one wall. The gruesome details of the couple's deaths were noted by Fosse, who implicated Hollywood as the murderer.

There were, of course, posthumous homages to Stratten: Bogdanovich's film; a television film, *Death of a Centerfold,* starring Jamie Lee Curtis as Stratten; a *Playboy* cable TV special; three in-depth magazine articles; and, finally, *Star 80.*

In *Star 80* Fosse latched onto three men—Snider, Hefner, and Bogdanovich—who each, in part, represented his own complex personality,

Dorothy Stratten, left, in Peter Bogdanovich's 1982 *They All Laughed (Steve Schapiro/Sygma)*. Mariel Hemingway, inset, underwent breast-enlargement surgery prior to being cast as the doomed centerfold Dorothy Stratten in Fosse's last film, *Star 80. (Copyright © 1983 The Ladd Company. All Rights Reserved)*

and a woman who was not so much a star in her own right as she was the sum total of these men's fantasies. Of these three, Fosse is most superficially compatible with Bogdanovich. Both developed stars from ingenues and girlfriends (in Bogdanovich's case, Cybill Shepherd), produced early films that were critical and box office successes (Bogdanovich's *Last Picture Show* and Fosse's *Cabaret*), and have similar stylized approaches to filmmaking. Both are also recognized for producing serious-minded films that have sometimes suffered at the box office because of their refusal to abide by formulaic storylines and "bankable" subjects.

Comparisons between Hefner and Fosse are not so obvious. Fosse was hardly exploitative of women; his reverence for them resulted in projects that illuminated their abilities and, for many, became star vehicles. But Hefner—and Snider—sought to re-create women. There is something cataclysmic about the rapid transformation of Dorothy Ruth Hoogstraten from the fresh-faced Dairy Queen countergirl in Vancouver to the crimson-lipped, bleached-blonde siren created by Hefner. Even before her spreads in the magazines, Dorothy had been taught how to please men by Snider, who dressed her in form-fitting (usually white) dresses and instructed her how to be graciously compliant. For a time, Paul decided Dorothy should be named Kristen Shields, even demanded that her family call her by that name. But it was "Stratten," pruned from the cumbersome Hoogstraten, that *Playboy* preferred. Even Bogdanovich, who passionately condemns the *Playboy* life-style in *The Killing of the Unicorn,* dropped "Dorothy" in favor of "D.R."

Ironically, it was Hefner, not Bogdanovich, who established Stratten's enigmatic appeal, roughly patterned after the image Snider had created for her. Here, once sees marked similarities between Hefner and Fosse. Jerry Orbach, who Fosse cast in the pivotal role of attorney Billy Flynn in *Chicago,* believes that Fosse "apologized" for the Hefner side of his personality in *Star 80.* "Fosse saw himself as Hefner a good deal of the time," says Orbach. "They were both guys who took girls from nowhere and made them somebodies. But, in the movie, Hefner comes out as something of a good guy, or at least neutral, whereas [Snider] is seen as crazy. I think Bobby empathized greatly with Hefner, and the movie was the perfect statement for him to make without saying [Hefner] was really him."

Carpenter, who was involved peripherally with the casting of some minor characters in the film, believes Fosse vilified Snider because he was dead. "As Fosse portrayed him in the film," she says, "he was so repugnant that you wondered what a girl like Dorothy saw in him. He had a vulnerable side, a sweeter aspect that Dorothy was attracted to.

Overall, I think the film was done with integrity and great artistic sensibility. My only criticism was the treatment of Snider. I think he was dramatically weakened."

If the Paul Snider of Carpenter's *Village Voice* article diverged drastically from Eric Roberts' interpretation of the role, it was because Fosse had personalized the character, aligned Snider with himself. The Fosse-Snider association is the most difficult of the three men involved with Stratten to discuss because Snider was such a repellent character; however much one may speak of Fosse's dark cynicism, he is generally remembered by those who knew him as a gentle, soft-spoken man with little resemblance to Eric Roberts's character. Yet Fosse's own self-hatred, evident throughout his life in his obsession with death and self-destruction, may have drawn him to a project focusing on a side of his personality he found abhorrent.

Even Fosse's behavior on the set of the film indicates his intense personal association with Snider. "One day I was having trouble with a

Paul contemplates a future without Dorothy in *Star 80*. *(Copyright © 1983 The Ladd Company. All Rights Reserved)*

scene," recalls Roberts. "I got very angry with myself and said, 'What the fuck am I doing here, playing this guy I don't even like, busting my balls and feeling depressed every day?' Fosse grabbed me, shook me, and said, 'Look at me, look at me! If I were not successful, this is what you're playing. Show me *me!*' It was the most personal direction I ever got from anyone."

In Kathy Henderson's book *First Stage: Profiles of the New American Actors,* Fosse, discussing Roberts' character in the film, says, "I thought the *Star 80* part was such a villainous role, the fellow should have some sort of likeability, the way Montgomery Clift did in *A Place in the Sun,* and Eric had that. Somehow, no matter how evil and sleazy the character was, I always seemed to sympathize. Somehow I felt sorry he was trapped."

Fosse's four-year Hollywood hiatus ended when he read Carpenter's article in the *Village Voice*. In Paul Snider he had found a character that might have been the ugly stepson of Fosse's autobiographic Joe Gideon in 1979's *All That Jazz*. Carpenter was in Albany, New York, researching a story on Jerry Falwell, when she received word from her agent that Fosse had expressed interest in her piece, which had been published only a few weeks prior. "We met at Sam Cohn's office, and Fosse was friendly, down to earth," Carpenter recalls. "It was understood that he would be writing the screenplay. I didn't know how much he would drop, if he would use only the idea or if he would go further. It became clear he was going to draw heavily from the factual elements of the story."

Fosse's meticulousness, his eye for detail and authenticity, was evident from the time the film began preproduction in late 1981. He dispatched first assistant director Wolfgang Glattes—who had worked with him on *Cabaret* and *All That Jazz*—to Vancouver to do research on Stratten's and Snider's backgrounds. During the numerous trips Glattes, who was also a co-producer along with Kenneth Utt, made to Vancouver, he drove to Stratten's home, talked to her high school teachers and principal, and looked up the bars Snider frequented. Later, when Fosse arrived in Vancouver, set designer Tony Walton recalls that Fosse took a particularly keen interest in "the sleazy strip clubs. He told us, 'This is where I'm going to die. I know it.' I was surprised at how candid he was about it. I think what impacted him the most about his own burlesque days was that heavy sexuality. He was constantly drawn back to it."

In the meantime, Peter Bogdanovich attempted to halt production of the film by having Stratten's family sign a statement saying they would not cooperate with interviews. They agreed, and Fosse did not attempt to dissuade them. Bogdanovich also approached Fosse directly to stop the film because, according to Fosse, 'You don't know the whole story.' When Fosse continued with preproduction—as Bogdanovich signed with William Morrow and Co. to write *his* version of the Stratten story—Bogdanovich told the *New York Post* he would sue for slander, because the film "contributes to the ghoulish atmosphere that caused Dorothy's death." An intriguing postscript is that, in January 1989, Bogdanovich married Dorothy Stratten's kid sister, Louise—at twenty, the same age as Dorothy was when she was killed.

In Los Angeles, Glattes located the West L.A. home by the freeway, where Snider killed Stratten. "It was spooky," Glattes recalls. "Nobody had been to that house in a long time. All this mail was stacked outside, which no one had bothered to pick up. I looked in the windows of the garage and the house, and you could still see the bullet holes in the walls. That blood was still on the ceiling; someone had tried to paint over it, but it came through."

Fosse wanted to use as many real locations as possible, so, when filming began, the exterior of the house and its corridors were included, along with the exterior of Stratten's family home in Vancouver and the Dairy Queen where Snider met her. From the beginning of *Star 80*'s three-month preproduction period, Fosse established a factual tone for the film, giving the finished product a cinema verité quality by using actual locations where Stratten and Snider lived and worked, and by talking to people who knew them.

Glattes, Roberts, and Fosse turned up further bizarre information on the story, such as discovering that the Mercedes with the "Star 80" license plates was still "running around L.A.," according to the Los Angeles Department of Motor Vehicles—eerily, still registered in Snider's name. In addition to the official report on the Stratten murder–Snider suicide, an earlier police report on the finding of the bodies stated that when the murders were discovered, everything in the apartment was arranged neatly, as if someone had come in afterwards and cleaned up. Speculation exists, however unsubstantiated, that Snider may have been set-up to be murdered, either to avenge a botched black-market job or because he owed someone money. Stratten may or may not have been an intended target; perhaps she just arrived at the house at the wrong time.

Although these findings were provocative, Fosse chose to follow Carpenter's account of the murder, which, in all probability, comes closest to accurately chronicling the events of August 14, 1980. Roberts, who auditioned for Fosse six times before winning the role over Richard Gere, was encouraged by Fosse to investigate Snider on his own. Roberts met with Snider's younger brother and describes him as "a calmer version of Paul with the same fashion sense." Alone and with Fosse, Roberts haunted the same nightclubs in Vancouver and Los Angeles frequented by Snider.

"I have a hard time with Paul Snider," says Roberts. "I hated playing him. I got a real sense of what it was like to be an outcast. I started dressing like Paul, talking like him, *thinking* like him. I hung out in the same nightclubs he did, and got to know these so-called real people who

went there. They gave me a horrible time, made me feel like shit. I'd bring my little reports back to Fosse. He'd wallow in them."

As Roberts continued to internalize the character, his behavior towards others on the set grew abusive. "Sometimes Eric would get into a little trouble," Fosse told *The Movies'* James N. Baker. "He would be less than polite to people on the set. I thought, 'Why is he doing this?' Then I realized that he was playing the part offscreen. He was making himself a bit of an outcast."

Despite Roberts' reservations about the part, he developed a strong rapport with Fosse. On their road trips to Vancouver, the two discussed the subjects of death, isolation, and love. Both men had, at different points in their lives, almost died—Fosse, with his near-fatal heart attack during *Chicago* rehearsals; Roberts, when he was nearly killed in a June 1981 automobile accident that put him in a three-day coma. They discussed out-of-body experiences and their subsequent fear of and fascination with death; "mental masturbations," Roberts calls them. Snider, whose utter rejection by everyone whose life-style he coveted drove him to his final act, was, of course, the core of these discussions. "I think Fosse had an enormous emotional and cerebral understanding of outcasts," Roberts believes. "Theoretically, we all know what it's like to not be allowed something. But when you're not allowed things a lot, or when someone you know is allowed them and you're not, there's jealousy—like Paul and Dorothy."

Having cast Roberts in the film's leading male role, Fosse was not as certain about who would play Stratten. The script, written by Fosse, focused intensely on Snider. The female lead therefore would have to convey an equally strong character without the benefit of a well-developed role. And, of course, she would have to physically resemble Stratten. Mariel Hemingway had received the script from her agent and indicated to Fosse she would like to read for the part. Fosse was concerned her image as established in *Personal Best* was too "tomboyish," but, at twenty, she was the right age and had the same wholesome blonde looks. Her film record at that point, including an Oscar nomination for *Manhattan,* was impressive. The only thing she didn't have was the *Playboy* proportions of Stratten. Although Hemingway told the *New York Post's* Stephen M. Silverman that the cosmetic surgery to swell her breasts from size 32 to 36 had "nothing to do with getting the part. . . . I did that for myself quite a while before the movie," it seems unlikely Fosse would

Fosse setting up a shot of Dorothy Stratten's Mercedes in *Star 80*. *(Copyright © 1983 The Ladd Company. All Rights Reserved)*

have cast a flat-chested actress, no matter how proficient, as a *Playboy* centerfold. Fosse himself told *People*: "It's the old boob question, you can't cast a girl unless she has them. . . . Her flat chestedness was one of my original objections to her." After the film was released he lamented, "Nobody talks about the movie, everyone talks about her boobs." Hemingway herself had no reservations about exposing her upper torso. She appeared bare-chested in *Vanity Fair* and went further with a now-famous nude split in *Playboy*.

Budgeted at $10 million, *Star 80* was produced under the aegis of The Ladd Company, a subsidiary studio of Warner Bros. Co-producer Wolfgang Glattes recalls that Fosse had a difficult time finding a studio to back him on the project. His reputation for scrupulous detail and over-shooting, in addition to the picture's subject matter, caused considerable speculation within the industry whether the film had commercial viabil-ity. But the fledgling Ladd Company, formed by producer Alan Ladd, Jr., was interested in securing controversial projects with big-name talent behind them. Shortly after the release of *Star 80,* the Ladd Company's deficits—none of its films was profitable—forced it to be absorbed by Warner Bros.

Fosse's production team was comprised of people he had worked with previously and trusted. The cast, besides Roberts and Hemingway, included former *Baby Doll* star Caroll Baker as Stratten's mother, Cliff Robertson as Hefner, and Roger Rees as the Bogdanovich-inspired Hol-lywood director. Fosse also used Hefner's brother Keith in a minor role as a *Playboy* photographer.

During preproduction, Fosse rehearsed Roberts and Hemingway for six weeks, blocking out the scenes and taping the floor as though marking a stage. In fact, Fosse attempted to keep the production as intimate as possible, establishing a continuity between scenes by filming the begin-ning and end of *Star 80* in sequence.

Because Fosse had already worked with Roberts while researching Snider, the two men had a strong relationship; however, Hemingway initially reacted strongly against Fosse's confrontational style of directing. According to Roberts, she broke down in tears during the first week of shooting in Vancouver, unnerved over Fosse's direction. "Fosse and I had already established a working relationship from being on the road for three weeks," says Roberts. "So when he yelled at me—and he could get pretty rough—I'd roll with it and say, 'okay, okay.' But he couldn't do that with Mariel; she's a very nice lady. Coming from that Hemingway background, things are done a certain way. Once he told her to 'get your fucking voice out of your face. Put it in your chest. I don't wanna hear this [imitates Hemingway's adolescent whine], I wanna hear *this* [uses his diaphragm to project].' She gets all teary and walks out. Two and a half hours later she comes back to the set and Fosse says, 'Okay, I can see I wasn't delicate enough in this situation, but you're gonna have to take it.' "

As he did with all his principal actors, Fosse worked to bring out Roberts's and Hemingway's idiosyncrasies and incorporate them into the actors' characters—and sometimes embarrassment, even shock, was his most effective strategy. The lovemaking scenes between Roberts and Hemingway were to be filmed with Roberts wearing a dance belt while under the sheets with Hemingway. Fosse, however, made Roberts remove the supporter, claiming the camera could see its outline through the sheet. "Well, I'm very embarrassed about taking it off, you know?" Roberts says. "I didn't understand why he couldn't just rearrange the sheets or something so that you couldn't see the goddamn belt underneath, but he insisted. Mariel also felt uncomfortable, so, trying to relieve the tension, I told her, 'If I get a hard-on, don't take it personally.' She didn't speak to me for two days." However explicit some of Stratten's *Playboy* photographs were, reportedly she felt awkward while having sex. By making Roberts remove his dance belt, Fosse could exploit Hemingway's own discomfort for a truer characterization.

Fosse was not above using more drastic measures; as he used animal intestines in *Cabaret* to get Marissa Berenson's reaction when she finds her dead dog, Fosse again resorted to real carnage in *Star 80*. Following the murder, there is a shot of Snider reaching out to touch Stratten's corpse. Fosse filmed it twice before screaming at Roberts, "What's happened to you? You've gone mechanical on me!" A break was called, and when the actor returned and filming was resumed, Stratten's "corpse" had been replaced by a bowl of cow brains. "It was awful," Roberts says, "really awful. I thought I was gonna get sick. That is, of course, what Fosse wanted. We did it in one take."

During production, shooting days often lasted up to fourteen hours. Fosse was tireless, rewriting daily. A manic energy set in among the cast and crew, and, as in other Fosse productions, no one seemed to mind the long days, especially Fosse. "Fosse expected nothing less of his actors than he himself could give," says Wolfgang Glattes. After one twelve-hour day, Roberts recalls retreating to his new home, address unknown to everyone connected with the film, and being abruptly interrupted. "I get home, strip, and am ready to hit the bed when I hear someone banging at my door. Since my girlfriend's the only one who knows where I live, I grab a hammer. I whip open the door with my hammer raised, and there's Bob Fosse standing there with a goddamn typewriter. 'Eric, put down that hammer,' he says. 'What are you trying to do, kill somebody?' And then he sort of chuckles. I said, 'Fosse, what the fuck are you doing here?' 'I type, you dance,' he says, walking in and setting up the typewriter."

Fosse's control of the script undoubtedly contributed to the development of the character of Snider as the film's keystone. Though *Star 80* abandons the quasi-documentary technique of *Lenny,* it does possess a compelling journalistic sensationalism that picks up momentum as the film nears the reenactment of Stratten's gruesome murder. The journalist we sometimes see taping conversations in *Star 80* could well be Teresa Carpenter, but Fosse is less than consistent in his use of this narrative device—point of view is one of *Star 80*'s chief problems, especially since the audience has so little empathy for Snider.

Early screenings in 1983 indicated audiences felt bludgeoned by the film's brutality. At a celebrity screening of about one hundred people, Roberts recalls dead silence for nearly thirty seconds after the film ended. "I was sitting next to Fosse, just scanning the audience's reaction, and I said to him, 'We got 'em, Fosse.' Rachel Welch came up to me later and said, 'My God, you were wonderful!' I thought the movie was going to be a hit."

That *Star 80* was a failure at the box office attests more to what mainstream film audiences do *not* want to see than it does to *Star 80*'s inconsistencies. "It's relatively tough to make a serious film today," Fosse told the *Cable Guide.* "Everyone wants to think things are great today, and I think they all want the *Rocky* story in some form. When I start working now it's in the back of my mind that the big hits are things like *Bachelor Party* . . . though the innocence and happy-ending pictures are in vogue, to make one takes somebody who really believes in that. And if I were to try to do one, I would be a hypocrite and therefore I couldn't do it well."

At a benefit held November 9, 1983 for New York's Post-Graduate Center for Mental Health, *Star 80* was enthusiastically received. Fosse and Gwen Verdon had had a twenty-five–year association with the organization, beginning as friends of its founder, Dr. Lewis Walberg, and, later, as trustees on its board of directors. Verdon was instrumental in the formation of the Center's Performing Artists Counseling Service, which continues to provide low-cost therapy to performing artists. (Fosse's will left $15,000 to be used at the Center's discretion.) The benefit screening, which Fosse claimed was a "present" to Verdon, began with a premovie cocktail party at Le Train Bleu in Bloomingdale's department store in New York City, followed by the screening, and dinner and dancing at Tavern on the Green. The event raised over $150,000 and, according to the Center's director of marketing, Esther Smith, was "a huge success."

The next day *Star 80* opened to decidedly mixed reviews. The *New York Post*'s Rex Reed called it a "bruising blockbuster of a film," while *New York Magazine*'s David Denby said "lurid yet tedious, grim yet unilluminating, *Star 80* sits badly, a small pool of dark, ill-smelling bile." Many critics were particularly harsh on Fosse's use of gratuitous violence, and audiences followed suit. "Most people I talked to who had seen it just couldn't take the bloodbath," says Wolfgang Glattes. "People walked out during the last fifteen minutes. Personally, I think it's the best film Fosse made, but word-of-mouth and the reviews killed it. People were scared away."

"He must have known not a lot of people would want to see such a story," believes John Lithgow, who continued to follow Fosse's career closely after appearing in *All That Jazz*. "[*Star 80*] exposed them to their own morbid sexual curiosity. Fosse was really challenging the audience as he rubbed our noses in it. If you had even come to see this movie, you were immediately suspect; you were fascinated by that lurid, sexual underbelly of society."

The notoriety of the Stratten-Snider story on film caused a immediate buzz behind the gates of the *Playboy* mansion. Fosse arranged a private screening for Hugh Hefner, who called it, "artful" but denounced Fosse's association between sex and violence, and especially how *Playboy* inadvertently promulgates the two. "If Dorothy had aspired to the Broadway stage, or to being a ballerina," Hefner told the *Post,* "many of the same things could have happened to her. But because she came to Hollywood and posed nude for *Playboy,* because of all the prejudices that exist toward that, there are all sorts of connections made between sex and violence."

In its first two weeks of release, the $10 million picture grossed only one million; by January it was pulled from wide release. Though *Star 80* made it onto several critics' "ten best" lists for 1983, when Oscar nominations were announced the film and its performers were conspicuously absent.

Perhaps author E. L. Doctorow, a long-time friend of Fosse's, best described the catharsis that was the film's reason for being for Fosse. In a *New York Times* article written shortly after Fosse's death, Doctorow commented: "The darkest of [Fosse's last three films] is the last because the performer now has no talent beyond beauty and no mind beyond innocence and no will to oppose except passively, a life of humiliation and a degrading death. *Star 80* is a despairing and absolute condemnation of the culture of sex in America that Fosse himself worked out of. It is an amazing transfiguring statement from the lithe little fellow with the choir-boy face who choreographed the 'Steam Heat' number in the musical *Pajama Game*."

BIG DEAL

Embittered by both public and critical reaction to his film, Fosse returned to Broadway the following year and began work on *Big Deal*. Although he was interested in directing a film musical of *Chicago,* with *Star 80*'s failure at the box office he could not find funding for the project, even though performers such as Liza Minnelli and Bette Midler had expressed interest in dong it. For a while he retired to his Long Island country home in Quogue, New York, where he continued to work on the always-in-progress Joffrey ballet in his newly installed dance studio. "It's going slower than I hoped," he told reporter Tom Hinckley. "For some reason, when you get older you start looking at how many cardinals and blue jays are in the feeder and not getting into the studio and sweating it out." Fosse told the *Boston Globe*'s Kevin Kelly two years later that his own insecurities as a jazz-trained dancer continued to thwart progress on the work: "I feel I really haven't fulfilled what I started out to do. I think I should have done more classical dancing. If I had my life to live over again, I would have gone the route of Jerry [Jerome Robbins], would have gone into ballet. . . . God, it's too late, too late now to do that. I can hardly move. I can't even tie my own shoes."

Recovering from the numbing rejection of *Star 80,* Fosse returned to old scripts written for a stage adaptation of *Big Deal on Madonna Street.* In 1967, Fosse had acquired the stage rights to the 1959 Italian crime caper, hoping to follow up his *Sweet Charity* success with another foreign-film–

Valerie Pettiford, Gary Chapman, and Barbara Yeager review the art of safecracking in *Big Deal*'s "Me and My Shadows." *(Martha Swope)*

inspired property. Like *Nights of Cabiria, Big Deal on Madonna Street* was a small film with a grand theme, one of achieving greatness in an ordinary world. If street urchin Cabiria's tragedy was her doomed pursuit of love, the six loveable burglars in Mario Monicelli's film are destined never to realize their fantasy of pulling off a big-time robbery. Although each man is, by turns, pathetic in his aspirations to achieve immortality, Monicelli uses fracturingly funny, Buster Keaton–inspired comic devices to avoid caricaturing them.

In the mid-Sixties, having already tried his hand at writing a libretto for *Sweet Charity,* Fosse continued to develop his own scripts with *Big Deal.* When the original company of *Sweet Charity* opened to favorable reviews, he returned to *Big Deal,* but could not come up with a composer. Periodically, between projects, he reconsidered it. In the mid-Seventies, he attempted to engage Stephen Sondheim to write the score. But Sondheim was busy writing the music for *Follies,* though he expressed interest in the project. While filming *Sweet Charity,* Fosse, expecting the musical to be a hit, attempted to sell *Big Deal* to Universal as his follow-up film musical. By that time, 1969, he had changed the locale from Italy

A bespectacled Fosse goes over *Big Deal* script revisions with Loretta Devine. *(Martha Swope)*

to Tijuana—even scouting locations there—and the Italians became Mexicans. The studio was intrigued until the film version *Sweet Charity* opened to indifferent reactions from critics and moviegoers.

In 1983 Fosse came upon the neglected script by accident while at his home in Quogue, squirreled away in the back of a desk drawer. Now some eighteen years old, the storyline, Fosse felt, would be better serviced by Depression-era Chicago Black than itinerant Mexicans. And instead of the Tijuana Brass sound, so popular in the late Sixties, the music would become Thirties and Forties standards such as Fosse remembered as a child. "Who's Your Little Who-zis?," "I'm Just Wild About Harry," "Happy Days Are Here Again," and "Everybody Loves My Baby" exemplified the genre of songs he wanted—simply constructed and hopeful in sentiment, perfect for big-band orchestrations and, always important, flexible enough to accommodate dance arrangements.

But from the beginning Fosse wanted original music, and sought out Peter Allen to compose a score mirroring the Depression era. Allen, whose song, "Everything Old Is New Again," accompanied Ann Reinking's and Erzsebet Foldi's top-hat-and-cane dance in *All That Jazz,* recalls four meetings with Fosse and producer Stuart Ostrow.

"I had already written two songs for *Big Deal* when the show got postponed. Assuming it would eventually be produced, I wrote two more. Then one day I read in a newspaper column that he had decided to use six songwriters, *including me.* That had never been mentioned in any of our prior meetings. I thought I would be doing the whole score, but Ostrow had neglected to tell me otherwise. I was very upset and pulled out." Instead, Allen began work on his own gangster musical, *Legs Diamond,* which included one song written for *Big Deal,* "Ain't I Somethin'?" Interestingly, when workshops for that show were held in 1986— after *Big Deal* had closed—Fosse attended one and expressed enthusiasm. "He was really wonderful," says Allen. "Fosse was one of the Nederlander Organization's [the producers of *Legs Diamond*] first choices to direct, but we were still raising money at the time. He told us to let him know when we were further along. After the workshop, he offered suggestions of things that could be cut."

After Allen backed out, Fosse abandoned the notion of a collaborative score and instead decided to compile vintage material himself. With orchestrator Ralph Burns he listened to hundreds of songs from the Thirties and Forties, finally selecting twenty-three he believed would best serve his libretto and choreography. Research assistants were hired to track down the songs' far-flung publishers, many of whom were no longer in existence, and negotiate royalties. Like Fosse's last Broadway production eight years before, *Dancin',* which also used pre-existing music, the cost of royalties per song rose to the six-figure range, making it one of the most expensive shows produced for Broadway's 1985–86 season. Although much of the budget was absorbed by Fosse's pyrotechnics ($850 was spent on equipment to enable scenes to "dissolve" and almost $30,000 was spent on a computerized lighting system) and the payroll, using the old music was actually more expensive than commissioning an original score. Budgeted at $4 million, some reports indicated *Big Deal* wound up costing its producers—the Shubert Organization, Roger Berlind, and Jerome Minskoff—nearly $7 million (Bernard Schoenfeld, chairman of the Shubert Organization, quotes $5.4 million).

Valerie Pettiford, a principal dancer and dance captain in the show, recalls that in the spring of 1985 Fosse called her to ask if she'd like to participate in a backer's audition for a new musical he was working on. Pettiford had danced for Fosse in the national tour of *Dancin'*, and jumped at the opportunity to work with him again. "There's something so soulful about his choreography," Pettiford describes, "to-the-earth, as they used to describe Martha Graham's dances. Every little nuance Bob gave you had a meaning. You never wondered, 'Why am I doing this?' " She, Barbara Yeager, and Lester Wilson danced for the backer's audition, and, in November, Fosse began casting.

As in all of Fosse's work, he sought out lead performers who could invest their characters with their own charisma. The predominately black cast was anchored by Cleavant Derricks and Loretta Devine, who had previously co-starred in Michael Bennett's equally cinematic musical *Dreamgirls* (Derricks won a Tony). As the down-on-his-luck boxer Charley, Derricks was modeled after many of Fosse's antiheroes from former projects. "I like scuzzy survivors," he told theater writer and critic Kevin Kelly when the show was in Boston, "guys who take risks, girls with free emotions." Charley ("Charley, My Boy" became his signature song) also personified Fosse's recurrent fascination with boxing. In both *Sweet Charity*'s "Rich Man's Frug" ("The Boxer") and *Dancin'*'s "Under the Double Eagle" the sound of a fight bell propelled his squat, swaggering men into the intricate footwork of pugilists. Frank Mastrocola, who danced for Fosse in *Pippin, Dancin',* and *Big Deal* notes the choreographer's concern with "sharpness, speed, and detail. It was based on his body as he saw it in the mirror—small, wiry, compact, energetic. It was choreography geared to the common man. He was really into athletes, especially fighters, and would talk about guys like Jack Dempsey."

Because Fosse perceived the career of dancers as being not so different from athletes, he adopted an overtly physical approach to problem-solving in his shows. Rehearsing a fight scene in *Big Deal* in which Mastrocola clouts Derricks on the head with a breakaway sugar bottle, Fosse became frustrated when Derricks complained the impact was injuring his head. "Bob really loved Cleavant," Mastrocola recalls, "but he couldn't understand why he didn't like the bottle. One night Bob comes into my dressing room and says, 'Frank, I have another kind of bottle to use that's suppose to be thinner, and I want you to try it on me before you try it on Cleavant.' He hands me the bottle and turns his back to me. He was wearing that silly hat he always wore, and took it off so I was facing the back of his bald head. All I could think of was, here I am, breaking a bottle over Bob Fosse's head. I whacked him with it, and it shattered. 'It's in,' he said, and put his hat back on."

Casting Loretta Devine as Lily, a maid with "free emotions," was, according to Devine, "a perfect coincidence." *Dreamgirls* was coming to an end on Broadway, and Devine put together a club act at New York's Don't Tell Mama cabaret called "I Could Have Been Dorothy Dandridge," hoping to increase her visibility and promote her range as a singer. She had heard Fosse was looking to cast a "Loretta Devine type" in the role, only someone who could also dance, and assumed she had the wrong body type for Lily. On the final night of her "Dorothy Dandridge" act, Fosse passed by Don't Tell Mama, saw that Devine was playing there, and went in. Later, she auditioned for him and got the role. "To the day he died, Fosse said he 'just happened' to be in the neighborhood when he saw me at the club that night," says Devine. "But I wonder."

Others cast in the show represented the best of black Broadway talent, and were drawn from the ranks of *Dreamgirls, The Tap Dance Kid, My One and Only,* and *Mama, I Want to Sing,* including Gary Chapman, Alde Lewis, Jr., Larry Marshall, Mel Johnson, Jr., Alan Weeks, Bernard J. Marsh, and Desiree Coleman. Coleman's charater was named Phoebe, as was Fosse's girlfriend at the time, Phoebe Ungerer. To stitch the various scenes together, Fosse employed the same type of narrative device he'd implemented in *Pippin.* Wayne Cilento, a veteran Fosse dancer, and Bruce Anthony Davis were cast as dual narrators. Enduring yet another career setback (or was it?), dethroned Miss America Vanessa Williams was cast as a third narrator, then written out of the script because it was believed two narrators were enough. The creative staff included set designer Peter Larkin, lighting designer (and executive producer) Jules Fisher, costume designer Patricia Zipprodt, conductor-arranger Gordon Lowry Harrel, orchestrator Ralph Burns, and sound designer Abe Jacob. Merely on the basis of its cast and crew, *Big Deal* was a musical to be reckoned with even before its rehearsals in December 1985.

Over eight hundred dancers were auditioned for the show in four days, which was not unusual for a Fosse musical. The late Phil Friedman, who retired as Fosse's stage manager shortly after *Big Deal* closed, attributed the flood of dancers to the career opportunities working for Fosse brought them. "A Fosse dancer could get other jobs, and often some of them even worked as choreographers, mostly in commercials. He was very good about recommending people, and he had a lot of connections. Dancers realized that being in a Fosse show was an investment in their careers. If he liked you, he helped you as much as he could."

Friedman said the *Big Deal* auditions were "not just cattle calls with a bunch of people on stage. Bobby had a great respect for actors and dancers, nobody was ever sloughed off." By this point in his career, Fosse's auditions were methodically run, beginning with a short, classical ballet routine, usually a combination of jumps or double air turns that dovetailed into a series of soft-shoe steps—a simple routine that separated trained dancers from the rest of the group.

Dance captain Pettiford taught Fosse hopefuls his trademark elbow-wrist-hand adagio, in which an arm begins hanging straight down the body and is gradually pulled up alongside it by the hand and wrist until the arm reaches above the head, fingers extended. (*All That Jazz*'s opening cattle-call segment features Fosse assistant Kathryn Doby demonstrating this combination.) "Bob always used to say he only had ten steps," Pettiford explains, "he just kept evolving them according to the nature of the show. They didn't become stale because of the way they were executed, and the kinds of dancers he chose. Every dance form has a rather small vocabulary. In ballet, for example, you have first position, second position, and so on, in order to get from point A to point B. Bob would take his own steps and build new dances from his technique. Most [Broadway] choreographers don't have their own technique."

Fosse began rehearsing his dancers without a script; rather, he had worked out choreographed scenes prior to rehearsals with assistant choreographer Christopher Chadman and dance arranger Gordon Harrell, and these became the framework of the show. With the principals, the process was different; they had scripts and were working toward character development. "My part's a little confused," Devine told Kevin Kelly in Boston, "but we're getting it." When interviewed for a *Dance Magazine* story on the show while it was previewing in Boston, narrator Wayne Cilento echoed many of the cast members' sentiments that, for all *Big Deal*'s choreographic detail, the script and Fosse's direction begged

Wayne Cilento (left) and Bruce Anthony Davis as the strutting narrators in *Big Deal*. (*Martha Swope*)

clarity. "I love this show," Cilento, a longtime Fosse dancer, emphasized, "but I'm having trouble with my part. I still haven't figured out why the narrators are integral to the show, and that's a fundamental problem when you're examining character motivation. I'm not sure I even *have* a character."

"I think as Bob's career progressed he was less concerned about pleasing others than he was about trusting his own instincts as a director and choreographer," says Frank Mastrocola. "By the time he did *Big Deal*, he was so far advanced beyond most people working in musical theater, except, perhaps, Michael Bennett. So when somebody said, 'Bob, I don't think this works,' unless he thought you really knew more about than he did, it was unlikely Fosse would believe you."

Early signs that the show was in trouble appeared shortly after its February 12, 1986, opening in Boston's Shubert Theatre, where the critics' opinions were mixed. *Variety* concluded its review by projecting, "it's nonstop hard work for everyone for the next six weeks." Although every Fosse musical from *Sweet Charity* through *Dancin'* had had trouble spots out of town, Fosse had listened patiently to producers' and critics' suggestions, rethought entire numbers, edited others completely, and ultimately constructed four-square hits. But on *Big Deal* he was resolute. Pettiford did not notice any dramatic changes in the musical from Boston to Broadway, "and that's exactly what the cast was waiting for . . . when you go out of town, it's expected you'll make a lot of changes. . . . Bob just did patchwork; he'd take out a word here, put in a sentence there."

"We knew we had a difficult show in Boston," says costume designer Patricia Zipprodt of her third Fosse musical. "He wore all the hats; the value of collaboration was not important to him. That made it difficult because everyone felt the show needed a lot of work."

Fosse's usually reliable audience did not turn out in Boston. The Shubert Theatre's 1,617 seats were never completely filled. In its third week, *Big Deal* was playing to only slightly more than half-capacity: the total was $239,280 out of a possible $441,374. The next week's receipts rose only slightly, to $260,374. In its last week, the show brought in just over $293,000, still a far cry from the makings of a box-office blockbuster. Alarmed at the prospects of a major financial catastrophe, Bernard Jacobs, president of the Shubert Organization, Gerald Shoenfeld, its chairman, and Sam Cohn, Fosse's agent, went to Boston to see *Big Deal*.

Their impressions and misgivings were summarized in a six-point letter drafted to Fosse on March 19, 1986. Suggestions included correcting sound problems (muddy in Boston); illuminating the set more (comparisons were made between Jules Fisher's lighting and a Reginald Marsh or Edward Hopper painting); providing more musical underscoring and "buttons," or emphatic closures, on some numbers; replacing the narrators, and adding more Fosse showstoppers. The letter was signed, "With great affection and friendship."

But Fosse resented the Shubert Organization's intervention, and reportedly broke down in tears during a rehearsal with the cast one day after the show had opened. "Rumors began circulating that the producers weren't supportive, that they were giving him a hard time," says Devine. "They wanted more dance numbers. I think Bob spent a lot of time trying to figure out how to make that happen, then just decided he liked it better his way."

"He could be hard as nails when it came to fighting for his material," Friedman recalled. "My theory about *Big Deal* is that he could not wear all those hats and edit himself. If he was the writer and didn't have a producer who was going to say yes or no, and didn't have a composer or lyricist, he had to go back to his hotel room every night and talk to himself. With *Big Deal,* there was nobody who would say no to him, and Bobby always needed someone to tell him no."

Neither would Fosse listen to his chiropractor and general practitioner, who continually advised him to slow down, stop smoking, and refrain from demonstrating dance combinations. By the time Kevin Kelly interviewed him after *Big Deal* had concluded rehearsals and was playing in Boston, he was harnessed into a foam brace for his sciatica. George Abbott, Fosse's first producer and forty years his senior, ran into him while the show was previewing on Broadway. "I was distressed that he was still smoking, and told him he'd better stop," says Abbott. "He just laughed." Shortly thereafter it was rumored that Gwen Verdon had taken over the technical direction of the show when a virus temporarily sidelined Fosse. Meanwhile, she was supervising rehearsals of the *Sweet Charity* revival a few blocks away at the Minskoff Theatre. She would later comment to the *Hamptons Newspaper Magazine* on the intervention of the Shubert Organization: "Bernard Jacobs and Gerald Shoenfeld are really money makers who've decided they're creative. . . . I think they've become seduced by their own sense of power. They're the Bobbsey Twins, or Siamese Twins really, joined at the hip and not the brain— because I don't think they've got a brain."

However vehemently those close to Fosse reacted toward the Shubert Organization, clearly Jacobs's and Shoenfeld's creative guidance was minimal. Their efforts to come to some sort of an agreement with Fosse over the production's overriding bleakness, and to temper his autocracy with outside assistance, were met with blunt enmity. In Boston, neither man was able to spend more than a few minutes with Fosse because, according to Jacobs, "he would go off with Herb Gardner [who, with

Steve Tesich, came in to administer to the book] or Jules Fisher, and we could never talk to him." The prevailing tension came to a head when the show moved to New York's Broadway Theatre, a Shubert house that had just undergone a $9 million refurbishing. To correct ongoing sound problems with the show, Jacobs and Shoenfeld enlisted Phil Ramone—the highly regarded music producer behind recordings by Paul McCartney, Barbra Streisand, Billy Joel, Carly Simon, and others—and sound board operator Steve Kennedy.

"[Fosse] said we had so many sound people there that he hoped we were finally satisfied," recalls Shoenfeld. "I responded that I thought we needed them because he was wearing out the carpet running back and forth between the orchestra pit and the sound console. He said, 'It's too bad the theater's not painted black.' I responded that his appreciation was overwhelming."

"I don't think the rumors are true that the Shubert Organization wasn't behind the show," claims Bert Fink, *Big Deal*'s press representative through Fred Nathan Associates. "They came up with the money for the commercial when it would have been just as easy to close the show. I will say that with this show there was a great suspicion between management and artist. That's a division you frequently have in the theater."

Fosse did follow through with some of the changes the Boston critics and the Shubert Organization suggested. Referring to *Big Deal*'s Boston reception, Fosse told the *New York Times*'s Leslie Bennetts, "I was hurt, but some of the criticism was accurate. In the rush to get things on, you think, 'Well, maybe that will be all right,' when you should have stopped and fixed it. And after they point it out, you go, 'Oh, God, of course!' A lot of things they were right about, and I think I've corrected most of those things. There have been a lot of changes."

In retrospect, this uncharacteristic admission of error hardly reflects *Big Deal*'s actual modifications from Boston to New York. If Fosse was eating humble pie for the *Times,* it was probably because word was already out that the show was in trouble, and, if he must promote it, Fosse would promote it as something different than what had been attacked in Boston. Actually, Fosse had done very little reworking. Though *Big Deal* arrived on Broadway April 10, 1987, with seventeen minutes shorn from its original length, book-related problems remained, the lighting was still pervasively dark, and the much-requested Fosse showstoppers were, with the exception of "Beat Me Daddy Eight to the Bar"—which began with gusty jazz riffs and quickly built into a terpsichorean torando—nowhere to be seen.

Although there is ample evidence available in print and film of critics' reaction to what was *wrong* with *Big Deal,* its all-too-brief Broadway run hastened an erroneous opinion that the show single-handedly plunged the American musical into its grave. Because Fosse had been the great progenitor of the Gower Champion–Jack Cole American dance musical, and because *Big Deal* was his much-heralded return to Broadway after an eight-year absence, expectations were high—perhaps too high—for him to produce another smash. Although Fosse claimed he was impervious to critics, Valerie Pettiford recalls that he felt insecure enough about his work to compare it with Peter Martin's choreography in *Song & Dance,* which had recently opened.

"Once during preproduction, Fosse said to the dancers, 'God, I just came from seeing a show. I think I'm going to have to start doing some tricks. I don't know if my choreography will hold up.' We just looked at him with these you've-got-to-be-kidding expressions on our faces. It struck me that his insecurity about his choreography was mind-boggling. We told him, 'Bob, that's the beauty of your work. You don't need tricks.' "

Unquestionably, *Big Deal* was served best by its choreography. If Fosse was worried that he could not conceive a ballet for Robert Joffrey that would last more than thirteen minutes, he instead choreographed a full-length jazz ballet for Broadway.

Through its shifting prisms of light, Fosse played with dance perspectives. The deceptively simple raked stage and platform designed by Peter Larkin as little more than black scaffolding allowed dancers nearly unencumbered space to move. At the same time, it alluded to the mean streets of Chicago and attendant dens of iniquity, achieving an ominous, other-worldly quality. For example, "Me and My Shadows," featuring a safecracker named Dancin' Dan (Gary Chapman) and his two assistants (Pettiford and Barbara Yeager), rises from the shadows to emerge as three forms slinking ghostlike into mobster immortality. In Pettiford and Yeager, Fosse found two women whose physical forms suggested the qualities of shadows, slithering forward and back in their gray unitards, at times nearly eclipsed by the more ample frame of Dancin' Dan. The women's splayed fingers and forward-thrust hips, along with the costume conceits of Dancin' Dan's spats and cane, evoked not so much flesh-and-blood characters as ancestors from another era—perhaps Fosse's Chicago burlesque.

In "Ain't We Got Fun," a wonderfully deadpan number, a chain gang of convicts crunch through a slow shuffle on sand boards, punctuating the lyrics, "Every mornin'/Every evenin'/Ain't we got . . ." with a shake of their shackles before finishing the verse with ". . . fun." "Now Is the Time for Love," one of the show's more sexually suggestive dances, featured performers on their backs on the floor with legs raised and splayed while behind them other dancers repeated the position standing up. The inversion and convolutions of body parts, a Fosse trademark, was as much a remark on sexual partnerings as it was an exhibit of less-is-more choreography. The number was not technically complex, but its visual impact was startlingly direct. If the book had not intruded, Fosse's dances spoke volumes in themselves. "Bob has, in effect, created an opera," said Gwen Verdon prior to *Big Deal*'s Broadway opening. "I think it's the best thing he's done, and that includes *Sweet Charity*."

The show's one and only showstopper, "Beat Me Daddy Eight to the Bar," satisfied audiences' hunger for a requisite bottom-of-the-first-act roof-raiser. Atop the scaffolding, a big band led by Bernard J. Marsh began the song with a somewhat straightforward arrangement that quickly broke into raucous jazz riffs as the dancers underneath the band picked out Fosse's choreography. The men's dramatic knee drops recalled Jack Cole's flashy nightclub choreography of the Forties and Fifties. The women's undulating hips and turned-in feet were an antithesis to ballet; here, body alignment had been shattered and reconstructed like a cubist painting.

Patricia Zipprodt recalls that because Fosse's choreography is centered low to the ground, costumes had to be especially flexible. "I remember that during *Sweet Charity* rehearsals, the men's trousers, which were made of wool, split not at the seams, but across the buns. It was hysteria time, so we got black spandex and made one pair for everyone just in time for the opening. By the time we got to *Big Deal* we'd learned our lesson painfully. I made pinstripe trousers using stretch fabric, dyed it to match each color suit, and we painted the pinstripes on *by hand*. Bob's the only choreographer I know whose leg and torso work puts this much stress on clothes. People were painting stripes on forever; it was very rigorous work."

When Tony Award nominations were announced May 6, 1986, *Big Deal* placed in five categories, including best musical, best book, best direction, best choreography, and best actor in a musical (Cleavant Derricks). It was a respectable share for a show blasted by most critics when it opened—echoing the Boston critics, New York reviewers had attacked the truncated musical arrangements, the terminally dark lighting, the scarcity of Fosse's showstopping choreography, and, especially,

Loretta Devine and Cleavant Derricks as Depression-era lovers in Fosse's 1986 *Big Deal*. (*Martha Swope*)

Fosse's book. Best summarizing the Broadway theater critics' consensus was Frank Rich's *New York Times* review: "[With 'Beat Me Daddy Eight to the Bar'] Mr. Fosse makes an audience remember what is (and has been) missing from virtually every other musical in town. . . . The dizzying sense of levitation that Mr. Fosse achieves in this dance is one of those unquantifiable elements . . . that defined the Broadway musical when it was a going concern. The disappointment of *Big Deal* is that even Mr. Fosse, one of the form's last great magicians, can conjure up that joy so rarely. . . . Given that Mr. Fosse had staged some of Broadway's funniest musicals . . . it's hard to understand how the book of *Big Deal* grew to be so ponderous and cheerless."

Not surprisingly, when the Tony Awards were presented June 1, 1986, Fosse was, in effect, shut out by his revival of *Sweet Charity,* which clinched the award for outstanding reproduction of a musical and three others, while *Big Deal* took home only one, for best choreography. The next day, the producers announced the show would close. "We thought the Tony would keep the show open till summer," says Devine. "It was really hard to believe we were closing. People were crying, it all seemed like such a waste. So much work had been put into this show. We knew it had problems, but the bottom line was that everyone believed in it, believed in Fosse. I mean, how could a Bob Fosse musical close so soon?" His last show, *Dancin',* had run a record-breaking 1,774 productions; *Big Deal* gasped its last breath after a mere 70.

"You can understand that Fosse thought this was his complete signature work," says the Shubert Organization's Gerald Shoenfeld. "No writers, lyricists, or composers to contend with, everything was his except the light, costumes, and scenic design. I cannot think of any situation where there was less intrusion, fewer meetings, fewer discussions, never saying no."

Publicist Bert Fink recalls seeing Fosse backstage after the final performance, as the set was being struck around him. "I had gone backstage to say good-bye to the cast. I'd heard Fosse wasn't going to show up because he was over at the Minskoff rehearsing *Sweet Charity*. But as I'm walking across the stage I see him standing right there talking to the crew. All around him guys were beginning to dismantle the set. It was just one of those moments that leaves a vivid impression with you forever—this Broadway genius standing amidst his last show. I wanted to say something to him, but I just couldn't. I was part of the management anyway, so I'm sure nothing I could've said would have persuaded him that I felt terrible too."

A few weeks later, Fosse threw a party for the cast at his summer home in Quogue, New York. Most of the performers attended, and both Valerie Pettiford and Frank Mastrocola observed that Fosse's mood during the evening shifted from fun-loving to despondent.

"God, did we have fun!" Pettiford recalls. "He had such a spread laid out for us. A little boat took us out on the lake, we played volleyball and pool—it was just this orgy of eating, drinking, singing, and dancing. He had built a new dance studio, and it had all the pictures of the show from the outside of the [Broadway Theatre]. . . . Fosse seemed fine. He was having a great time playing games. Then, about an hour or two after dinner, we all got very sentimental and cried, Bob included. By the end of it, he was really depressed."

Big Deal also marked the end of Phil Friedman's career, whose employment as stage manager of Fosse's shows began nearly thirty years before with *The Conquering Hero*. "It was a bittersweet night," Friedman recalled shortly before his death in 1988. "It affected me a little bit more than most because my career was ended; I ended it by retiring. And there were all these people I had worked with all my life at this party, having a wonderful time. We were all visiting—you know how show folks are when you haven't seen each other for a long time. You pick up the friendship as if it were yesterday." As he recalled the cast from the show, his voice caught, and he said haltingly. "Well, that happened at this party, and it crossed my mind a number of times that this might be the last time. . . . Now I'm no longer a part of the theater, and my extended family no longer exists. But they were all there that night."

"When I saw [Fosse] again," Pettiford says, "he was rehearsing a new project he was very secretive about. Barbara Yeager and I were auditioning for *West Side Story* that spring, and we saw his name on the roster at the Minskoff studios. We thought, 'Hmmm, Bob's back in the studio again. Wonder what he's doing?' So the next day we visited him, and he loved it. We had the best time, and later met him over at Charlies [a popular Broadway restaurant]. We sat and talked and reminisced. He told us stories about *Star 80*; he always had the best stories to tell. We kind of eased into talking about *Big Deal*. It was obvious none of us had ever gotten over it. If I remember correctly, he said he wished he could have done more for the cast—especially the principals. He wished he could have put them on the level of Gwen or Ann Reinking or Ben Vereen. . . . He told us he'd been asked to do *Dancin' Too,* and that he'd also been asked to direct *Big Deal* in London, and was considering it. Then Barbara and I looked at him and said, 'Bob, to hell with all this Broadway stuff. Let's go make a film.' He just laughed and said, 'Yeah, that'd be a great idea.' "

Fosse's easy rapport with his dancers leaves one to ponder the possibilities of *Dancin' Too,* *Dancin's* proposed sequel. Although the Shubert Organization had also heard Fosse was at work on it, neither Jacobs nor Shoenfeld believed he would have approached them about financing it after the *Big Deal* debacle. He was much more viable to produce as a choreographer and director than as a writer, however, and with the astounding success of *Dancin',* it seems likely Fosse would have found no trouble securing a producer, despite *Big Deal's* multimillion-dollar loss. As to whether that show would have worked in London, it's likely Fosse would have taken the risk because he believed so steadfastly in it, and would have relished the opportunity to have the last word on the Boston and New York critics.

Big Deal's New York production was a fascinating failure. The few pirated videotapes that exist of the production reveal the work of a bolder Bob Fosse, reconciling old Chicago vaudevillian and burlesque theater forms while bringing post–*Sweet Charity* musicals up to date with choreography that was so integrated into the show's structure, many people failed to notice it. Despite the promise of a new Fosse musical, Fosse film producer Wolfgang Glattes believes he was due to return to the screen with *Chicago.* Fosse had had preliminary discussions with Madonna, though he denied that they were business-oriented.

"Madonna called me out of the blue and said she'd like to meet me," Fosse told a *Hollywood Reporter* reporter, when spotted having lunch with the singer-dancer-actress at the Westbury Hotel. "Who am I to turn down Madonna? So we met and talked, and I found her charming." According to Liz Rosenberg, Madonna's publicist, she and Fosse met to discuss the film version of *Chicago,* in which she would play Roxie Hart. "She wishes she would have had the opportunity to have worked with him," Rosenberg states.

No matter what particular project Fosse would have done next, it seems unlikely he would have embarked on anything as downbeat as *Star 80* or as gloomy as *Big Deal.* Though Fosse had exorcised his own demons in these projects, he was always a showman. If he became acclimated to the typewriter, it was nonetheless a different affinity from that which he shared with the derby and cane. What *is* apparent is that Fosse would not have abandoned show business for an early retirement. His need for self-expression was too great to be muffled by even the most vociferous skeptics of his work. As he posited to Kevin Kelly during *Big Deal's* rehearsals: "I'm fighting indifference, cynicism. My own indifference. My own cynicism. And what's out there that's indifferent and cynical. That's always been a battle for me. At a certain point I feel, 'I really don't like what's around, so I'll go out and show 'em.' Then I think, 'They'll chop off my head, so why should I?' And I think, 'I know who and what I am. Why do I have to go out there and have them say either the terrible things or the good things? Why?' "

Despite *Big Deal*'s disappointment, Bob Fosse's career did not end anticlimatically. In early 1984 plans commenced to mount a revival of *Sweet Charity*. It would prove to be the definitive production of the show, garnering praise from critics and audiences alike. The film's cult status gave way to a renewed appreciation of Fosse's considerable achievements with the stage musical.

Joseph Harris, one the show's original producers (he had also helped produce Fosse's 1975 Broadway musical *Chicago*), had approached Fosse about the idea, but he was involved with *Big Deal,* and did not believe he could direct two shows at the same time. Also, because the original choreography for *Sweet Charity* had not been notated clearly—an assistant who had taken notes on the dances in 1966 could not figure them out for the 1986 production—all the dances would have to be reconstructed from memory, by using raw footage taped from a Japanese tour of the show, and from the Universal film. It was a Herculean endeavor, especially when Fosse was not nearly as concerned with reviving his old choreography as presenting new material. Verdon helped persuade him to agree to the revival, however, and eventually he participated as production supervisor.

While Fosse began rehearsals for *Big Deal,* Verdon called every dancer still ambulatory who was in the original company to help her reconstruct the dances. She, Chris Chadman, and Mimi Quillin (two of Fosse's favorite dancers) worked out rough approximations of the original numbers, notating them for rehearsals in Los Angeles, where many of the dancers had already assembled. John Bowab was credited as the revival's director, though many of the dancers recall that Verdon seemed at the helm. Fosse was especially concerned about the show's star, and voiced reservations about the producers' choice, Debbie Allen, whose credits included Anita in the Broadway revival of *West Side Story* and television's *Fame* (a featured role, choreographer, director, and producer).

Allen's personality and dance "attack" resemble Chita Rivera's—powerful, self-confident, muscular—qualities seemingly at odds with Charity's vulnerability. But arguably, her ethnicity—Allen is black—added yet another dimension to the character, one never directly addressed in the revival; and, of greater importance, Allen's name was recognized by millions of faithful *Fame* viewers, insuring large box-office grosses. Fosse flew to California to meet her, where she read for him and they worked on a couple of numbers. She impressed Fosse as an intuitive, well-schooled dancer, but on the other hand, she gave the role a feisty street-toughness. Former Charity Shirley MacLaine recalls seeing Fosse as he was going into the West Coast rehearsals of the show. "I asked how things were going, and he said [referring to Allen], 'I'm working with a powerhouse. How can I teach her vulnerability?' "

Once Fosse was satisfied that Allen was the right choice to play Charity, he returned to New York and *Big Deal*. He did not fly back to Los Angeles until rehearsals for *Sweet Charity* began in late spring 1985. Dana Moore recalls how drastically the choreography and direction changed upon his arrival.

"It was an amazing time," Moore says. "He was only there four and a half days, but he never stopped working. He would give the cast five-minute breaks, but he never took one. Gwen and Chris [Chadman] had sketched everything out, and when Bob came out we presented it to him. I remember he looked very depressed, smoked, hung his head down, and mumbled under his breath. During a break he talked to Gwen. The next thing I knew we were starting back at the beginning of the show. He reworked everything one moment at a time. He would explain things to us, define details in a combination. As soon as he started working on it, it all came together; you understood it.

"I don't want to slight Gwen, because she is a genius in her own right, but when Bob came in he cleaned everything up. He got us involved emotionally *and* physically."

The four and a half days Fosse spent working on the show reignited his interest in it; by the time the show opened on the West Coast in the fall of 1985, with Bowab listed as director, it was clear Fosse's input had brought *Sweet Charity* back to the stage from near-obscurity. When the show finally arrived on Broadway in 1986, Fosse was fully credited as director and choreographer.

Although Verdon and Fosse formally separated in 1971, they continued to remain friends throughout Fosse's relationships with Ann Reinking, Jessica Lange, Julie Hagerty, Phoebe Ungerer, and others. Reinking even assumed Verdon's role in *Chicago* and, in the revival of *Sweet Charity,* replaced Allen. The creative alliance between them survived the degeneration of their marriage, with Verdon functioning as his assistant in *Dancin'*

and *All That Jazz*. But during the rehearsals for *Sweet Charity* in Los Angeles, they appeared to rekindle an emotional, if not sexual, fire that contributed to the show's esprit de corps; the loving, committed atmosphere in which the efforts of two mature artists revived their biggest hit inspired their performers to strive for the standards of Fosse-Verdon excellence.

"Their relationship was such a mystery to me," says Moore. "It was loving, unselfish, and truthful. If they would allow their outside lives to interfere, [their relationship] would probably have been a mess, but when they were working with each other, they didn't deal with themselves as a romantic couple, except on a creative level. . . . People would say, 'Oh, she just kisses the ground he walks on. It's so embarrassing.' I never really saw that. I always thought he gave her as much back; he kissed the ground *she* walked on.' "

Donna McKechnie, who had danced for Fosse in *How to Succeed in Business Without Really Trying* on Broadway and portrayed Charity in the revival's national tour, comments on the Verdon-Fosse collaboration, "I was always really impressed by their marriage. I remembered them working together in *How to Succeed . . .* and envying their collaboration. Twenty-five years later, when I played Charity in the national tour of the Broadway revival, you could see that that joy of creating was still there. As a woman, I related very emotionally to Gwen [McKechnie had been married to and divorced from Michael Bennett and, with him, created the Tony Award–winning role of Cassie in *A Chorus Line*]. She would tell me things about Charity, and tears would come to her eyes. I got through the first act one day during rehearsals, and I was so relieved that I'd done it without falling down that, spontaneously, I hugged her and said, 'Oh, thank you, Gwen.' She got very emotional, and I realized how hard doing this show again must be for her."

Sweet Charity was a hit all over again when it opened in Los Angeles and San Francisco, playing to packed houses and garnering rave reviews. The cast, especially Allen, Bebe Neuwirth, Alison Williams, and Michael Rupert, received outstanding notices. The show had a long hiatus before arriving in New York, since Fosse was unable to supervise rehearsals while working on *Big Deal*. It finally opened on Broadway in April 1986 on the heels of *Big Deal*'s scathing reviews. And though the New York critics, led by Frank Rich's guardedly enthusiastic *New York Times* review of *Sweet Charity,* echoed the sentiments of their West Coast colleagues, their accolades were of little solace to Fosse.

"Bob had quit drinking and smoking for *Big Deal*," says Moore, "but after *Big Deal* he started smoking again. [The critics' reactions to it] knocked all the wind out of his sails. He had a bad cold and wore two sweaters. I was glad he had *Sweet Charity* to keep him occupied. He came into our rehearsals the day after the *Big Deal* reviews came out and worked us all the way through. He sort of jokingly dismissed the reviews for *Big Deal* by saying, 'Well, wasn't that fun?' Nobody, of course, brought it up. The issue was never directly addressed. Instead, Bob just threw himself into the rehearsal feverishly. It was definitely one of the best ones we'd had. We worked around the clock; there were no breaks that day.''

Unfortunately, the early promises of a smash run for the show went unfulfilled after Allen left *Sweet Charity* when her six-month contract expired in October 1986. Although the musical won three Tonys—best revival, best supporting actress in a musical (Bebe Neuwirth), and costume design (Patricia Zipprodt)—it spent the remainder of the run in Broadway's cavernous Minskoff Theater playing to less-than-capacity houses. The box-office lull could be attributed, in part, to casting Ann Reinking as Allen's replacement. While Reinking is, next to Verdon,

On the first day of *Sweet Charity*'s Broadway rehearsal, the creative staff meet for a press conference. From left, Gwen Verdon, composer Cy Coleman, male lead Michael Rupert, new Charity Debbie Allen, and Bob Fosse. *(AP/Wide World Photo)*

Fosse's greatest Pygmalion success, her interpretation of the role was lackluster. As a dancer, she was arguably the finest technician to succeed Verdon, because Reinking's ballet background, Fosse's jazz technique, and her projected vulnerability onstage made her especially well-suited for the requirements of the part. But vocally Reinking was inferior to both Verdon and Allen (whose voice was her best asset), and, as an actress, she was never a convincing Harlequin. In her short bleached-blonde wig with a tarty red bow and tight black dress, Reinking looked like a Fredericks of Hollywood mannequin. Her stint was overshadowed by disagreements among management, which refused to change the souvenir program featuring photos of Allen as Charity. The most publicity Reinking received in the role was when a stagehand used hydrogen peroxide to rinse out a beer bottle prop Charity uses in the closet scene, and forgot to empty it. When Reinking took a swig of the "beer," the peroxide ulcerated the inside of her mouth and she ran off the stage. Despite rumors of sabotage, the incident was labeled an accident, and Reinking returned to the stage after a lengthy intermission.

Producers hoped to recoup their losses from the Broadway production by mounting a national tour with a Charity of equal star-power as Allen. Donna McKechnie was in New York reprising her role of Cassie in *A Chorus Line,* and Fosse went to see her two or three times a week. Despite tension between Michael Bennett and Bob Fosse dating back to *A Chorus Line*'s Tony triumph over *Chicago* in 1975, McKechnie believed Fosse was eager to put the past behind him. He called her after seeing her performance "comeback" as Cassie in 1986 and complimented her on the role, but did not mention casting her as Charity. She was convinced he wasn't interested and called her agent at William Morris to tell him she didn't think Fosse wanted her for the tour. But McKechnie was informed that Fosse already had called William Morris to negotiate her contract. She would be his next—and last—Charity.

Although the show was to have a lengthy tour, box-office receipts in Toronto were less than expected, and when *Sweet Charity* moved on to Washington, D.C., advance ticket sales were discouraging. Opening night in October 1986, Fosse spoke to his cast about the possibility that the show might fold.

" 'It's not your job to be producer,' " McKechnie remembers Fosse told the company that day. " 'Your job is to be up on stage doing your work. Keep worrying about getting better, not just on stage, but in your lives. Be happy and strive to be better people. Save your money.' Who talks like this? It was so touching and fatherly. 'What more can I do?' Bobby said, 'I can't get out on the street and sell tickets!' " The national company toured only three months, and *Sweet Charity*'s revival never

recouped its investment despite strong box-office sales during Allen's run.

McKechnie had been interviewed by a reporter earlier that week about the differences between working with Michael Bennett and Fosse. When she got a copy of the article the day of *Charity*'s opening, her comments had been misconstrued, implying that she was critical of Fosse's work. Feeling terrible about the piece, she approached Fosse half an hour before curtain time.

"I blurted the whole thing to him," says McKechnie, "about how guilty I felt that this reporter had stated things about him that were not from my point of view. I was almost in tears about it. Bob just looked at me and said, 'Well, then, I won't read it,' and put his arms around me in the alcove by the orchestra. It was a rare, warm personal hug. See, Fosse didn't like to be touched. He was protective that way. It was not easy for him to be affectionate with people he didn't know well. Then, he squeezed my arm and said, 'Good luck tonight, Donna,' and left. It made me feel really good."

While McKechnie went back to her dressing room, Fosse approached the orchestra pit, where assistant dance captain Chet Walker was consulting with the conductor about last-minute arrangement changes. It was unusual for Fosse to speak directly to the conductor, but after he was satisfied his suggestions were understood, he walked up the aisle and out

Dana Moore (center) demonstrates the Fosse style's turned-in wrists and knocked knees in "The Aloof" from *Sweet Charity*'s "Rich Man's Frug." (*Jack Mitchell*)

of the theater. Verdon, who was waiting for him, watched him leave, sensing something was wrong. "Wait for me, I'm coming with you," she reportedly called to him, but he kept walking until he was outside. A few minutes later, in front of the hotel lobby next door to the theater, Fosse, with Verdon at his side, suffered a massive heart attack.

"When I came offstage," says McKechnie of her opening night performance, "I had mixed feelings about how I had done. I walked into my dressing room and Cy Coleman and Joe Harris were there. I thought, 'Oh, shit, we're closing.' Joe said, 'I have some bad news for you,' and I said, 'I know,' thinking he meant the show was closing. He said, 'You do? How could you?' I told him I'd kind of seen it coming, and he had this grief-stricken look on his face. He said, 'Donna, Bob's dead.'

"I had no idea who he meant. I said, 'Bob who? Bob Hope?' And then I knew he meant *Bobby*!" McKechnie's voice breaks and she begins to cry. "I looked at Cy. I couldn't believe it. My mind flashed back on Bob's vitality and that little hug he'd given me. It was like he'd been trying to get it all in before he died. It was as if he *knew* he was going to die.

"After Joe and Cy told me the facts, I asked how Gwen was. Cy said, 'She's at the hotel, but she wanted us to be here with you when you got offstage.' It's amazing to me that she would think of me at that moment. It was important to her that they were in my dressing room when I came backstage. I told them to please go back and take care of her."

Some months later, McKechnie suffered the losses of both Bennett (to AIDS) and her father. At a memorial service for Bennett in New York, she eulogized him, but also mourned the passing of an era of musical theater on Broadway. After the service, the *Chorus Line* alumni decided to meet at Columbus Restaurant on the Upper West Side "to have our own little party for Michael." McKechnie was en route to the restaurant when, walking around the corner of Sixty-ninth Street and Columbus Avenue, Gwen Verdon appeared.

"I realized the last time I'd seen her was the night Bobby died," McKechnie says. "She hadn't wanted anyone to call her; I think she needed to be alone for a while. We fell into each others arms and I started weeping. It was like everything that had been building up inside me from so many people who were close to me dying just surfaced. Gwen was working to keep herself together, too, and I said, 'Gwen, how are you? We're so worried about you. Are you okay?' She said, 'Just barely.' It was obvious she didn't really want to talk about it out there on the street. She was very upset. 'He lives inside you,' she said. I told her, 'Yes, I know.' It was like a Pinter exchange. Then she disappeared."

CURTAIN CALLS

After you've gone
And left me cryin'
After you've gone
There's no denyin'
You'll feel blue
You'll feel sad
You'll miss the bestest pal you ever had

> —"*After You've Gone*"
> by Creamer and Layton

On Wednesday, September 23, 1987, twenty-three minutes after the curtain went up on the Washington, D.C. premiere of his *Sweet Charity* revival, Fosse lay dead of a massive heart attack at George Washington University Hospital. Following a brief viewing of the body at a Washington, D.C., funeral home, his remains were disposed of, as he had requested, at the Trinity Crematory in New York City.

At his death, Bob Fosse was worth an estimated $3,745,000, a figure that hardly reflects his contributions as an artist. The Fosse will, however, is an intriguing summation of his life. Its contents reflect his show business philosophy and his fondness for and dedication to the performers, writers, friends, and family who were so much a part of his career.

Fosse had made preparations long before his passing to ensure that there would be no mournful tidings. In his will he bequeathed $25,000, or $378.79 a piece, to sixty-six friends saying: "I have made this provision so that when my friends receive this bequest they will go out and have dinner on me. They all have at one time or another been very kind to me. I thank them."

"He always used to say, 'I'll buy you dinner,' " says Ben Vereen, "and he finally did."

Included in the sixty-six were many dancers, actors, writers, and

Gwen Verdon with estranged husband Fosse and their daughter, Nicole, at the *Dancin'* Tavern on the Green party. *(AP/Wide World Photo)*

"techies" who had worked with Fosse, such as Kandy Brown, Chris Chadman, Cy Coleman, Cleavant Derricks, Loretta Devine, Kathryn Doby, E. L. Doctorow, Vicki Fredericks, Phil Friedman, Dustin Hoffman, Jessica Lange, Janet Leigh, Liza Minnelli, Leland Palmer, Ann Reinking, John Rubenstein, Roy Scheider, Neil Simon, Ben Vereen, and Tony Walton. Other noteworthy names to appear were composer Ralph Burns, entertainment reporters Chris Chase and Gene Shalit, director-choreographers Stanley Donen and Jerome Robbins, and actors Ben Gazzara, Melanie Griffith, and Buddy Hackett. The ex-girlfriends included, in addition to Reinking and Lange, Liz Canney and Julie Hagerty. His companion for the past several years, twenty-six-year-old Phoebe Ungerer, received a bequest of $7,500.

Sam Cohn, the legendary International Creative Management agent who represented Fosse throughout the latter half of his career, was given the "right, title, and interest in and to" Fosse's Long Island restaurant, the Laundry, which he acquired in the early 1980s. His sister and only living relative, Marianne Dimos, received $20,000. Organizations he supported for many years, the Heart Fund and the Postgraduate Center for Mental Health, were each bequeathed $15,000. Indicative of how much Fosse valued loyalty and friendship were his distributions of $15,000 each to his long-time assistant Cathy Nicolas and his good friend and colleague Herb Gardner. Despite matrimonial disputes, Fosse remained close to his first wife, Mary Ann Niles, and left her $15,000 as well. Coincidentally, she died a few days after Fosse.

Trustees of the Fosse estate, Gwen Verdon and Nicole Fosse, shared the remainder of his net worth, valued at $1 million.

The Fosse legacy will continue through a $100,000 "Bob Fosse Theatre Scholarship." In his will, Fosse instructed that the money was to be "used exclusively to provide financial assistance to deserving individuals for the education and training in the theatrical arts." Fosse the philanthropist never gave up hope that the American musical theater would be revitalized by the thousands of aspiring young people who each year cast their bids at showbiz immortality.

Sadly, it is Fosse's own contributions as a director and choreographer for the stage that have gone unrecorded. Although video cassettes exist of all of his film work from *Kiss Me Kate*'s "From This Moment On" to *Star 80,* none of his Broadway shows was filmed, with the exception of an inferior-grade Showtime cable television presentation of *Pippin.* Even the New York Public Library at Lincoln Center's Theatre on Film and Tape Project—which, since 1970, has attempted to videotape Broadway shows—has nothing available of Fosse's Broadway musicals. Dance, one of the most ephemeral of the arts, proved especially so for the man who most popularized it on the Broadway stage.

The videocassette of *Pippin,* however flawed, is an essential inclusion in the Fosse library of his filmed dances. It was not supervised by Fosse; Kathryn Doby, his long-time assistant, who was in *Pippin's* original company, directed and choreographed the 1983 Showtime special at the Hamilton Place Theatre in Ontario, Canada. At the time the television deal was made, Fosse was working on another project, and trusted Doby to re-create his work. She sent him videotapes of rehearsals for his inspection and suggestions, and during the last week of rehearsals, Fosse went up to Canada and tightened the show. But according to the *Pippin* contract for the television production, its producer, David Sheehan, had artistic control of the final cut; not Fosse.

The controversy stemmed from twenty-three missing minutes of the show that were edited in order to keep it at the maximum running length for the cable presentation: an hour and fifty-two minutes. According to Doby, "[Sheehan's] ego was telling him that he was going to show Fosse how to edit a film." Editing disagreements were coupled with technical ineptitude; after editing one number, Doby discovered later that some of Sheehan's staff had taped over it. "Hours of footage that was all edited—ruined," Doby sighs. "It was outrageous, awful. After a while, both Bob and I gave up." Frank Mastrocola, one of the Players in the Showtime presentation, says Fosse sent the cast members letters apologizing for the final cut. "In the letter he wrote us," says Mastrocola, "he stated he was under the assumption he was going to have the final say in the film before it was released. As it turned out, he didn't. He was very upset and tried to stop the release. When he couldn't do it, he sent the letter, which at least let us know this *Pippin* was not his approved version." Surprisingly, *Pippin* shorn of nearly half an hour still holds up well, despite its choppiness.

Fosse's creative output is best seen through those who are his torch

Fosse in 1975 (*Photofest*)

bearers. Today, these people are legion, and include virtually everyone who ever worked for him in Hollywood or on Broadway. Leland Palmer, who retired from show business after her performance in *All That Jazz,* found a loss in her own life with Fosse's passing. "I had given it up," she says. "Bob was the first and last person I ever worked for professionally. My choice to give up my career was tied to the reality of *All That Jazz.* I made a positive, wonderful working relationship with this person. Now it was part of my past, and his life was over."

"You pass on what you learn from them," says Donna McKechnie, whose own career includes shows by Fosse, Michael Bennett, Abe Burrows, George Abbott, and Frank Loesser. Like Fosse protégés Gwen Verdon, Ann Reinking, Chris Chadman, and Wayne Cilento, McKechnie teaches classes to students interested in discovering the Fosse technique. But without hard taskmasters such as Bennett and Fosse, she notes, "the caliber of dancing on Broadway has fallen considerably."

Former Fosse assistants Gene Foote and John Sharpe have mounted successful productions of Fosse shows across the country and around the world. Sharpe believes the era of the director-choreographer, represented by Fosse and Bennett, has come to an end—at least for the time being— with the advent of the European "popera." "There's very little call for someone to serve that position," Sharpe believes. "The English Broadway shows are closer to opera, like [Frank] Loesser's *Most Happy Fella.* There is a renaissance in music and lyrics; the approach to musicals today is less physical. You don't find people writing things like *Sweet Charity* and *Li'l Abner* anymore. Therefore, director-choreographers don't have much challenge, except to create their own work."

Some, in fact, have done just that. One of the best examples of Fosse protégés is Graciela Daniele, whose 1987 theater-dance work *Tango Aspasionado* owed a considerable debt to Fosse's slithering, sinister chore-ography. Daniele continues to mount inspired dances that range from Broadway revivals (*Zorba*) to film (*The Pirates of Penzance, Naked Tango*) and concert stage dance (American Ballroom Theatre). If her "style" per se is not a facsimile of Fosse's (or Michael Bennett's, whom she assisted), he no doubt would have admired her ability to choreograph so many different styles of dance; his own range was admittedly limited.

For many who worked with Fosse during his peak years in the Seventies, their recollections of him are equated with the prevailing belief among many of its director-choreographers at the time that dancers had to work beyond their physical capacity to turn in exemplary work. For some, like Ben Vereen and Ann Reinking, the results were career advance-ments. Others, like Sandahl Bergman, were forced to reassess their performing careers after years working for driven directors Michael Bennett and Fosse had led to premature burnout.

"For me, success is equated with pain during the Seventies," says Bergman reflectively. "You had to suffer to be good. My work ethic at the time was, If it didn't hurt, you weren't doing it right. Michael and Bobby were so obsessed, and they created that obsession in their dancers. It became a sickness. The over and over and over relentlessness of the rehearsals were, in many ways, destructive to us. In those days, there was no margin for error; 100 percent not enough." For Bennett and Fosse, she believes, "that's where the drugs and drinking came in. You can't treat the body like a machine."

Unquestionably, both Fosse's and Bennett's reliance on stimulants was partly responsible for their work habits and periods of severe emotional instability. Fosse's deep-seated insecurities forced him to work harder and explore in depth long-held opinions on mortality and sex. The result was increasingly introspective work and, predictably, gravitation toward those people most associated with ideas and concepts: writers.

At his memorial on October 30, 1987, at Broadway's Palace Theatre, many of Fosse's writer friends in attendance spoke fondly of his attempts to bring them into his rarefied world of dance. At Fosse's home in Long Island, he began, at the suggestion of E. L. Doctorow, a class called Dancing for Writers, which eventually included in its membership Doctorow, Herb Gardner, Peter Maas, Pete Hamill, Paddy Chayefsky, and Fosse's agent Sam Cohn.

"After Fosse started writing movies," recalled Doctorow, "I told him I was going to take up tap dancing. Looking me over he agreed it was a splendid idea. I asked him if he would design a course of instruction called Dancing for Writers. He said he would. On my next birthday he

Fosse and Bette Midler attend the 1973 *After Dark* Ruby Awards. Fosse wanted Midler to co-star with Liza Minnelli in a never-made film version of his 1975 Broadway musical *Chicago. (Ron Galella)*

presented me with a pair of Capezios with taps, white gloves, a white scarf, and enameled walking stick and a sweatshirt that said 'Broadway.' At this point I realized that I would have to practice."

One autumn, at a surprise birthday party for Fosse at his studio in Quogue, the writers greeted him positioned in costume at the barre. "Now you'd figure that spotting, say, Sam Cohn in a tutu would trigger a surefire guffaw," Peter Maas said at the memorial. "But when Fosse saw us, his eyes teared up. 'Gee,' he said, 'this is really sweet of you.' "

Although he did not always succeed in his own efforts as a writer, clearly Fosse was stimulated by those who put their thoughts to paper. Among the nondance projects he, at one time or another, considered filming was Herb Gardner's play *The Goodbye People* and E. L. Doctorow's best-selling novel *Loon Lake*. If it would have materialized, the film version of *Chicago* no doubt would have been written (or co-written) by Fosse. At his death, he also had been asked to direct one of the three segments in the film *New York Stories,* which, when it was released in early 1989, included stories directed by Martin Scorsese, Woody Allen, and Francis Ford Coppola.

Dancer-turned-writer Shirley MacLaine shares Fosse's affinity for nonverbal communication. "I saw him working his way up from seed to thoughts," she says. "As a dancer, you think with your feet and go all the way up. In the process, you end up wanting to express yourself with thought instead of movement. He wanted to be an intellect, and all the guys he hung out with wanted to hoof."

MacLaine also believes that, along with his writing, Fosse was working toward reconciling the masculine and feminine sides of his personality, which, in his stage work, became exercises in sexually suggestive choreography. "What he was trying to do," she says, "is figure out his own feminine energy. This came from his burlesque orientation—how to tease and postpone pleasure from a feminine perspective. He was an expert at the ménage à trois psyche. What did it mean? It was always two women and a man."

The closest Fosse ever gets to providing an answer is in a brief but telling fantasy scene in *All That Jazz*. Confessing his sex life to angel of death Jessica Lange, Fosse alter ego Joe Gideon recalls living briefly—and blissfully—with two women. But one day, Gideon says, he came home to find a letter from one of them stating she had left the arrangement because "I cannot bear to share you with anyone else." Observing him knowingly, Lange's character asks, "How do you know the letter was to you?"

The suggestion that the *idea* of the ménage à trois is of greater sexual appeal than its *reality* may be found in *Cabaret* and *Lenny,* too. The physical attraction between Max and Brian can be expressed only through their mutual infatuation with Sally. But when the three finally have an opportunity to have sex together (illustrated in the film through a slow dance in which Sally, Max, and Brian sway with their arms draped around each others' shoulders), the friendships, made carnal, quickly disintegrate. In *Lenny,* Honey Bruce is pressured by husband Lenny to enliven their sex life by taking on another woman in bed as he watches. But the encounter only confuses Honey in her own tormented bisexuality, and ultimately leads to Lenny rejecting her as a lesbian.

Between admittedly self-referential projects that revealed his interest in directing, choreographing, writing, sex, and death, Fosse sporadically found time to perform. Although he claimed a 1963 revival of *Pal Joey* was his stage farewell, Fosse was lured back to the limelight for Stanley Donen's 1974 film musical adaptation of the popular French children's fable, *The Little Prince.* The film, about a pilot grounded in the desert and his adventures with an intergalactic child, boasted a score by Freder-

Fosse played the Snake in Stanley Donen's failed 1974 movie musical adaptation of *The Little Prince. (Courtesy Paramount Pictures Corporation. Copyright © 1974 by Stanley Donen Films, Inc.)*

ick Loewe and Alan Jay Lerner and Fosse's choreography. Donen, who brought Fosse to Hollywood in the early Fifties, also wanted him to play the role of the Snake, but, at forty-five, Fosse believed he was too old, and recommended other candidates. Finally, he consented; his sinuous dance cameo became the film's highlight.

"I was starting to feel fat and rich, and I thought I'd better get in a studio and take off five pounds and find out how an actor feels," Fosse admitted to the *Los Angeles Times* in 1975. "It had been a long time since I'd faced what it was like to be in front of a camera, or on the stage." *The Little Prince* was not a hit, but Fosse grudgingly admitted he enjoyed watching his dance, which featured him in his requisite tight black pants, black ruffled tuxedo shirt, black leather gloves, and cigarette dangling. Whether he's wriggling across the craggy limb of a sun-bleached tree or shuffling along in a sand dance across the desert floor, the Snake is as seductive a serpent as the reptile that tempted Eve. Though he had another, nondance, cameo as a drug addict in 1977's *Thieves*, *The Little Prince* is his definitive film performance as a mature dancer.

As a director, however, his pièce de résistance was his own memorial in 1987. Fosse did not believe in wasting funerals on the dead. If *All That Jazz* forecast with alarming accuracy Fosse's premature death, his real grand finale was a memorial service and party, with its director-choreographer in absentia. Who but Fosse would have staged a musical on Halloween Eve, at the majestic Palace Theatre, where one of his

Bob Fosse played a junkie in *Thieves* with Marlo Thomas. *(AP/Wide World Photos)*

greatest efforts, *Sweet Charity*, once played? Who but Fosse would have followed it up with a caviar-and-champagne party at Central Park's Tavern on the Green, across the street from Gwen Verdon's and Nicole Fosse's spacious Central Park West penthouse?

The celebration began in the early afternoon. The public memorial at the Palace had been announced in the *New York Times,* and a throng of Fosse fans queued up around the theater, later filling the house to standing room only. The audience was an assorted lot: friends and family sat in the front, near the orchestra pit in a cordoned-off section; Fosse fanatics swapped stories in the balcony; and curious passers-by wondered what all the fuss was about.

A hush fell over the Palace as its blood-red velvet curtain rose over a large screen. To the lyrics of "I Want to Be a Dancin' Man," photos of a young Bobby Fosse in top hat and tails were projected on the screen. They segued to clips from his MGM film work and, finally, his own films. The audience applauded appreciatively at favorite Fosse dances such as *Sweet Charity*'s "Big Spender," *Cabaret*'s "Money, Money," and *All That Jazz*'s "Everything Old Is New Again." It remained rapt when excerpts from his nonmusical films, *Lenny* and *Star 80,* unspooled. In a few short minutes, the film retrospective, compiled by Gwen Verdon, captured the evolution of a remarkably clear-sighted director-choreographer, who frequently used music and dance to illuminate hard truths about performing—on stage, at work, in the bedroom and in life.

Speakers, not surprisingly, included a great many writers, such as Noel Behn, Peter Stone, Pete Hamill, Steve Tesich, Peter Maas, E. L. Doctorow, Neil Simon, and Herb Gardner. Everyone had humorous recollections that had less to do with Fosse as he appeared to his public than a soul-searching, deeply insecure perfectionist who appreciated a good joke, pretty women, and untapped talent—as the Dancing for Writers class illustrates. Composers and lyricists John Kander and Fred Ebb, Peter Allen, and Cy Coleman recounted their own anecdotes about Fosse's approach to music, his disdain for ballads, and his often abrupt omissions of their favorite songs from his shows. Coleman performed a song parody written by David Zippel whose lyrics humorously depict a director (Fosse) mercilessly pruning the score of his latest out-of-town musical: "Pardon me, Cy/But we've just said goodbye/To your fav'rite song . . ./Call it coincidence/Call it a joke/(When) twelve hundred people/Go out for a smoke. . . ." Other speakers included director Stanley Donen, actor Roy Scheider, and singer Loretta Devine, who, with musical arranger Gordon Harrell, ended the memorial with a stirring rendition of "Life Is Just a Bowl of Cherries," from *Big Deal*. At the rear of the theater, Gwen Verdon thanked everyone for coming as they filed out. She was smiling and convivial, seemingly intent on keeping the service as "up" as possible.

Actress Alyson Reed, who performed for Fosse in *Dancin'*, was crying silently at the end of the tribute. "I looked around me," she later said, "and here was all of Broadway mourning not just the man but the era he represented. With Michael [Bennett] and Gower [Champion] gone, the Fosse memorial was like this wake for all Broadway director-choreographers. My training with Bob and Michael was my foundation as an actor. So, for me, that day was the end of one stage of my career. It was me letting it go."

If dancers were strangely absent from the Palace's memorial to Fosse, they threw themselves whole-heartedly into the Tavern on the Green party later in the day. The guest list was dictated by those Fosse had named in his will; in all, around seventy-five people turned out for the festivities. "If you thought you were Bob Fosse's friend," says Graciela Daniele, "you would find out once and for all at the party. He only invited people he really liked."

The Central Park restaurant, situated among a thatch of trees slathered in white electric lights, has always been one of New York City's most glittering celebrity haunts. That evening, however, Tavern on the Green was illuminated by Fosse's aura. On the tables, guests found tiny top hats, white gloves and little laugh boxes. When they were opened, miniature hands applauded above the words, "give yourself a hand."

Tony Walton, one of the guests, remembers how Fosse's "leading ladies," Verdon, Nicole Fosse, and Ann Reinking, helped conjure an evening of magic as Fosse would have wanted it. "Nicole and Gwen got up on stage and did a dance," he says. "They were joined later by Ann Reinking, who performed an Irish jig. The whole evening took on a kind of New Orleans jazz celebration quality. There was absolutely no feeling of doom and gloom or ending about it. Nicole went down into the audience and grabbed some of the writers who were in his dance class, including Herb Gardner, who had just come out of traction, because he'd broken his arm, his leg, his knee—everything. He was whirling around the dance floor with his wife, silently screaming. The dance floor was small, and jam-packed with these wonderful dancers who had worked with Fosse."

Among the mimes and magicians entertaining the guests, Fosse's ghost was almost palpable in the room that night, says Ben Vereen. "I could feel his presence in the corner, just watching us all and smiling. Bob really loved to party and have a good time.

"Toward the end of the evening it really got down. We danced and danced and danced. The band would sort of let down, and I'd tell 'em to keep the music goin', keep the music goin'. It was like we *had* to keep the energy up because we were afraid of losing it and crying. I left when the party was at its peak, because I wanted him to be vivid in my mind as someone alive."

Vereen, who appeared in *Sweet Charity, Pippin,* and *All That Jazz*—and was coached by Fosse, a "doctor" for musicals in trouble, in the Broadway disaster *Grind*—carries forth Fosse's legacy today. His nightclub act, in fact, features a tribute to Fosse in which Vereen performs dances from various Fosse shows. Shirley MacLaine, too, acknowledges Fosse in a dance segment from her own one-woman show. So do Chita Rivera, Juliet Prowse, and Ann Reinking. Fosse's style has been absorbed and assimilated into the repertory of most dance stars, the few that remain.

Equally important progenitors of his work are those who have taken his choreography and applied it to their own esthetics. Graciela Daniele is one promising up-and-comer, so is former *Pippin* dancer Justin Ross, whose downtown club and Off-Broadway staging of fringe theater "spectacles" such as Theater-Off-Park's *I Could Go On Lip-Synching* starring John Epperson, reveal an innovative young director-choreographer redefining the concept of cabaret with Fosse-inspired less-is-more staging. Tony Stevens, Wayne Cilento, and Christopher Chadman—all former Fosse dancers and assistants—continue to choreograph for musical theater, although, to date none of them have had a breakthrough hit of Fosse caliber. Even Ann Reinking, who once claimed she had no desire to choreograph, has ventured into dancemaking. In part, the decision to choreograph comes from the realization that a dancer's days are numbered. Gwen Verdon once commented that a dancer dies twice, the first time when the body does not respond to the brain.

Those who are perhaps best suited to promote Fosse's dance technique are Verdon and Nicole Fosse. Admittedly Fosse's best student, Verdon continues to teach and discuss Fosse's choreography, although she has not danced on Broadway since 1975's *Chicago*. Her own career has reflected a hard-won determination not to quit when the legs won't dance, as her performances in *Cocoon* and *Cocoon II,* among other films, indicate. A licensed theatrical electrician who remodels old barns and stables, Verdon, now a great-grandmother, is as irrepressible as her stage characters.

In her roomy Central Park West penthouse, comfortably furnished with antiques, and its adjacent herb garden on the terrace, Verdon's life seems contentedly removed from show business. Unlike Fosse's former cluttered Central Park South apartment with its modern decor and Broadway memorabilia, Verdon's home is absent of anything about her career. There are no Tony Awards on the mantel or posters from her many hit shows on the walls. Instead, curious pen-and-ink drawings done by Nicole as a child adorn the room. "Nicole is everything to her now," says Donna McKechnie, who worked with Verdon in the 1987 national tour of *Sweet Charity*. "Gwen is a very private person who loves her work and her family and tries to keep them separate."

Nicole Fosse, today in her mid-twenties, dances in the chorus of Andrew Lloyd Webber's Broadway musical *Phantom of the Opera* and has

Nicole Fosse applies makeup before her stage debut in an Atlantic City production of *Can-Can* in 1982, the show that launched her mother's career. *(Jack Vartoogian)*

also appeared in Richard Attenborough's film version of *A Chorus Line* and a 1982 Atlantic City production of *Can-Can,* the musical that launched her mother's career.

Throughout her teen years, Nicole was intent on becoming a ballerina. She studied at North Carolina School of the Arts and the New York School of Ballet before apprenticing at the Cleveland Ballet. But her time there was frustrating; she danced as a mouse in the company's *Nutcracker,* and, after a year, saw no larger roles forthcoming. Lou Conte, artistic director of Chicago's Hubbard Street Dance Company, recalls Gwen Verdon approaching him about getting Nicole an audition with his troupe. According to Conte, Verdon, who now sits on the company's advisory board, told him, "Nicole wants to be a ballet dancer but she doesn't have the ability. But I think she does have the ability to be a dancer in a nonclassical mode." Although Conte agreed to arranging an audition, he says, "nothing ever came of it. I think it was all Gwen's idea that her daughter audition. Who knew if she was even interested?"

Nicole is pragmatic about her career and retiring about her parents. In two interviews I did with her for *Dance Magazine,* I found she flinches at the inevitable "what's-it-like-to-be-the-offspring-of-two-stars" question, though she freely speaks about her parents when the subject of dance arises.

"It took my mother forever to get cast in nondancing roles," she told me in 1988. "When you go in to read for film roles and the casting agent sees 'dancer' on your resume, automatically he or she thinks that's all you do. I mean, yes, I am a dancer, but I also sing and act, and I'll even do your apartment." In the mid–Eighties, Nicole decided to pursue a degree in interior design. "I like knowing there's something else I can do where I don't have to kick my legs around," she said shortly after she began dancing in *Phantom of the Opera.* As if presuming reporters' assumptions of nepotism, Nicole Fosse makes it clear that, with or without dancing and her famous parents, she would still have a career.

"She's studying architecture at Parsons," Fosse boasted to the *New York Times* of his daughter's aspirations in 1986. "She said, 'Not everyone's a star, and you've got to have something to fall back on.'"

Reactions to Bob Fosse's death were predictable: Everyone was saddened, no one surprised. For a man flirting with death throughout his career, Fosse finally decided to take his last curtain call. If his death on a sidewalk in Washington, D.C., was not exactly like the elaborate production number staged for a dying Joe Gideon in *All That Jazz,* there were the undeniable theatrics of having just left a last rehearsal of *Sweet Charity* before its opening night. And, of course, of having Gwen Verdon at his side when he collapsed.

"I was devastated when I heard of it," says John Lithgow. "I think most people felt there was an inevitability about it, since he was dancing with death for years. And as upset as I was about it, in many ways, it was long overdue for him. He had kept a standing date with death for so many years, this time he finally answered her call."

"I was very sad to hear about Bob's death," recalls *The Pajama Game* composer Richard Adler, "though I kind of expected it. Other people have said it too, but I'll reiterate that his death was unnecessary; he just didn't care."

Not everyone who worked with Fosse took his death matter-of-factly. Shirley MacLaine says she felt like "someone had thrown wet cement over me," and Debbie Reynolds remembers "feeling like a page from my history as an actress had been ripped out of the book." For many who had worked with him, Fosse represented not just a fellow performer, choreographer, or director, but a man whose outlook on the world colored their own perceptions. And while he may have discussed suicide and engineered his own heart attacks, Fosse always came back from the dead to prove everyone—even himself—wrong.

Eric Roberts was in his apartment on Sunset Boulevard when his manager called him to tell him about Fosse's death. "I immediately went outside," says Roberts. "It was about 11 P.M., and I went to the church where he and I rehearsed [*Star 80*] so much. I did what we mortals do when we've lost something we're not ready to lose. I was so angry because he didn't have to die. It's the only thing about his life that I can't forgive. Basically, I believe he killed himself, and I was insulted that he didn't care enough about the people who loved and respected him to stop that from happening. To my mind, living's the hard part. Dying is easy."

"They say underneath a cynical soul is a sentimental heart," Louise Quick says. "I think that was very true of Bob." Quick, who worked with Fosse on all three of his "triple crown" projects of 1972 and 1973—*Cabaret, Pippin,* and *Liza with a Z*—observed how expectations put on him to constantly top himself only succeeded in causing him to doubt his achievements. For someone who spent decades trying to move past song and dance in order to challenge himself with choreographing, directing, and writing, Fosse never developed as a full-fledged Renaissance man.

Nineteen-year-old Nicole Fosse caught in jeté on the beach at Atlantic City, 1982. (*Jack Vartoogian*)

But, in the end, he *was* a master of his craft. "I think Bob's world-weariness was justifiably earned," says Quick. "He, like so many of us, expected more from a world that is just so . . . fucked up. And like all of us, he got tired of having to put up with so much bullshit. One day Bob just said to hell with it. I think he must have been at odds with himself though, because he never stopped observing people, and there was always so much compassion. He was a very giving man. Maybe in the end, he believed he'd given too much."

Mama, that boy in the sleek scarlet tights
That I kept tryin' to dance like for days and for nights?
The one that could leap-and-stop like an impala
Or stand still and twitch in one spot like a swallow?
That one that I told you until you got fed up
The one with the strange little jerks and gyrations
Suggested incredible sex situations
Then could make you break up just by rolling his shoulder?
Stood like the Salvador Dalis? I told ya!
Oh, you never listen, that slip of red lightning
Just wiggling his hips and relaxing and tightening
His knees alternatively, the one that I said
Made me have to go into theatre? He's dead.

Oh, weep for fair Balder, oh weep for wee Pan,
That serious satyr, that humorous man.
Of the tiniest movement could make a great dance,
Of the slide of a shoe, of a shift of his pants.
Oh, the girls with mascara all running like rain:
No one will see them like he did again.
All the sexual violence he forced into form!
All the graceful finesse he whipped into a storm!
Taught the ugliest duckling to fake like a swan!
All the street agitation he stung with *elan!*
And above all, below all the shame of our nights,
Made the tawdriest rituals memorable rites.

—Robert Patrick, 1987

BIBLIOGRAPHY

Alpert, Hollis. *Fellini: A Life*. New York: Paragon House, 1986.

Bordman, Gerald. *The Concise Oxford Companion to American Theatre*. New York: Oxford University Press, 1987.

Croce, Arlene. *Afterimages*. New York: Alfred A. Knopf, 1977.

D'Emilio, John and Estelle B. Freedman. *Intimate Matters: A History of Sexuality in America*. New York: Harper & Row, 1988.

Fava, Claudio G. and Aldo Vigano. *The Films of Federico Fellini*. New Jersey: Citadel Press, 1981.

Gottfried, Martin. *Broadway Musicals*. New York: Abradale Press/Harry N. Abrams, 1979.

Guernsey, Otis, Jr. *Broadway Song & Story*. New York: Dodd, Mead & Company, 1985.

Henderson, Kathy. *First Stage: Profiles of the New American Actors*. New York: Quill, 1985.

Hirschhorn, Clive. *The Hollywood Musical*. New York: Crown, 1981.

Isherwood, Christopher. *The Berlin Stories*. New York: New Directions, 1954.

Kislan, Richard. *Hoofing on Broadway*. New York: Prentice Hall Press, 1987.

La Fosse, Robert, with Andrew Mark Wentink, *Nothing to Hide,* New York: Donald I. Fine, 1987.

Loney, Glenn. *Twentieth Century Theatre, Volumes 1 and 2*. New York: Facts on File, 1983.

————. *Unsung Genius: The Passion of Jack Cole*. New York: Franklin Watts, 1984.

Mayer, Harold M. and Richard C. Wade. *Chicago: Growth of a Metropolis*. Chicago: University of Chicago Press, 1969.

Migdoll, Herbert. *Dancers Dancing*. New York: Harry N. Abrams, 1978.

Miller, Arthur. *Death of a Salesman*. New York: Viking Press, 1949.

Scililiano, Enzo. *Pasolini: A Biography*. New York: Random House, 1982.

Segel, Harold B. *Turn-of-the-Century Cabaret*. New York: Columbia University Press, 1987.

Terkel, Studs. *Division Street: America*. New York: Pantheon Books, 1967.

Thomas, Tony. *That's Dancing!* New York: Harry N. Abrams, 1984.

INDEX

An italic number indicates a page with a photograph.